Oh, Jerry!

Copyright © 2022 Piotr Gibas and Werner Skalla. All rights reserved.

Published by Skapago Publishing, Furth im Wald, Germany.
1st edition published in June 2022

No part of this publication may be reproduced, stored in a retrieval system, or transmitted in any form or by any means, electronic, mechanical, photocopying, recording, scanning, or otherwise, except as permitted by law, without the prior written permission of the Publisher. Requests to the Publisher for permission can be addressed to jerry@skapago.eu.

Links published in this book are accessible at the time of publication. The publisher cannot guarantee accessibility in the future.

Picture credits:
Photography © Piotr Gibas except:
Introduction – young people singing © Everett Collection / Shutterstock.com
Chapter 1 – horse being taught reading © Oleg Golovnev / Shutterstock.com
Chapter 2 – girl in front of the blackboard © Tom Wang / Shutterstock.com
Chapter 4 – high heels © Gábor Szűts / Unsplash
Chapter 5 – Terracotta Warriors © Aaron Greenwood / Unsplash
Chapter 5 – shocked young woman © Krakenimages.com / Shutterstock.com
Chapter 5 – flooded trucks © Jéan Béller / Unsplash
Chapter 6 – wedding cake on the floot © Gladius Stock / Shutterstock.com
Chapter 7 – Great Wall of China © Joel Danielson / Unsplash
Chapter 8 – Koala © David Clode / Unsplash
Chapter 10 – horses © CanuckStock / Shutterstock.com
Chapter 10 – dentist © Hananeko_Studio / Shutterstock.com
Chapter 12 – cow © Cranach / Shutterstock.com
Chapter 12 – woman knocking on the door © Nitiphonphat / Shutterstock.com

Cover designed by Abdulrahman Aburahmah

ISBN: 978-3-945174-16-6

Free bonus materials to this book: https://www.skapago.eu/jerry/bonus/ →

Learn other languages with Skapago
German: Jens und Jakob, ISBN 978-3-945174-06-7
Swedish: Alfred the Ghost, ISBN 978-3-945174-10-4
Norwegian: The Mystery of Nils, ISBN 978-3-945174-00-5

Other languages at www.skapago.eu

Oh, Jerry!

Part 1 – Chinese Course for Beginners
Learn Chinese. Enjoy the Story.

Texts & Photography by
Piotr Gibas

Co-created by
Grainger Lanneau

Illustrations by
Abdulrahman Aburahmah

Edited by
Werner Skalla
Nic Song

published by
Skapago
www.skapago.eu/jerry

Contents

Chapter	Page	Grammar / Conversation Topics
Let's get started	7	
1	16	*You good!* or how to say *hello*, Questions with 呢 ne, How to use 是 shì, Asking questions with 吗 ma, Negative 不 bù, Question word 谁 shéi/shuí, Chinese names
2	26	And what about 呢 ne?, What? 什么 Shénme?, Plural, or the lack thereof, 也 yě, Eating cooked rice by default: verbs, Other uses of 好 hǎo, Let's 吧 ba!, 要不要 yào bú yào want no want?, 没有问题 méi yǒu wèntí – No problem
3	38	More ways to be: why we need very 很 hěn, Alternating questions, How to describe stuff, How and why to use 都 dōu, Four character expressions 成语 chéngyǔ, Possession, Family members 家人 jiā rén, Nationalities and languages, To know how, Connecting words in a sentence
4	54	Little great particle 的 de, 在 zài to be present, Particle 啊 a, The verb 骑 qí.
5	64	How to complete things, 就 jiù and 才 cái: Two opposite things that mean almost exactly the same ..., Where are you from, again?, Numbers, "Three pieces of person"?, How to say a lot, 就 jiù again The curious incident of 老 lǎo
6	84	How many? Question word 几 jǐ, Only 只 zhǐ, 没关系 méi guānxi – it doesn't matter, Let's get professional, The story of a little sound: 儿 er, Where on earth, or how to use 哪儿／哪里 nǎ'er/ nǎlǐ?, Why do we use "that"?, The opposite of 好 hǎo, "To know" something or somebody?
7	100	Inside, Person Place Action, How to say "how?", How to tell the date, The (not so) delicate matter of asking about age ..., How to change things, Too good, How is it?, The verb "to give" 给 gěi, Very very, Telling the time, How to exaggerate a little bit, The Rule, This way
8	120	Some useful time expressions, But I thought ..., Lonely verbs, We love Jerry SO much, What will the future bring?, How to be more expressive, Completing things (part 2), Alone, Let's talk about money
9	136	Time: 时间 shíjiān versus 时候 shíhou, Time Place Action, More time expressions, Still on top, Must, What if?, Wishing and thinking, Completing things (3)
10	152	More and more, To be or to live somewhere, Already 已经 yǐjing, Three kinds of "can", With, Alone or together?, Orders and suggestions,
11	164	Want, Postpositions: table on, Subordinate Clause?, If, The curious matter of the word 几 jǐ, Like versus would like,
12	178	Verb complements, First and again, Some, How to use the toilet, 对 duì "right"
13	192	Language, When things happen, Running away, Making exceptions, Quickly about finishing things, Comparisons
Epilogue	212	
Word list	216	
Key to the exercises	245	

Things to help you

You will find texts from the book as audio files, pronunciation explanations on video, additional exercises, a vocabulary trainer, and much more — most of it for free, at www.skapago.eu/jerry.

People to help you

It might be difficult for you to learn a new language all on your own. Personally I believe you should get support from a teacher.

Now, you might accuse me of being biased and just want to sell you our courses since Skapago is an online language school. So I'll be the first to admit that other schools have great teachers, too, so feel free to get in touch with one of our competitors.

Our teachers will talk to you through Skype and use a video conference, so you can join our live individual classes wherever you are in the world. You can schedule a free demo lesson here: www.skapago.eu

Mistackes

You won't believe how many times we read through this book before we dared to publish it. Still, we cannot guarantee that the book contains no mistakes. Should you find one, please send an e-mail to: jerry@skapago.eu. Jerry will send you a personal thank you message!

The best Chinese textbook ever?

When we started working on this book, our ambition was to make the best Chinese textbook ever, but well, let's keep our feet on the ground. Let us know what you think! Are there exercises you don't like, explanations you don't understand, texts that are boring, images you find ugly? If you have comments or ideas for improvement, or if you just want to say hello to Jerry – don't hesitate and send an e-mail to: jerry@skapago.eu

Chinese is ridiculously simple.

You don't believe me?
Look:

He eats	他吃	*He eat*
He is eating	他正在吃	*He right now eat*
He ate	他吃了	*He eat complete*
He has eaten	他吃过	*He eat "pass"* (as in *to pass* through a valley)

Look how the verb *eat* changes in English. In Chinese, the verb 吃 *to eat* stays the same in all circumstances.

Let's look at another example.

He is my classmate.	他是我的同学。	*He is my classmate.*
I don't like him.	我不喜欢他。	*I don't like he.*
His attitude is bad.	他的态度不好。	*He's attitude is bad.*

See how *he* can have different forms in English - not in Chinese: always the same word 他.

So far for the good news. You might have spotted the bad news by now: Chinese does not use our alphabet. Instead, every single word has its own character, and there is no connection to the pronunciation. Many Chinese dictionaries include 40,000 characters. I know what you might be thinking, that's way too many!

But don't freak out just yet! It is not as horrible as it sounds.

Firstly, unless you are planning on learning the periodic table or read journals in medicine, there are a ton of characters that you are not required to learn. How many words do you know in the English language? Probably not all of them (if you do then congratulations). There is a lot of specialized vocabulary that you will never encounter.

Secondly, there is a trick to learning Chinese characters: many big and complicated characters are made up of small and simple characters.
Look at this character:

赢 **To win**

You might be thinking: "Oh no! How can I write something like that?" It looks really complicated.
However, this character is made up of simpler characters as can be seen below.

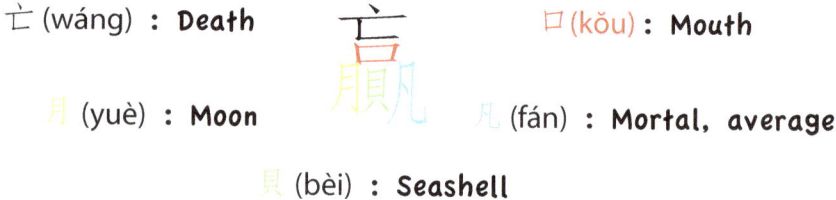

亡 (wáng) : **Death** 　　　　　口 (kǒu) : **Mouth**

月 (yuè) : **Moon** 　　　　　凡 (fán) : **Mortal, average**

贝 (bèi) : **Seashell**

Not always are these combinations 100% intuitive – what do seashells have to do with winning? But still, knowing these details will help you remember characters that look super complicated at first glance. In this book we will first show you the simple characters to build a foundation, then move on to the complicated characters.

Thirdly, there is a stroke order for all of these characters. The order of strokes shows the order of how a character is written and that there is methodological approach to it rather than simply "drawing". This makes remembering how to write a character so much easier. For every character we will show you how it is written in a video explanation. You can find these videos at www.skapago.eu/jerry/bonus.

How to pronounce Chinese?

Learning Chinese is like learning songs: not just texts, but also melodies, and the two of them are inseparable. Why? Because in Chinese every word has a **tone** (kind of like pitches in music). For example the word **zhuo** has no meaning without the tone, and people in China will not understand what you are saying unless you pronounce it in the correct tone. Then, **zhuo** means *a table*. The meaning of the words changes completely if you apply the wrong tone, even if the pronunciation of the words is the same otherwise.

American students practicing Chinese tones

Fortunately, Chinese has only 4 tones , i.e. "melodies" a word can have: a level tone, a rising tone, a low tone and a falling tone. Check our video at www.skapago.eu/jerry/bonus to see how this works. Don't skip this because tone pronunciation is very, very important.

For example: 厉害 **lì hài** (falling tone) means *awesome* and 里海 **Lǐhǎi** (low tone) means the Caspian Sea. **Shui Jiao** means *dumplings* or *to sleep*, depending on the tone. If you go to a restaurant and you tell the waiter you want **shui jiao** incorrectly, he will advise you to go home and rest.

The best way when you memorize vocabulary is to say the word out aloud in the correct tone: Learn it like a song - text and melody together, not just one of them. If you ask me, "what tone is **zhuo** for *table* in," I will need to say it first and then I will tell you. Always say the word correctly, and then you will remember it! For checking if you are saying words correctly, see the videos at www.skapago.eu/jerry/bonus.

Some subtle pronunciation differences

Like all languages, Chinese has a few sounds that don't exist in English, and you will have to learn how to produce these sounds. Go to www.skapago.eu/jerry/bonus to see video explanations about these sounds.

Now the 100 Dollar question!

How do you know how to pronounce a Chinese word when you only see the character – since the character has absolutely nothing to do with the pronunciation?

The answer is …

Pinyin 拼音

Pinyin is a Chinese term that literally means *to split sound*. Pinyin uses our alphabet to write Chinese. For example *hello* 你好 in pinyin is **nǐ hǎo**.

The strange little curves on the **ǐ** and the **ǎ** indicate what tone you have to use. So pinyin is super helpful! Therefore we will always introduce new vocabulary not only in characters, but also in pinyin.

However there are quite a few letters with sounds that are different than what English speakers would usually assume. Take a look at the pinyin chart at our website www.skapago.eu/jerry/bonus and see the videos for how they are pronounced.

There you have it, the easy and difficult parts of learning Chinese. Hopefully you feel more comfortable as well as more aware of the feasible challenge that lies ahead.

Oh, there is one more thing: in modern day Chinese, the writing system has been split into two groups.

Traditional vs. simplified characters:

Traditional characters have been used in China for thousands of years. They have many strokes and are more likely to have pictographic meanings.

Simplification of Chinese characters was a long campaign and debate that began in the 20th century. In order to decrease illiteracy rates, scholars and intellectuals decreased the number of strokes in complicated looking characters, but not all characters were changed. See examples below.

CAR / CHARIOT

This character looks like a chariot going left or right from a bird's eye view.

The simplified version of the character *car* or *chariot* lost its symmetry and doesn't look much like a chariot anymore. On the other hand, it is easier to write.

LOVE

This character has another character 心 (*heart*) inside.

The simplified version of *love* has no heart on the inside. Many critics of simplified characters will say "how can you love without a heart?" That is the problem of the simplified characters – they lose a lot of the original meaning.

Should I study traditional or simplified characters?

It ultimately depends. If you only want to communicate and just go to Mainland China then simplified is a better fit. If you plan on understanding Chinese culture and plan on going to Taiwan, Hong Kong, or Macao, then it is better to learn traditional characters.

In this book we present both versions. In the chapter texts, the characters that are the same in traditional and simplified versions will always be printed in black, the specifically simplified ones in grey. In the word lists we show both versions. If you change your mind at some point, no problem – you can always learn the other variation as well. In grammar explanations and exercises we use simplified characters.

A bit more about Chinese characters

妈妈骑马。马慢。妈妈骂马。

Pinyin transcription:
mā ma qí mǎ.   mǎ màn.   mā ma mà mǎ.

When you look at the pinyin text, do you notice anything interesting? That's right, the recurring syllable **ma**. It appears here with three different tone marks (**mā, mǎ, mà**) and with no mark at all (**ma**). In each case when the tone mark is different, **ma** means something else.

Now, look at the Chinese characters. Do you see any recurring elements? That's right, all of these characters except one (慢) are similar: they all contain the same element (马). If you look again at the pinyin text and match the characters with the transcription, you will notice that all of the characters with the same element are pronounced **ma**, except for one (骑 **qí**); every time when the tone on **ma** is different, a different character is used.

Chinese characters often, but not always, contain two elements: *phonetic* (suggesting the pronunciation) and *semantic* (suggesting the meaning).

All three characters in the text pronounced **ma** share the same *phonetic* element. Can you guess which one? Of course, it is the element 马. A simple and a basic element like this is called a *key* or a *radical*. There are about 240 radicals and all Chinese characters are built from one or more of them.

马 **mǎ** means *horse*.
妈 **mā** means *mother*; 马 serves as the phonetic element, suggesting the pronunciation; the key 女 **nǚ** means *woman* and serves as the semantic element (most mothers are women); knowing these two things, we can guess both the meaning and the pronunciation of the character;
骂 **mà** means *to curse*; the semantic element here is 口 **kǒu**, which means *mouth*; you can see that it is used twice on top of the phonetic element 马 **mǎ** – two mouths suggest a lot of noise being made!

So far so good. How about 骑? Why does it contain the *horse* element (马) but is not pronounced **ma**? It is because in this character, 马 has a semantic function; 骑 **qí** means *to ride*; the phonetic element is 奇 (**qí**). Thus, **qí** with a horse element suggests an action related to horses.

This should give you an idea of how Chinese characters are build. The last one in our sentence is 慢 (**màn**). Again, we have two elements here, phonetic 曼 (**màn**) and semantic 忄 **xīn**, meaning *the heart*. 慢 **màn** means *slow* and the heart element indicates an action performed slowly and patiently. The heart radical is used in a lot of characters expressing emotions, feelings, etc.

Would you be able to guess the meaning of 慢 **màn** if you knew the meaning of the components beforehand? Of course not. But the knowledge of these things helps to make sense of Chinese characters in the process of learning them.

However, you should be able now to translate our little sentence. Can you try?

妈妈骑马。　　马慢。　　妈妈骂马。
mā ma qí mǎ.　　**mǎ màn.**　　**mā ma mà mǎ.**

Mother　ride　horse.　　Horse slow.　　Mother　curse horse.
(Mom rides a horse. The horse is slow. Mom curses the horse.)

But now, since we have been talking about horses so much – lets's finally meet Jerry, the horse!

> **The mythical horse**
>
> The 马 character abstractly resembles a horse. 马 is a radical in its own right. The traditional 馬 contains 灬, which stands for "fire" (火 **huǒ**). In ancient China horses were believed to be semi-mythical creatures related to fire. Horses ran so fast as if they were on fire. In the simplified form 马 the four dots 灬 become a line 一.

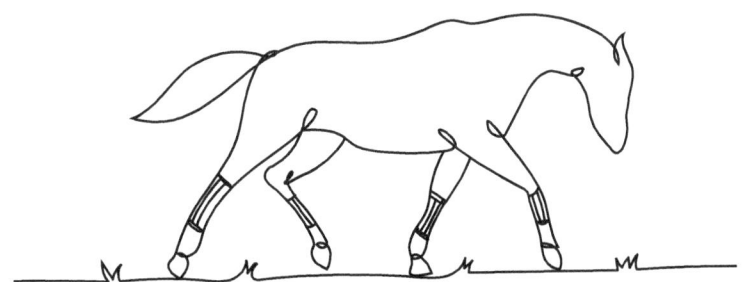

Ready for chapter 1?

Let's do this!

Resources you will need:

- **audio files**
- **pronunciation videos**
- **... and much more**

for free & up to date

at

www.skapago.eu/jerry/bonus/

What to do with the text on the next page
Please watch our video at
www.skapago.eu/jerry/bonus

This is how we structure the text and the word lists:

Grey characters have a traditional version that differs from the simplified version.
↓

For black characters, the simplified and traditional versions are identical.
↓

学生：老师好！
Xuésheng: Lǎoshī hǎo! ← pinyin
Student(s): Teacher good! ← literal translation
Students: Hello teacher! ← translation to "real" English

pinyin transliteration and English meaning; type the number into our app for a video that explains the writing. More information: www.skapago.eu/jerry/bonus

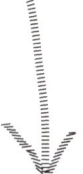

traditional version → 老師
simplified version → 老师

lǎoshī 247
teacher

explanation → "old" + "master" = "teacher"

Part 1

老师： 大家好！我姓齐，我是老师。
Lǎoshī: Dàjiā hǎo! Wǒ xìng Qí, wǒ shì lǎoshī.
Teacher: Everybody good! I last name Qi, I am teacher.
Teacher: Hello everybody! My name is Qi, I am a teacher.

学生： 老师好！
Xuésheng: Lǎoshī hǎo!
Student(s): Teacher good!
Students: Hello teacher!

老师： 请问， 你贵姓？
Lǎoshī: Qǐngwèn, nǐ guì xìng?
Teacher: May I ask, you noble last name?
Teacher: May I ask, what is your last name?

请问， 你贵姓？

他呢？ And he?

老 **lǎo** 108
old

often used to express respect

師 **shī** 109
师
master

老師 **lǎoshī**
老师 teacher

"old" + "master" = "teacher"

大 **dà** 101
big

a person standing with legs and arms extended out to the side

家 **jiā** 102
home, family

roof 宀 mián over a pig 豕 shī. Village people often lived with farm animals under one roof, and the pig has always been China's favorite!

大家 **dàjiā**
everybody

"big" + "family" = "everybody"

好 **hǎo** 103
good, well

女 nǚ "woman" radical and child 子 zǐ "son;" a mother and child together is considered a good thing. 女 nǚ looks like a woman standing up with arms out, the pointy chest on the left; 子 resembles an infant, with the contour of the head, arms stretched out, and the lower body.

大家好 **dà jiā hǎo**
hello everybody

我 **wǒ** 104
I

Two elements combined together: a hand 手 shǒu holding a spear 戈 gē. Originally, 我 did not mean "I," but "us" and indicated a community. The hand holding a spear with a banner or a standard attached to it was a point of reference during a battle – it was "us" represented by the standard versus "them", the enemy.

姓 **xìng** 105
surname

The woman radical is on the left. In ancient times Chinese names were passed down along maternal lines. 生 shēng on the right means "to give birth," but here it serves as a phonetic element and suggests the pronunciation of the character (xìng and shēng sound similar).

齊 / 齐 **qí** 106
orderly, correct, tidy; *Chinese family name*

see the note about names

是 **shì** 107
to be sth./sb.

老師好 / 老师好 **lǎoshī hǎo**
Hello teacher

學 / 学 **xué** 123
to study

子 zǐ "child" element represents a boy studying under a roof (at school); the top of the traditional character is believed to be a phonetic element; the pronunciation has changed since ancient times, therefore this element is now invalid.

生 **shēng** 124
to give birth; an adept

學生 / 学生 **xuésheng**
student

"to study" + "an adept" = "student." 生 shēng often serves as a suffix: when it follows another character meaning a skill or a practice (e.g. 学 xué "to study"), 生 indicates a person specialized at that particular skill.

請 / 请 **qǐng** 110
to ask for; to invite; to request; please

The radical 讠(言) yán on the left means "speech," "words," or "language." Grabbing someone's attention often involves speech. 青 qīng on the right side means "azure," but it often serves as a phonetic element. Almost all characters with this element are pronounced qing or jing.

問 / 问 **wèn** 111
to ask a question

There is a 口 kǒu "mouth" inside the "gate" 门 [門] mén, because we need a mouth to ask a question; 门 [門] serves as a phonetic element, because mén sounds similar to wèn.

請問 / 请问 **qǐngwèn**
excuse me, may I ask

"to ask for" + "to ask a questiion" = "please, may I ask" → "excuse me"

你 **nǐ** 114
you

Radical 亻 on the left is a short form of the character 人 rén, which means "person" or "human being;" this radical often indicates that the character represents a human being.

貴 / 贵 **guì** 115
expensive; noble; honorable

The upper part of the character is a container, which is filled with the precious shells that we see in the bottom part: element 贝 (貝) bèi means "cowry shell." In ancient China, cowry shells were often used as currency; hence the radical often appears in characters that deal with wealth, jewels, and treasures.

王小猫：我姓王。我叫王小猫。
Wáng Xiǎomāo: Wǒ xìng Wáng. Wǒ jiào Wáng Xiǎomāo.
Wang Little Cat: I last name Wang. I call Wang Little Cat.
Wang Xiaomao: My last name is Wang. My full name is "Wang Little Cat".

老师： 他是谁呢？
Lǎoshī: Tā shì shéi ne?
Teacher: He is who and what about?
Teacher: And who is he?

小 **xiǎo** 112
small

We often use 小 to express familiarity with someone or to indicate that something is lovey or cute, but sometimes 小 may also mean condescension or disrespect. When we have a friend whose last name is e.g. 王 Wáng, we will call him 老王 Lǎo Wáng if he is older than us or if we want to show him respect and high esteem, and 小王 Xiǎo Wáng when he is younger and we want to express our familiarity with him. 小人 xiǎo rén, however, is not a little or a lovely person, but an insult: a "petty person," "a commoner," an "uneducated boor." Similar, 小子 xiǎozǐ "little son" actually refers to a sly, crafty or naughty person.

貓
猫
māo 113
cat

Beautiful character. The traditional form has a special radical 豸 zhì "insect without feet" that is used in characters indicating cat-like creatures, e.g. panthers; in simplified forms, it has been replaced with a more general 犭(犬) quǎn "dog," now used in characters indicating all sorts of beasts. 苗 miáo suggests the pronunciation (similar to māo); by itself, it means "sprout" and consists of a grass radical 艹(艸) cǎo and 田 tián "field". Lovely!

小貓
小猫
xiǎo māo
little cat; kitten; *here: a given name*

王 **wáng** 116
king

A monarch's duty was to be the intermediary between heaven, earth and humanity, represented through the horizontal lines; the vertical line connects those three strata. Wáng is one of the most popular Chinese last names.

他 **tā** 117
he

Another example of a character with the radical 亻(人) rén designating a human.

她 **tā** 118
she

It is the same word as "he" above, with the same pronunciation, but we write it differently to indicate a different meaning: we use 女 nǚ "woman" instead of 亻, so we get the character 她 tā, which means "she" – a female 3rd person pronoun.

誰
谁
shéi/shuí 119
who

Another character with the 讠(言) yán "speech" radical, this time because it is a question word and we need speech to ask a question. 隹 zhuī on the right side means "bird with a short tail" (really!). It serves as a phonetic element: zhuī sounds similar to shéi/shuí.

呢 **ne** 120
and what about?

We see a 口 kǒu "mouth" radical, because this question particle has no particular meaning and serves only as a part of speech, modifying the meaning of the sentence. 尼 ní is phonetic (similar to ne).

You good! or how to say *hello*

你好 **nǐ hǎo**: This phrase literally means *you good*. It can be translated as *you are good* or *you are well*. While the English *you* can mean one person or many persons, the Chinese 你 **nǐ** implies only one person. So when you say 你好 **nǐ hǎo**, you are saying *hello* to only one person.

To say *hello* to a group of people or to another person, we change the word in front of 好 **hǎo** depending on whom we want to greet:

    你们好 **nǐmen hǎo**: *You [plural] good (Hello you all!)*
    大家好 **dàjiā hǎo**: *Everybody good (Hello everybody!)*
    老师好 **lǎoshī hǎo**: *Teacher good (Hello teacher!)*

There are two ways of asking someone's name in Chinese. One is the casual 你叫什么名字 **nǐ jiào shénme míngzi** (literally: *You called what name*). This is an informal question that we may use only e.g. with people of the same age as ourselves.

叫 **jiào** is a verb* and means *to call* or *to be called*. To introduce ourselves, we simply replace the question word after 叫 **jiào** with our answer:

    我叫 ... **wǒ jiào** ... *I [am] called ... (My name is ...)*

We can include both our last and given names.

The extremely formal way of asking someone's name is 你贵姓 **nǐ guì xìng** – *what is your last name*. 贵 **guì** normally means *expensive*, but in this context it means *noble*. 姓 **xìng** can be both a noun** (*surname*) or a verb (*to be surnamed*). The structure of the sentence 你贵姓 **nǐ guì xìng** literally means *your noble surname*. Nowadays, we ask for people's names in this way when we meet strangers. However, in less formal situations, for example among university students, our Chinese speaking peers would find it strange if we ask them 你贵姓 **nǐ guì xìng**. If we are still curious and want to specifically ask them about their *last* names, we can say 你姓什么? **nǐ xìng shénme?** literally: *You last name what?*

To answer this question, we wouldn't say *我贵姓王 ~~wǒ guì xìng Wáng~~ *My noble surname is Wang*. We must drop the 贵 **guì** and simply say 我姓王 **wǒ xìng Wáng** *My surname [is] Wang*. 姓 **xìng** works as a verb here and means *to be surnamed*, so the sentence is literally translated as *I am surnamed Wang*.

men 133
suffix used after a personal pronoun*** to indicate plural

We see the "man" 亻(人) rén radical on the left, because 们 is a pronoun – it refers to human beings; 门 mén is for pronunciation.

nǐmen
114, 128
you (plural)

---

* A **verb** is a word that tells you what someone does: *eat, sleep, work, fly, love* ... these are all verbs.

** A **noun** is a word that stands for a specific thing or person, e.g. *cheese, newspaper, teacher, Jerry* ...

*** A **pronoun** is a word that replaces a person or a thing: *I, you, he, she, it* ...

Asking questions with 呢 ne

呢 **ne** is a particle* used to turn statements into open questions. 呢 **ne** is often translated as *what about*, *how about*, or *and*. It is always at the end of the sentence.

* *Particles* are words that have no meaning on their own, but instead they have specific grammatical functions in a sentence.

我姓王，你呢？ **wǒ xìng Wáng, nǐ ne?**
I last name Wang, you *and [what about]*?
(My last name is Wang, what about you?)

他是谁呢？ **tā shì shéi ne?**
He is who *and [what about]*?
(And who is he? / How about him, who is he?)

我是学生，他呢？ **wǒ shì xuésheng, tā ne?**
I am student, he *and [what about]*?"
(I am a student, and what about him?)

我是学生，他呢？

Part 2

王小猫：他不是人！他是马。
Wáng Xiǎomāo: Tā bú shì rén! Tā shì mǎ.
Wang Little Cat: He no is person! He is horse.
Wang Xiaomao: He is not a human! He is a horse.

老师：他是学生吗？
Lǎoshī: Tā shì xuésheng ma?
Teacher: He is student [question]?
Teacher: Is he a student?

王小猫：他不是学生。
Wáng Xiǎomāo: Tā bú shì xuésheng.
Wang Little Cat: He no is student.
Wang Xiaomao: He is not a student.

老师：他叫什么名字？
Lǎoshī: Tā jiào shénme míngzi?
Teacher: He call what name?
Teacher: What is his name?

王小猫：他叫 Jerry。
Wáng Xiǎomāo: Tā jiào Jerry.
Wang Little Cat: He call Jerry.
Wang Xiaomao: His name is Jerry.

不 **bù** 121
no, not

人 **rén** 122
person, human being

looks like a walking man

馬
马 **mǎ** 3
horse

嗎
吗 **ma** 125
question particle

I need a 口 kǒu "mouth" to ask questions. 马 (馬) mǎ is phonetic.

叫 **jiào** 126
to call

I need a mouth 口 kǒu to call.

甚/什
麼
么 **shén** 127
what?

me 128
what?

幺 yāo in the traditional form 麼 means something tiny, . 麻 má ("hemp") is phonetic (sounds similar to "me"); the simplified form lost the phonetic part.

什麼
什么 **shénme**
what?

A dialect word, used in spoken modern Mandarin. In dialects, (in contrast to literary Chinese) there are words made of more than one syllable, e.g. "shénme" = "shén" + "me;" separately they have no meaning of their own. The characters used to write "shénme" were adopted to represent the sound of this vernacular word.

名 **míng** 129
name

字 **zì** 130
word, character

名字 **míngzi**
name

"name" + "character" = personal name = characters to write it

21

How to use 是 shì

是 **shì** has a couple of different meanings. One of them is equivalent to the English word *am*, *is* or *are*. For example:
> 我是马 **wǒ shì mǎ** *I am a horse.*
> 他是马 **tā shì mǎ** *He is a horse.*

However, the basic meaning of 是 **shì** is *to be so* and it can also be used to answer *yes* or *no* questions. Therefore it is often translated as *yes*, e. g. when someone asks Jerry whether he is a horse, he can answer:
> 是，我是马 **shì, wǒ shì mǎ** *Yes, I am a horse.*
> or literally: *It is so, I am a horse.*

Asking questions with 吗 ma

With the particle 吗 **ma** we can turn any statement into a question. The particle works like a question mark at the end of a sentence:
> 他叫 Jerry **tā jiào Jerry** *He is called Jerry.*

> → 他叫 Jerry 吗？ **tā jiào Jerry ma?**
> *He [is] called Jerry [question?]*
> ("Is he called Jerry?")

> 你是学生 **nǐ shì xuésheng** *You are a student.*
> → 你是学生吗？ **nǐ shì xuésheng ma?**
> *You are student [question]?*
> (Are you a student?)

Note that 吗 **ma** doesn't have a tone. To learn how to pronounce it, please watch the video at www.skapago.eu/jerry/bonus.

Negative 不 bù

不 **bù** is often translated as *no* or *not*. It is the negation for being or doing something, but not e.g. for having something (we will talk about this in chapter 2). We would use 不 **bù** to say someone or something is not something (i.e. sentences with 是 **shì**):

他不是人 **tā bú shì rén** *He not is person. (He is not a person.)*
我不是马 **wǒ bú shì mǎ** *I not am horse. (I am not a horse.)*

Unlike in English, we always put 不 **bù** before the verb or phrase that we want to negate.

他不叫 Jerry **tā bú jiào Jerry**
He not called Jerry. (He is not called Jerry.)
我不姓王 **wǒ bú xìng Wáng**
I not last name Wang. (My last name is not Wang.)

Note about pronunciation:

When 不 **bù** comes before a word with a fourth tone, it changes into a second tone [**bú**], so the sentence **wǒ bù shì mǎ** will be pronounced [**wǒ bú shì mǎ**]. Please watch the video at www.skapago.eu/jerry/bonus for details.

Question word 谁 shéi/shuí

谁 **shéi/shuí** (both pronunciations are correct, **shéi** is more common) means *who* and it is a question word.

To ask a question, we replace the object we want to ask about with 谁 **shéi/shuí**:
他是 Jerry **tā shì Jerry** *He is Jerry.*
他是谁？ **tā shì shéi?** *Literally: He is who? → Who is he?*

他是谁？

Chinese names

Chinese names consists of two, maximum three characters (four character names are extremely rare). The surname (姓 **xìng**) always comes first! Whenever you see a Chinese name, such as **Yao Ming** or **Xi Jinping**, the first word is invariably the last name (surname). The reason for this is logical: The surname is much more important than the given name; people are first of all born with their surnames and given names are secondary.
By the way this even applies to titles: we have to say 齐老师 **Qí lǎoshī** *Qí teacher* in this order. You will learn more about this in chapter 3.

1. Read the following tongue twister to practice pinyin and your tones.

bàba de bàba pà bàba de māma

māma de māma pà māma de bàba

2. Convert the following pinyin phrases into characters and say them aloud!

a) dàjiā hǎo

b) wǒ shì lǎoshī

c) tā bú shì rén

d) tā shì xuésheng ma

e) tā shì shéi

Convert the following Chinese phrases into pinyin and say them aloud!

f) 我姓王。

g) 他叫什么名字?

h) 我是老师。

i) 请问，你贵姓?

j) 你是学生吗?

3. Fill in the blank.

a) 他 ____ Jerry。   (His name is Jerry.)

b) 我 ____ 人 。   (I am a person.)

c) 我 ____ 老师。   (I am not a teacher.)

d) 他是 ____ ?   (Who is he?)

4. Compose sentences with the vocabulary. Put the words into the right order and provide pinyin:

a) What is your name?
名字 / 你 / 什么 / 叫

b) Who is she?
谁 / 是 / 她

There is not much space here. That's because I encourage you to write the exercises on a separate piece of paper and not into the book. That way you can do them again if you get them wrong or when you want to repeat them (yes, you should do that). You can find the solutions on page 245.

c) I am a student.
学生 / 我 / 是

d) I am not a teacher.
不 / 老师 / 我 / 是

e) Excuse me, are you a good person?
吗 / 问 / 是 / 好 / 你 / 人 / 请

5. Which one makes sense? Choose 吗/呢:
a) 他不是人吗/呢？
b) 他叫什么名字吗/呢？
c) 你是谁吗/呢？
d) 他是学生，你吗/呢？
e) 你姓王吗/呢？
f) 谁叫Jerry吗/呢？
g) 谁是老师吗/呢？
h) 谁姓齐吗/呢？
i) 你贵姓吗/呢？
j) 你是王小猫吗/呢？

Fortune cookie:

筷子 **kuàizi**
chopsticks

131, 132

6. Questions from the text: answer the following questions in Chinese.
a) Jerry是学生吗？
b) Jerry是人吗？
c) 齐老师是人吗？

7. Transcribe these sentences into pinyin, mark the tones, and translate:
a) 齐老师不是好人
b) Jerry是好学生
c) 王小猫不是小猫，她叫小猫
d) 她不叫小马，她叫小猫
e) 学生不是老人
f) 小马问小猫：Jerry是谁？
g) 请问，你学什么？

More exercises online at www.skapago.eu/jerry/bonus

2

我们喝啤酒吧!
Let's drink beer!

Part 1

齐老师: 王小猫，你做什么呢?
Qí lǎoshī: Wáng Xiǎomāo, nǐ zuò shénme ne?
Qi Teacher: Wang Little Cat, you do what [right] now?
Teacher Qi: Wang Xiaomao, what are you doing?

王小猫: 我吃饭呢。
Wáng Xiǎomāo: Wǒ chī fàn ne.
Wang Little Cat: I eat cooked rice [right] now.
Wang Xiaomao: I am eating.

齐老师: 好吃吗?
Qí lǎoshī: Hǎo chī ma?
Qi Teacher: Good [to] eat [question]?
Teacher Qi: Is it tasty?

王小猫: 好吃! 老师，你要吃吗?
Wáng Xiǎomāo: Hǎo chī! Lǎoshī, nǐ yào chī ma?
Wang Little Cat: Good [to] eat! Teacher, you want eat [question]?
Wang Xiaomao: It is tasty! Teacher, do you want to eat?

齐老师: 我不要吃。我不饿。
Qí lǎoshī: Wǒ bú yào chī. Wǒ bú è.
Qi Teacher: I no want eat. I no hungry.
Teacher Qi: I don't. I am not hungry.

做 **zuò** 201
to do, to make

呢 **ne** 120
right now; at this moment

see grammar explanations

吃 **chī** 202
to eat

The 口 kǒu "mouth" wants food and 乞 qǐ is for pronunciation, but it also means "to beg," so in 吃 we see a mouth that begs!

飯 **fàn** 203
饭 cooked rice; food

飠 is a radical that means "food", 反 fǎn is phonetic.

吃飯 **chī fàn**
吃饭 to eat

"to eat" + "cooked rice" = "to eat"

好吃 **hǎo chī**
好吃 tasty; delicious

"good" + "to eat" = "good to eat"
see grammar explanations

要 **yào** 204
to want

Jerry 呢？他要不要吃？
Jerry　　ne?　　Tā yào bú yào chī?
Jerry and [what about]? He want no want eat?
What about Jerry? Does he want to eat?

饿
饿　　è 205
　　hungry

饣 shí "food" on the left, 我 wǒ is phonetic (è sounds a bit like wǒ).

我吃饭呢。

And what about 呢 ne?

As we learned in Chapter 1, 呢 **ne** is a particle that converts sentences into questions, meaning *And what about ...?* However, 呢 **ne** has a few other meanings, and sometimes it is not a question at all. For example, 呢 **ne** can mean *at this moment, right now*:

你做什么呢？ **nǐ zuò shénme ne?**

You do what right now? (What are you doing right now?)

我吃饭呢 **wǒ chī fàn ne**

I eat right now (I'm eating right now)

Usually in English we translate it with the present continuous tense: **I am reading, drinking beer**, etc. 呢 **ne** indicates that the action is happening right now.

The question, 你做什么呢？ **nǐ zuò shénme ne?** could still be translated *And what about you, what are you doing?* The meaning depends on the context:

你吃什么呢？ **nǐ chī shénme ne?**

You eat what right now? (What are you eating?)

我吃草。你吃什么呢？ **wǒ chī cǎo. Nǐ chī shénme ne?**

I eat grass. You eat what [and what about]?
(I'm eating grass, and what about you, what are you eating?)

What? 什么 Shénme?

什么 **shénme** *what* is a question word. We saw it in 你叫什么名字 **nǐ jiào shénme míngzi** *You [are] called [by] what name*. For the answer, we do not change the word order; we just replace 什么 **shénme** with the answer:

    她做什么？**tā zuò shénme?**   →   她吃饭. **tā chī fàn.**
    question   answer
    She does what?   →   *She eats.*

Or more specific:

    她做什么？**tā zuò shénme?**   →   她做饭 **tā zuò fàn.**
    She does/makes what?   →   *She makes cooked rice.*
                                                      = *She is preparing a meal.*

做 **zuò** can mean *to do* and *to make*; 做饭 **zuò fàn** *to make food* means *to cook*.

In English, we should say *what does she do/make?* because we use a different word order when we ask questions and when we answer them (the question word will go to the front and we need to use the auxiliary verb *to do*), but in Chinese the question has exactly the same structure as the answer (we don't add more words and the word order remains intact):

    你吃什么？**nǐ chī shénme?**   →   我吃草 **wǒ chī cǎo.**
    You eat what?   →   *I eat grass.*
    (What do you eat?)

    他看什么？**nǐ kàn shénme?**   →   我看书 **wǒ kàn shū.**
    You read what?   →   *I read [a] book.*
    (What do you read?)

    你看什么书？**nǐ kàn shénme shū?** → 我看好书 **wǒ kàn hǎo shū**
    You read what book?   →   *I read [a] good book.*
    (What book do you read?)

The question has exactly the same structure as the answer: we put 什么 **shénme** at the place where we would expect the word we are asking for in the answer.

他看什么书？

Plural, or the lack thereof

In general, Chinese has no plural. Whenever we see a Chinese noun (a word indicating a person, an animal, or an object), it can be both singular and plural, e.g. 人 **rén** *person* or *people*; 学生 **xuésheng** *student* or *students*. The specific number is usually clear from the context e.g.

    我是学生 **wǒ shì xuésheng**

    I am a student (it is clear that I am only one student).

    我们是学生 **wǒmen shì xuésheng**

    We are students (it is clear that we are more than one student).

We use the suffix* - 们 **men** to form personal pronouns in the plural:

    我 **wǒ** + 们 **men** → 我们 **wǒmen** *we*
    你们 **nǐmen** *you all*
    他们 **tāmen** *they*
    她们 **tāmen** *"female they"* (only for a 100% female group)

(Note: the pronunciation is exactly the same for **tā**, but the characters differ. We use 他 **tā** for men, 她 **tā** for women and 它 **tā** (822) for animals and objects.)

* A **suffix** is a syllable we put at the end of a word to change the meaning. For example -*ing* in English is a suffix. It changes the verb *to mean* into the noun *meaning*.

Part 2

—Jerry也不要吃。 Jerry不吃饭，他吃草。
- **Jerry   yě   bú yào chī.   Jerry   bù   chī fàn,   tā chī cǎo.**
- Jerry   also   no want eat.   Jerry   no eat cooked rice, he eat grass.
- Jerry doesn't want to eat, either.   Jerry does not eat rice, he eats grass.

—他做什么呢？他看书吗？
- **Tā zuò shénme ne?   Tā kàn shū ma?**
- He do what and [what about]? He read book [question]?
- And what is he doing?   Is he reading?

—他不看书！老师，你看！Jerry喝啤酒呢！
- **Tā bú kàn shū!   Lǎoshī,   nǐ kàn!   Jerry   hē píjiǔ ne!**
- He no read book!   Teacher,   you look!   Jerry   drink beer [right] now!
- He isn't reading!   Teacher, look!   Jerry is drinking beer!

—没有问题！来，我们上课吧！
- **Méi yǒu wèntí!   Lái,   wǒmen shàng kè ba!**
- No have question!   Come,   we   go [to] class [suggestion]!
- No problem!   Come, let's start class!

也　**yě** 206
also, too, either

草　**cǎo** 207
grass

The top part 艹 is a short form of the radical 艸 cǎo "grass." Every time we see this radical, we can assume that the character is some sort of a plant. 早 zǎo ("early," "morning") on the bottom is for the pronunciation (cǎo → zǎo).

看　**kàn** 208
to watch, to look at, to read, to visit (to see somebody)

Upper part: "hand" 手 shǒu, lower part: 目 mù "eye" → we take our eye in our hand to take a closer look at things.

也 yě

也 **yě** means *also*, *too* or *either*. Remember to always put it in front of a verb:

我也是马 **wǒ yě shì mǎ**
I also am horse (I am a horse, too)

他也不是人 **tā yě bú shì rén**
He also not is person (He is not a person, either)

你也吃饭吗？**nǐ yě chī fàn ma?**
You also eat rice [question] (Are you eating, too?)

As you can see, in English we can put *too* or *also* in different places in the sentence. In Chinese, the position of 也 **yě** (or any other adverb) is fixed!

---

* An adverb is a word modifying the verb, describing how the action is performed

書
书

shū 209
book

The 聿 element in the traditional form 書 represents a pen, whereas the simplified form 书 looks more like a stack of books.

看書
看书

kàn shū
to read, to study

to read silently + books = to read

喝

hē 210
to drink

口 kǒu "mouth" on the left - we need it for drinking!

啤

pí 211
beer

Imitates the sound of the English word "beer." 口 kǒu "mouth" radical, 卑 bēi for pronunciation.

酒

jiǔ 212
wine, alcoholic beverage

Ancient character that means any kind of alcoholic beverage. 氵 is a short form of the beautiful radical 水 shuǐ "water" (氵 = three drops of water). 酉 yǒu is an ancient vessel for holding wine. For different kinds of wine, we just put the "kind" in front of 酒.

啤酒

píjiǔ
beer

"beer" + "wine" = beer (Western style); the syllable pí alone can have many different meanings, so we use píjiǔ when we talk about beer, not pí alone.

沒
没

méi 213
there is not

有

yǒu 214
to have; there is

題
题

tí 215
subject, topic

問題
问题

wèntí 111, 215
question, problem

"to ask" + "topic" = question

沒有問題
没有问题

méi yǒu wèntí
no problem

有 yǒu "to have" is always optional after 沒 méi, which by itself means "not have;" see grammar explanations.

來
来

lái 216
to come, to arrive; *often used to invite somebody to do something: "let's"*

們
们

men 133
suffix used after a personal pronoun to indicate plural

亻 rén "man" radical, because 们 is a pronoun; 門 mén is for pronunciation.

我們
我们

wǒmen
we, us

上

shàng 217
on; to be on top; to get onto; to come on top; to mount; to climb; to ascend

課
课

kè 218
lesson, class

上課
上课

shàng kè
to go to/be in class, start/have class

吧

ba 219
Particle expressing a wish, a suggestion, or a guess

Like other particles, it has the 口 kǒu "mouth" radical; 巴 bā is for pronunciation.

Eating cooked rice by default: verbs

In English, it is enough to say *I eat* or *I like to eat*, but in Chinese we usually need to specify what we eat. The word 吃 **chī** *eat* on its own does not really mean anything. In Chinese, every verb has a default object. For example, the default object of 吃 **chī** is 饭 **fàn** *cooked rice*. 吃饭 **chī fàn** *eat cooked rice* actually means *to eat* in general (technically, we see a verb with a specific object, but we do not translate the object). So, when I say 我吃饭 **wǒ chī fàn**, it literally means *I eat cooked rice*, but in fact it simply means *I eat*.

We can see another example in this chapter: 看书 **kàn shū**. Literally, it means *to read books*, but actually it means *to read*, or, by extension, *to study*. 书 **shū** *books; written documents* is the default object of 看 **kàn**.

Of course, we can eat or watch other things. Then, we change the object:
  我吃草 **wǒ chī cǎo** *I eat grass*
  你吃人 **nǐ chī rén** *You eat people*
  他看Jerry **tā kàn Jerry** *He is watching Jerry*

The mandatory object often helps us determine the meaning of the main verb. 看 **kàn** has many meanings (*to read (silently)*, *to watch*, *to look at*, *to visit*) and it is the object that helps us determine which one we want to pick.

If we want to ask a question, we put the question word in place of the object:
  你吃什么 **nǐ chī shénme** *You eat what?* (*What are you eating?*)
  他看谁? **tā kàn shéi** *He sees who?* (*Whom is he watching/visiting?*)

上 **shàng** and 来 **lái** are verbs of motion (they indicate a movement), which do not need default objects; the destination is usually clear from the context.

上 **shàng** is a very important and a very special word. It means *to be on top* or *to climb on top* of something. 上课 **shàng kè** literally means *to go onto the class/lesson*. We can translate it *to start class, to go to class, to have class,* or *to be in class*, depending on what we want to emphasize.
We will learn many more ways of using 上 **shàng** later (chapter 11).

来 **lái** is another special verb. It means *to come*, but we can often use it as an invitation or to express an urgent wish:
  来，我们吃饭吧！ **lái, wǒmen chī fàn ba**
  Come, we eat [suggestion] (*Come on, let's eat!*)

---

*A **verb** is an action—something we do, and an **object** is the thing upon which we act, e.g. *I eat "something,"* e.g. "rice."

Other uses of 好 hǎo

好 **hǎo** can mean different things depending on where we put it in the sentence. If we put it in front of a verb, it means that the action is good or easy to do, and the two characters (好 **hǎo** and the verb) together become an adjective:

好吃 **hǎo chī** → *good to eat* → *tasty*
好看 **hǎo kàn** → *good to look at / good to watch / good to read*
→ *good-looking, handsome, interesting* (about a book or a movie)
好学 **hǎo xué** → *good to study* → *easy (to learn)*

If we want to say something is not tasty/good-looking/easy to learn, we just add 不 **bù**: 不 + 好吃／好看／好学.

不好吃 **bù hǎo chī** *not tasty*
不好看 **bù hǎo kàn** *not good looking*
不好学 **bù hǎo xué** *not easy to learn*

Let's 吧 ba!

Like 吗 **ma** and 呢 **ne**, 吧 **ba** always appears at the end of the sentence. It is an extremely useful particle that indicates some sort of suggestion, possibility, wish, light command, guess, etc. It may be a question or a statement, e.g.

Suggestion, wish or light command:

我们上课吧 **wǒmen shàng kè ba**
We go to class [suggestion] (Let's start class!)

你吃吧 **nǐ chī ba** *You eat [suggestion] (Please, eat!)*

In commands, we can use verbs without objects. When we see a "bare" (object-less) verb, it usually is a command, e.g. 吃 **chī** *Eat!* We can use the object, also, the command may sound rude without it.

Possibility or guess (question form):

他是老师吧 **tā shì lǎoshī ba**
He is a teacher [suggestion/guess]
(He must be a teacher? / I guess he is a teacher?)

她是老师吧

他不是人吧 **tā bù shì rén ba**
He not is a person [suggestion/guess]
(I guess he is not a human being? / He may not be a human?)

你是齐老师吧 **nǐ shì Qí lǎoshī ba**
You are Qi Teacher [suggestion/guess]
(You must be teacher Qi? / I guess you are teacher Qi?)

要不要 yào bú yào *want no want?*

We can create questions by putting 吗 **ma** at the end of the sentence. But we can also skip 吗 **ma** and ask questions by alternating the verb with the negation 不 **bù**:

我是学生 **wǒ shì xuésheng** *I am a student*
→ 你是不是学生 **nǐ shì bú shì xuésheng**

Literally: *You are not are a student?* (Are you (or are you not) a student?)
[instead of 你是学生吗? **nǐ shì xuésheng ma** *You are a student [question]?*]

If we have a verb with an object, we can repeat the whole thing:

我吃饭 **wǒ chī fàn** *I eat (rice)*
→ 你吃饭不吃饭？ **nǐ chī fàn bù chī fàn**

Literally: *You eat rice not eat rice?* (Are you eating?)
[instead of 你吃饭吗？ **nǐ chī fàn ma** *You eat rice [question]?*

But it is easier to skip the object and repeat the verb alone:

你吃不吃饭？ **nǐ chī bù chī fàn** *you eat not eat rice?*

We can alternate any verb in the same way. Whether we use 吗 **ma** or alternate the verb, the meaning of the sentence is the same.

要不要 **yào bú yào** is an extremely useful phrase. It means *do you want to?*, but also *will you?* or *are you going to?*, or less formally *do you feel like?*

We can also ask 要吗？ **yào ma?** *wanna ...?*
To answer *no*, we simply say 不要 **bú yào**, which is the most common way to say *no* to anything in Chinese.
The verb 要 **yào** is one of the most versatile Chinese verbs, and it means *to want*, but also *to need, to have to (do something), must*, and also *to be going to / to intend to (do something)*. We will learn more about it in chapter 11.

没有问题 méi yǒu wèntí No problem

有 **yǒu** means *to have*; it also means *there is/are*.

> 我有马 **wǒ yǒu mǎ** *I have horses.*

> 我们大学有马 **wǒmen dàxué yǒu mǎ**
> Literally: *Our university has horses. (There are horses at our university.)*

没有 **méi yǒu** means *to not have*. 没 **méi** is the negation for the verb *to have*. It is absolutely illegal to say ~~不有~~ **bù yǒu**.

We can use 吗 **ma** to ask questions with 有 **yǒu** *to have*. We can also alternate 有 **yǒu** using the negation with 没 **méi**:

> 有没有问题? **yǒu méi yǒu wèntí?**
> Literally: *Have not have questions? (Are there any questions?)*

instead of:

> 有问题吗? **yǒu wèntí ma** *Have questions [question]?*

The expression 有(没有) **yǒu méi yǒu** *have not have* (*Is there …? Do you have …?*) is extremely common in Chinese. 没有 **méi yǒu** simply means *there is not*, so we will use it all the time. Imagine you come to a store:

> 有没有啤酒? **yǒu méi yǒu píjiǔ?**
> *Have no have beer? (Is there beer?)*
> 没有 **méi yǒu** *No have. (There isn't.)*

Since the only function of 没 **méi** is to negate the verb 有 **yǒu**, we can even skip 有 **yǒu** to say *there is not*; 没 **méi** is enough to express *there is no …* E.g. we don't need to say: 没有问题 **méi yǒu wèntí** *not have questions*; it is much more common to say 没问题 **méi wèntí** *no questions*, just as in English, when we say *(there is) no problem*.

Fortune cookie:

酱油 jiàngyóu soy sauce

1. Read the following tongue twister to practice pinyin and your tones.

吃葡萄不吐葡萄皮

chī pútao bù tǔ pútao pí

不吃葡萄倒吐葡萄皮

bù chī pútao dào tǔ pútao pí

"Eat grapes [but do] not spit out the grape skin,
[Do] not eat [the] grapes but spit out the grape skin."

2. Convert the following pinyin phrases into Chinese characters.
a) wǒ chī fàn ne
b) méi wèntí
c) nǐ bù chī ma?
d) tā bú kàn shū
e) wǒmen shàng kè
f) wǒ yào wèn wèntí

3. Convert the following Chinese phrases into pinyin.
a) 我不吃，我不饿。
b) 我问你。
c) 人不是马，马也不是人。
d) 他不看书。
e) Jerry喝啤酒。
f) 我要吃猫

4. Fill in the blank.

a) 他看___呢 (He is now reading a book)

b) 她___啤酒！(She drinks beer)

c) 我们___饭！ (We have a meal)

d) 你有___吗？ (Do you have a question?)

e) 你们要 ___ 她吗？ (Do you all want to see her?)

5. Write one sentence about what the persons on the image are doing.

Example:

Jerry吃草呢。

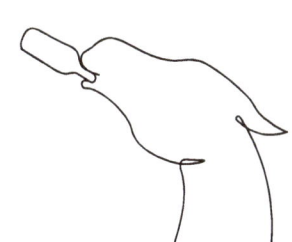
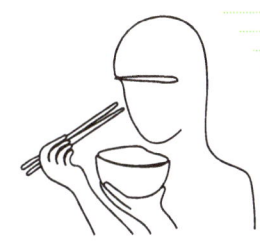

_____   _____   _____

6. These phrases below are incorrect; please write them in proper Chinese:
a) 我吃饭也
b) 老师王喝啤酒呢
c) 我不学生
d) 他是谁吗
e) 我贵姓齐
f) 谁是她？
g) 他们要不要来吗？

7. Questions from the text: answer the following questions in Chinese.
a) Jerry喝啤酒吗？
b) 齐老师饿吗？
c) 王小猫吃不吃草？
d) Jerry是不是马？
e) 王小猫做什么呢？
f) Jerry做什么呢？
g) Jerry 要不要吃饭？
h) 老师有没有问题？

8. Put words in the right order:
a) 吃不吃 / 老师 / 呢/饭 / 王？
b) 什么 / 你 / 做 / 呢
c) 也 / 小猫 / 草 / 齐 / 吃
d) 人 / 是 / 也 / 我 / 不
e) 吃 / 饭 / 什么 / 你
f) 啤酒 / 也 / 喝 / 我们 / 呢
g) 要 / 喝/你们/不要 / 啤酒

学不学中文?
To study or not to study Chinese?

Part 1

早上， 齐老师， 王小猫和 Jerry 都来上课。
Zǎoshang, Qí lǎoshī, Wáng Xiǎomāo hé Jerry dōu lái shàng kè.
Morning, Qi Teacher, Wang Little Cat and Jerry all come attend class.
In the morning, teacher Qi, Wang Xiaomao, and Jerry come to class.

齐老师： 王小猫，你好吗？
Qí lǎoshī: Wáng Xiǎomāo, nǐ hǎo ma?
Qi Teacher: Wang Little Cat, you good [question]?
Teacher Qi: Wang Xiaomao, how are you?

王小猫：我很好， 谢谢！ 老师好吗？
Wáng Xiǎomāo: Wǒ hěn hǎo, xiè xie! Lǎoshī hǎo ma?
Wang Little Cat: I very good, thank you! Teacher good [question]?
Wang Xiaomao: I am fine, thank you. How are you, teacher?

— 马马虎虎。我很忙， 也很老。
— **Mǎmǎ hūhū. Wǒ hěn máng, yě hěn lǎo.**
— Horse horse tiger tiger. I very busy, also very old.
— So so. I am busy and old.

王小猫，你忙不忙？
Wáng Xiǎomāo, nǐ máng bù máng?
Wang Little Cat, you busy no busy?
Wang Xiaomao, are you busy?

早 **zǎo** 301
early; morning

the sun 日 rì rising on top

早上 **zǎoshàng** 217
morning; in the morning

上 is a postposition (unlike a preposition, it comes after a noun) and means "on," so we use 早上 to say something is happening "in the morning," but it can also just mean "morning." For "good morning," we say "早上好！" or "(你)早！"

和 **hé** 302
and, with

Radical 禾 hé is a blade of rice with the grain on it; 和 means "harmony," but because of the pronunciation (hé) this character was "borrowed" to spell the conjunction "and," which is also pronounced hé.

都 **dōu** 303
all

The radical 阝 yì is a short version of 邑 and it means "city;" 都 is originally pronounced dū and it means "capital city;" the character, because of similar pronunciation, was borrowed to represent dōu.

38

hěn 304
very

Radical 彳 is known as "double standing man," because it is similar to 亻 "a standing man," but in fact it means "to take many small steps;" 艮 gěn is for pronunciation (gěn → hěn).

謝
谢 **xiè** 305
to thank

讠 yán (言) "speech" radical: an obvious choice, we need words to say *thanks*; 射 shè "to shoot" for pronunciation (shè → xiè).

謝謝
谢谢 **xièxie**
thanks

 hǔ 306
tiger

虎 means "tiger," but hǔ can mean many things, e.g. "amber;" therefore, to say "tiger" and avoid confusion, we must say 老虎 lǎohǔ "old tiger." 老 in this case is an expression of respect, like in 老师 lǎoshī.

馬馬
虎虎
马马
虎虎 **mǎ mǎ hū hū**
so-so; fifty-fifty; mediocre; average

"horse horse tiger tiger;" note that 虎 hǔ changes the tone here and is pronounced hū.

忙 **máng** 307
busy

忄 is a short form of 心 xīn "heart," a radical often used to express emotions and states of mind; "busy" is a stressful condition that affects peoples' hearts; 亡 wáng "to die" is for pronunciation (wáng → máng).

你忙不忙？

—我不忙，也不老。
- **Wǒ bù máng, yě bù lǎo.**
- I no busy, also no old.
- I am not busy and I am not old.

老师，你为什么忙呢？
Lǎoshī, nǐ wèishénme máng ne?
Teacher, you why busy [and what about]?
Teacher, why are you busy?

—因为我学马的心理和爱好。
- **Yīnwèi wǒ xué mǎ de xīnlǐ hé àihào.**
- Because I study horse's psychology and hobbies.
- Because I study the psychology and hobbies of horses.

為 为 為什麼 为什么
wèi 308
for the sake of; to do; to act; to be

wèi shénme 127, 128
why? *Literally: for the sake of what?*

因 因為 因为
yīn 309
cause; reason

yīnwèi
because

"the reason" + "for the sake of which" = because

的
de 310
possessive particle; of/'s

白 bái on the left means "white;" 的 originally pronounced dì means "clear" and "white;" the character was borrowed because of the sound to express possession or belonging (see grammar explanations)

心
xīn 311
heart; mind

One of the most beautiful and memorable characters, which looks almost like a beating heart. It is very common and we have just seen it in 忙 máng "busy".

理
lǐ 312
reason; logic; cause; truth; right; law; principles; texture

心理
xīnlǐ
psychology

"heart/mind" + "inner ruling principles" = "the true structure of the mind"

愛 爱
ài 313
to love

It's unclear what has been accomplished by simplifying this character. The traditional form contains the "heart" 心 xīn grasped from both sides by claws (爪 and 夂); the simplified form contains nothing and it isn't even much simpler. Maybe 友 yǒu "friend" suggests a meaning close to "love"?

好
hào 103
to like; to be fond of

Note that this familiar character is pronounced here in the 4th tone (hào) instead of the usual hǎo; together with the tone, the meaning changes also, and 好 hào now is a verb.

愛好 爱好
àihào
hobby; interest; love

"to love" + "to like" = "things to love and like"

More ways *to be*: why we need *very* 很 hěn

You might not be aware of it, but in English we use the verb *to be* in two ways:
- to indicate what things or who people are, e.g. *I am a teacher*
- to describe what things or people are like, e.g. *I am old*.

In English, in both cases we use *to be*, but in Chinese we distinguish between these situations. In the first case, we use 是 **shì**, which we also translate as *to be*:

> 我是老师 **wǒ shì lǎoshī** *I am a teacher*.

But in the second case, we just use an adjective – it is not necessary to have a verb *to be* in such cases in Chinese:

> 我老 **wǒ lǎo** literally: *I old (I am old)*

This adjective in a Chinese sentence acts as a verb *to be old*. This function of an adjective is called a ***predicative*** and it exists also in English, but in English we still use the verb *to be*.

In such sentences in Chinese, we don't use 是 **shì**; we will typically use 很 **hěn** in front of the adjective in order to give it more emphasis. 很 **hěn** normally means *very*, but in this kind of sentence it is not quite as strong. For example, when someone says: 我很老 **wǒ hěn lǎo**, it just means *I'm old*, not necessarily *I'm very old*. Without 很 **hěn**, the sentence is still correct, but it seems incomplete and may sound a bit confusing.

We don't need to worry about how to translate 很 **hěn**, but we must remember to never use 是 **shì** in sentences where we describe something or someone.

So, when we want to say *Jerry is beautiful*, we will say Jerry 很美 **Jerry hěn měi**, because we are describing him; but to say *Jerry is a beautiful horse*, we will say Jerry 是美马 **Jerry shì měi mǎ**, because we are saying who he is.

We don't use 很 **hěn** in questions:

> Jerry 美吗? **Jerry měi ma?**
> *Jerry beautiful [question]? Is Jerry beautiful?*

Same in negations: no 很 **hěn**, we just put 不 **bù** in front of the adjective:

> 王小猫不美 **Wáng Xiǎomāo bù měi** *Wang Xiaomao [is] not beautiful*.

Alternating questions

As we saw in the previous chapters,, instead of using 吗 **ma** to ask questions we can use 不 **bù** and alternate:

你好 **nǐ hǎo** *You well (You are well)*
→ 你好不好？ **nǐ hǎo bù hǎo?**
You well not well? (Are you (or are you not) well?)
(instead of 你好吗 **nǐ hǎo ma?** *You well [question]?*

We can do this with any predicatives:

王小猫美不美？ **Wáng Xiǎomāo měi bù měi?**
Wang Xiaomao beautiful not beautiful? (Is Wang Xiaomao beautiful?)

老师忙不忙？ **lǎoshī máng bù máng?**
Teacher busy not busy? (Is the teacher busy?)

How to describe stuff

Same as in English, a description in Chinese always comes before the person or object we want to describe:

好 **hǎo** *good* + 人 **rén** *person* → 好人 **hǎo rén** *good person*

我 **wǒ** *I* + 妈妈 **māma** *mom* → 我妈妈 **wǒ māma** *I mom (my mom)*

中国 **zhōngguó** *China* + 学生 **xuésheng** *student*
→ 中国学生 **zhōngguó xuésheng** *Chinese student*

Many words in Chinese are created by combining syllables according to this pattern:

小 **xiǎo** *little* + 猫 **māo** *cat* → 小猫 **xiǎo māo** *little cat, kitten*

学 **xué** *to study* + 生 **shēng** *an adept* → 学生 **xuésheng** *student*

中 **zhōng** *middle* + 国 **guó** *country* + 人 **rén** *person*
→ 中国人 **zhōngguó rén** *Chinese people*

There are no exceptions from this rule; therefore, even personal names in Chinese always come before titles. Unlike the English *Teacher Qi*, in Chinese we must say *Qi Teacher* (齐老师 **Qí lǎoshī**).

How and why to use 都 dōu

The little word 都 **dōu** means *all* or *both*, but we use it differently than in English. We must always put it before the verb:

王小猫，齐老师和 Jerry 都来上课。
Wáng Xiǎomāo, Qí lǎoshī hé Jerry dōu lái shàng kè.
Wang Xiaomao, Qi Teacher, and Jerry all come to class.
Wang Xiaomao, Teacher Qi and Jerry all come to class.

学生都吃饭 **xuésheng dōu chī fàn** *Students all eat (All students eat).*

大家都看 Jerry **dà jiā dōu kàn Jerry**
Everybody all watches Jerry (Everybody is watching Jerry)
→ in English, we don't use "all" at all.

We use 都 **dōu** much more often in Chinese than we would use *all* or *both* in English. In English, we can often skip **all** and just say *Everybody is looking at Jerry* or *People come to class*, but in Chinese it is in each case more natural to add 都 **dōu**, so we say literally *Everybody is all watching Jerry*. In Chinese, where nouns have no plural, 都 **dōu** emphasizes that the action is performed by more than one person.

In English, we can put *all* in different places, but not so in Chinese! A clear example of this is when we translate 都 **dōu** as *both*:

Jerry 和王小猫都吃草 **Jerry hé Wáng Xiǎomāo dōu chī cǎo**
Jerry and Wang Xiaomao both eat grass.

We may never translate literally and say ~~都Jerry和王小猫吃草 dōu Jerry hé Wáng Xiǎomāo chī cǎo~~.

This is extremely important. If we put 都 **dōu** in a different place, the sentence will make no sense.

> Imagine Chinese sentences like a train. In every coach only certain pieces of information can book a seat. For example, the coach before the verb is always reserved for words like 都 **dōu** (these words are called **adverbs**, we will learn more about them in chapter 8).

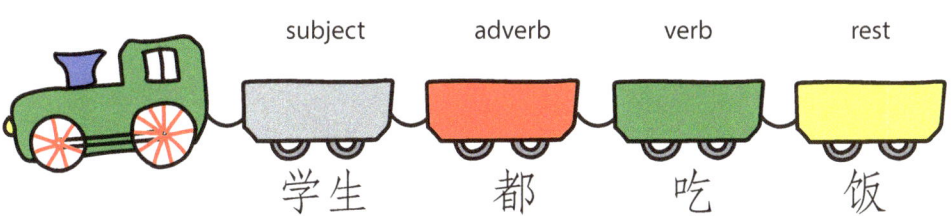

43

Four character expressions 成语 chéngyǔ

马马虎虎 **mǎ mǎ hū hū** is an example of a particular kind of Chinese expressions, which as a rule use only four characters to express an often-elaborate idea. This example literally means *horse horse tiger tiger*, which makes it neither a horse nor a tiger, but perhaps a bit of both, fifty-fifty. We often use it to express that things are going just so-so, or that something, e.g. food or a movie, is very average. Such compositions of four characters are called 成语 **chéngyǔ** *fixed phrases*. There are thousands of them, they are immensely popular, and they usually have a historical background to justify their meaning. Chinese speakers will be very pleased and impressed if you use a 成语 **chéngyǔ** in a daily conversation.

成

chéng 333 to become; to form; to fix; to establish; ready-made

语 语 成语 成语

yǔ 334 language; speech

chéngyǔ idiom; set phrase

Possession

Simply put, 的 **de** is a particle that expresses possession and can often be translated as the English *'s*. For example:

    马的爱好 **mǎ de àihào** *horses' interests*
    = *the interests that belong to horses, i.e. that horses possess;*
    → *the hobbies of horses*

    老师的马 **lǎoshī de mǎ** *teacher's horse (the horse of the teacher)*
    小猫的饭 **xiǎo māo de fàn** *little cat's food (the food of little cat)*

We will learn a lot more about 的 **de** in the chapters 4 and 11.

Part 2

齐老师：王小猫，你学什么呢？
- **Qí lǎoshī: Wáng Xiǎomāo, nǐ xué shénme ne?**
- Qi Teacher: Wang Little Cat,   you study what [and what about]?
- Teacher Qi: How about you, Wang Xiaomao, what do you study?

一我学中文。
- **Wǒ xué zhōngwén.**
-   I study Chinese language.
-   I study Chinese.

一你为什么学中文呢？你不是中国人吗？
- **Nǐ wèishénme xué zhōngwén ne?   Nǐ bú shì Zhōngguó rén ma?**
- You why study Chinese language [and what about]? You no are China person [question]?
- And why do you study Chinese?   Are you not Chinese?

一不是。我爸爸妈妈是中国人。
- **Bú shì.   Wǒ bàba   māma shì Zhōngguórén.**
-   No am.   I   dad   mom   are China people.
-   I am not.   My parents are Chinese.

中　　**zhōng** 314
　　　middle; center;
　　　Chinese

A square box crossed in the middle - a representation of "the middle;" this combined with 国 guó ("state", "country") forms the word "China" 中国 zhōngguó "The Middle Kingdom," and in abbreviations 中 often stands for "China" or "Chinese."

文　　**wén** 315
　　　language; letters; script

more about this character in chapter 13.

中文　　**zhōngwén**
　　　　Chinese language

"Middle (Kingdom)" + "language" = Chinese language

 **guó** 316
country; state

Cities and states in China were surrounded by a wall (radical 口). 或 huò in the traditional form is for pronunciation (huò → guó). In the simplified version 玉 yù "jade,": something precious within the walls.

中國
中国　　**zhōngguó**
　　　　China

"middle" + "state" = China

 zhōngguórén
Chinese person;
Chinese people

"China" + "person" = Chinese person (people); remember there is no plural in Chinese!

 bà 317
father

父 fù on top means "father" (more formally) and suggests the meaning of 爸; 巴 bā is for pronunciation (bā → bà; we saw this phonetic element earlier in 吧).

 bàba
dad

Bà can mean many things so we repeat it to emphasise the meaning.

媽
妈　　**mā** 1
　　　mother

"woman" 女 nǚ for the meaning, 马 mǎ for pronunciation

媽媽
 māma
mom

— 你是哪国人?
- **Nǐ shì nǎ guó rén?**
- You are which country person?
- Which country are you from?

— 我是美国人。
- **Wǒ shì Měiguórén.**
- I am America person.
- I am American.

— 你爸爸妈妈不会说中文吗?
- **Nǐ bàba māma bú huì shuō zhōngwén ma?**
- You dad mom no can speak Chinese language [question]?
- Your parents cannot speak Chinese?

— 他们会说中文,可是我不说中文,
- **Tāmen huì shuō zhōngwén, kěshì wǒ bù shuō zhōngwén,**
- They can speak Chinese language, but I no speak Chinese language,
- They can speak Chinese, but I don't speak Chinese,

我说英文。
wǒ shuō yīngwén.
I speak English language.
I speak English.

—Jerry 会说中文, 也会说英文。
- **Jerry huì shuō zhōngwén, yě huì shuō yīngwén.**
- Jerry can speak Chinese language, also can speak English language.
- Jerry can speak Chinese and also English.

哪 **nǎ** 318
which?

 kǒu "mouth": we are dealing with a question particle; 那 is pronounced nà, but it also means "that."

美 **měi** 319
beautiful

羊 yáng "sheep" and 大 dà "big." Are big sheeps beautiful? Well, the character actually depicts a man with a sheepskin hat, which used to be a fancy headdress to have.

美國　**měiguó**
美国　America

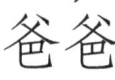

"beautiful" + "country" = America. Why? See grammar notes.

爸爸　**bàba māma**
媽媽　parents
爸爸
妈妈

As comprehensive as can be; however, note that we have to say "father" first before "mother." "妈妈爸爸" māma bàba does not exist. If we want to insist, we need to use 和 hé: 妈妈和爸爸 māma hé bàba "mom and dad."

會　**huì** 320
会　to know how; can

See grammar explanation.

說
说
shuō 321
to speak

讠 yán (言) "speech" radical. 兑 duì is for pronunciation, because 说 is also pronounced shuì.

可
可是
kě 322
but; however

kěshì 322, 107
but; however

可 kě on its own has many meanings and only one of them is "but;" when we combine it with 是 shì, the meaning is clear.

英
yīng 323
hero; English; flower

Meanings "hero," but also "flower", hence the 艹 cǎo "grass" radical; 央 yāng is for pronunciation (yāng → yīng). Because 英国 yīngguó means "England" (see grammar notes) 英 can can also be used as an adjective "English."

英文
yīngwén 315
English language

Family members 家人 jiā rén

In Chinese we must use more specific ways to refer to your siblings than just *brothers/sisters*, as well as to members of the paternal/maternal side of the family.

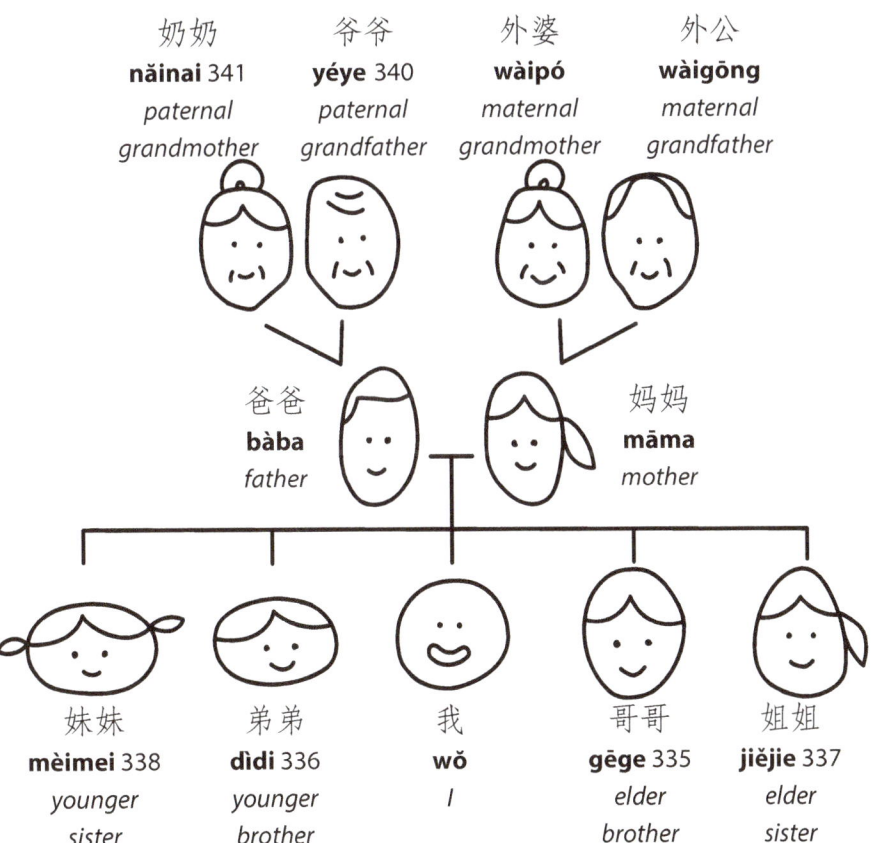

A general term for *siblings* is 兄弟姐妹 **xiōngdì jiěmèi** (339, 336, 348, 338) *elder and younger brothers, elder and younger sisters*. 兄 **xiōng** is a more formal form of 哥 **gē** *elder brother*.

For *parents*, we say 爸爸妈妈 **bàba māma** *father-mother*, with the word for *father* always coming first!

公
外公
gōng 342
lord

wàigōng 325
maternal grandfather

婆
外婆
pó 343
old woman; husband's mother

wàipó
maternal grandmother

47

Nationalities and languages

Following the rule about describing things, we can see how the names of countries, nationalities, and languages are formed.

国（國） **guó** means *kingdom* or *country*. Although not used for all of them, 国 **guó** is included in the names of many countries. We can just describe what kind of country we mean by putting the description in front of 国 **guó**:

  中国 **zhōngguó** *China*
  英国 **yīngguó** *England*
  美国 **měiguó** *United States*

These names literally mean *middle country*, *hero country*, and *beautiful country*, respectively. If we add 法国 **fǎguó** (344) *country of law* (France) and 德国 **déguó** (345) *country of virtue* (Germany) to this list, we may start wondering what the heck is going on, but actually, these names are just abbreviations: 英国 **yīngguó** is short of 英格兰 **yīnggélán**, 美国 **měiguó** of 亚美利加 **yàměilìjiā** (*America*), 法国 **fǎguó** of 法兰西 **fǎlánxī** (*France*) and 德国 **déguó** of 德意志 **déyìzhì** (*Deutsch ~ German*)!

As we can see, names of foreign countries in Chinese are basically made up and mimic the sounds of the original languages. Only some countries neighboring China and with whom China was historically involved have "native" Chinese names, e.g. 日本 **rìběn** (346, 347) *Japan* → *the sun* + *origin* → *country where the sun is born* → *Country of the Rising Sun* (Japan is located to the East of China).

The same attributive rule applies to nationalities. We describe the *person* 人 **rén** by using the name of the country she comes from:

  中国人 **zhōngguórén**: *China + person → Chinese (person)*
  美国人 **měiguórén**: *America + person → American (person)*
  英国人 **yīngguórén**: *England + person → English (person)*
  日本人 **rìběnrén**: *Japan + person → Japanese (person)*

Similarly with the names of languages. 文 **wén** means *language*, so instead of 国 **guó** or 人 **rén** we must describe 文 **wén**:

  中文 **zhōngwén** *Chinese (language)*
  英文 **yīngwén** *English (language)*
  日文 **rìwén** *Japanese (language)*

Before the Qín Dynasty (221-207 BCE), the territory occupied by today's China was divided into many little states (*kingdoms*); those located in the Central Plains along the Yellow River were the center of Chinese civilization, and they were called *central plains*; therefore, the term 中国 **Zhōngguó** *Middle Kingdom* has nothing to do with the idea that China is the center of the world.

Please note that in English, *Chinese* or *English* can refer both to people and language, e.g. *I am Chinese, but I speak English*; in Chinese, we always need to specify whether we mean a person or a language by using 人 **rén** or 文 **wén** after the attributive, respectively.

If we want to ask where someone comes from, we use the question word 哪 **nǎ** *which*:

你是哪国人？ **nǐ shì nǎ guó rén?** literally *you are which country person?*

外国人 **wàiguó rén** is the standard way to say *foreigner*. 外 **wài** means *outside* or *outer*; 国 **guó** *country*; 人 **rén** *person*. It can be roughly translated as *foreign country person*. On the other hand, 老外 **lǎowài** is a slang way to say *foreigner*. But don't worry, Chinese speakers insist it is not offensive. You will learn more about 老外 **lǎowài** in chapter 5.

豆 **dòu** 331
beans

腐 **fǔ** 332
rotten; corrupt; spoiled

豆腐 **dòufu**
bean curd; tofu

To know how

会 **huì** expresses the ability to do something:

我会说中文 **wǒ huì shuō zhōngwén** *I can speak Chinese*

王小猫不会做饭 **Wáng Xiǎomāo bú huì zuò fàn**
Wang Xiaomao no can make food (Wang Xiaomao can't cook)

你会骑马吗？ **nǐ huì qí mǎ ma?**
You can ride horses [question]? (Can you ride horses?)

你会不会看中文书？ **nǐ huì bú huì kàn zhōngwén shū?**
You can no can read Chinese language books?
(Can you read books in Chinese?)

Fortune cookie:

豆腐 **dòufu**
tofu

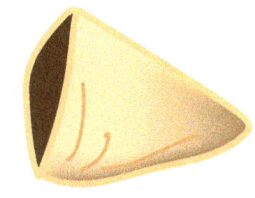

Part 3

—Jerry 很酷！他学什么？
- **Jerry hěn kù! Tā xué shénme?**
- Jerry very cool! He study what?
- Jerry is cool! What does he study?

—Jerry 学人的爱好。
- **Jerry xué rén de àihào.**
- Jerry study people's hobbies.
- Jerry studies the hobbies of people.

—老师，你爸爸妈妈也是中国人吗？
- **Lǎoshī, nǐ bàba māma yě shì Zhōngguórén ma?**
- Teacher, you dad mom also are China people [question]?
- Teacher, are your parents Chinese, too?

—不是。我爸爸妈妈是外国人。
- **Bú shì. Wǒ bàba māma shì wàiguórén.**
- No are. I dad mom are outside country people.
- No. My parents are foreigners.

我也是"老外"。
Wǒ yě shì "lǎowài."
I also am "old out."
I am an "outsider," also.

—可是你是中文老师！
- **Kěshì nǐ shì zhōngwén lǎoshī!**
- But you are Chinese language teacher!
- But you are a Chinese teacher!

—下课！
- **Xià kè!**
- Off class!
- The class is off!

酷 **kù** 324
cool

酉 yǒu is a wine vessel (remember 酒 jiǔ "wine"?); 告 gào is for pronunciation (gào → kù); 酷 originally means "strong and stimulating," like an intoxicating and fragrant substance; but Chinese kù also sounds similar to English "cool," and that's how we get today's meaning.

外 **wài** 325
outside; foreign

外國
外国 **wàiguó**
325, 316
foreign country

"outside" + "country" = foreign country

外國
人
外国
人 **wàiguórén**
325, 316, 122
foreigner

"outside" + "country" + "person" = foreigner

老外 **lǎowài** 108. 325
foreigner; outsider

"old" + "out" = outsider; 老 lǎo has a double function here, it also expresses respect; this term for foreigner is casual and slightly derogatory; see grammar notes.

— 真的吗? 为什么?
— **Zhēn de ma?　Wèishénme?**
— Really [question]? Why?
— Really?　　　　Why?

— 算了! Jerry，我们去喝啤酒吧!
— **Suàn le!　Jerry,　wǒmen qù hē píjiǔ ba!**
— Count [complete]! Jerry, we go drink beer [suggestion]!
— Forget it.　　Jerry, let's go get some beer!

Connecting words in a sentence

One of the most common meanings of 和 **hé** is *and*, but we can only use it to connect people or things, e.g. Jerry 和我 **Jerry hé wǒ** *Jerry and I*. If we want to connect actions, e.g. *I eat and read*, or descriptions, e.g. *I am old and ugly*, we cannot use 和 **hé**, we must use 也 **yě** *also*:

我不美，（我）也很老 **wǒ bù měi, (wǒ) yě hěn lǎo**
I not beautiful, (I) also very old
(I am ugly and [also] old)

In Chinese, when we say *not beautiful*, very often it actually means *ugly*; similarly, *not good → bad; not small → big* etc.)

我吃饭，也喝啤酒 **wǒ chī fàn, yě hē píjiǔ**
I eat rice, also drink beer. (I eat and [also] drink beer.)

Usually, we can just list the things we do without any connecting words, so the list of different things we do becomes one action:

早上，Jerry和我都做饭，看书，说中文
zǎoshàng, Jerry hé wǒ dōu zuò fàn, kàn shū, shuō zhōngwén
Morning on, Jerry and I both make rice, read books, speak Chinese.
(In the morning, both Jerry and I cook, read, [and] speak Chinese.)

下　**xià** 326
down; under; to go down; to descend; to get off

下 is the opposite of 上 **shàng**; we can see the little element is under (下) and not over (上) the horizontal line.

下课　**xià kè** 326, 218
to get off class; to finish class

真　**zhēn** 327
real; true

真的　**zhēnde** 327, 310
really

"real" + "'s" = "real's [kind]" → "something real" → "really"

算　**suàn** 328
to count; to calculate

⺮ (竹) zhú "bamboo" radical; the accounts used to be made with the help of bamboo strips

了　**le** 329
aspect particle indicating the action has been completed

for more information about 了 le see chapter 7

算了　**suàn le**
nevermind; forget it!

"the accounts have been completed"

去　**qù** 330
to go

51

1. Read the tongue twister below out loud.

Xiǎojiě xiǎojiě, bié shēng qì,   Miss miss don't be pissed
míngtiān dài nǐ qù kàn xì.   Tomorrow [I] take you [to] watch [a] play
Wǒ zuò yǐzi, nǐ zuò dì;   I sit [on the] chair, you sit [on the] floor
wǒ chī xiāngjiāo, nǐ chī pí.   I eat [the] banana, you eat [the] peel.

2. Nations: Where are these persons from?

3. Translation from English to Chinese:
a) Forget it! My older brother wants to eat grass!
b) My father, mother and I all study Chinese.
c) I can speak Chinese and I can also speak Japanese.
d) Why do you not drink beer?
e) Cooking is my hobby.

4. Convert the following pinyin phrases into Chinese characters.

a) wǒ bù chī cǎo
b) wǒ bàba māma shì zhōngguó rén
c) wǒ bù shuō zhōngwén, wǒ shuō yīngwén
d) nǐ xué shénme
e) nǐ māma máng ma?
f) wǒ ài zuò fàn

5. Convert the following Chinese phrases into pinyin.
a) 你忙不忙？
b) 我很忙，他也很忙
c) 他也是老外
d) 你是英文老师
e) 你好吗？
f) 我请Jerry吃中国早饭，可是他不要吃饭，他要吃草。

6. Translate the following Chinese phrases into English.
a) 马马虎虎
b) 我是老外
c) 你是中文老师
d) 我学猫的心理
e) 老虎不吃猫，老虎吃人
f) 中文字不好学

7. Where to put 都?
a) __我们__很忙 (We're all busy)
b) __他们__是__老外 (All of them are foreigners)
c) __妈妈和爸爸__吃__豆腐 (Both mom and dad eat tofu)
d) __英文和中文__Jerry__会__说 (Jerry can speak both English and Chinese)
e) __王小猫和齐老师__不__喝啤酒 (Wang Xiaomao and teacher Qi both don't drink beer)

8. Tell us about yourself! Answer the following questions below in Chinese!
a) 你是哪国人？   e) 你爸爸妈妈是哪国人？
b) 你是学生吗？   f) 你学什么？
c) 你会说中文吗？   g) 你有什么爱好？
d) 你喝不喝啤酒？

9. Questions from the text: answer the following questions in Chinese.
a) 齐老师为什么忙？
b) 王小猫学什么？
c) 王小猫是哪国人？她是不是中国人？
d) Jerry学什么？
e) 齐老师是中国人吗？

10. Match the sentences using 可是 *but*. Find a suitable sentence on the right to connect with a sentence on the left:
a) 我的猫很酷。   她不老。
b) 我哥哥很好看。   它有心理问题。
c) 我的马不是人。   它爱喝啤酒。
d) 中文很不好学。   马不吃老虎。
e) 她是老外。   我爱学中文。
f) 老虎吃马。   爸爸妈妈都不爱他。

> Remember that we use 他 **tā** for men, 们 **tā** for women and 它 **tā** (822) for animals and objects.

11. Use 很 or 是:
a) 老虎__饿   h) 我的学生__老外
b) 老外__酷   i) 美国__大
c) 老师__外国人   j) 中国饭__好吃
d) 啤酒__贵   k) 你__忙
e) 王小猫__学生   l) 草__好看
f) 我__中国人   m) 他的中文__好
g) 我妈妈__美   n) 我__爸爸

老师不在
Teacher is not here

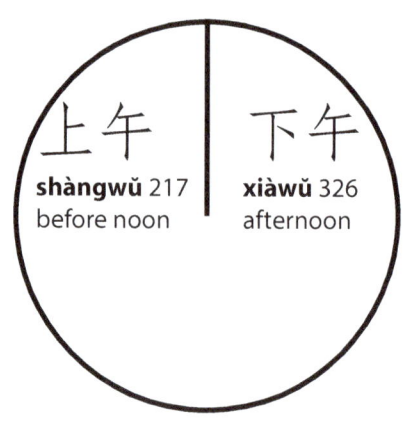

shàngwǔ 217
before noon

xiàwǔ 326
afternoon

下午新的同学来上中文课。
Xiàwǔ xīn de tóngxué lái shàng zhōngwén kè.
Afternoon new['s] classmate come attend Chinese language class.
In the afternoon, a new classmate comes to Chinese class.

他姓马。 他不认识齐老师。
Tā xìng Mǎ. Tā bú rènshi Qí lǎoshī.
He last name Ma. He no know Qi Teacher.
His last name is Ma. He does not know teacher Qi.

马先生：请问， 你姓不姓齐？
Mǎ xiānsheng: Qǐng wèn, nǐ xìng bú xìng Qí?
Ma Mister: Please ask, you last name no last name Qi?
Mr. Ma: Excuse me, is your last name Qi?

王小猫：我不姓齐， 我姓王。
Wáng Xiǎomāo: Wǒ bú xìng Qí, wǒ xìng Wáng.
Wang Little Cat: I no last name Qi, I last name Wang.
Wang Xiaomao: No, my last name is not Qi, my last name is Wang.

—你是不是老师？
— **Nǐ shì bú shì lǎoshī?**
— You are no are teacher?
— Are you a teacher?

午 **wǔ** 401
noon

下午 **xiàwǔ** 326, 401
afternoon; PM

to go down + noon = afternoon

新 **xīn** 431
new

同 **tóng** 402
same; alike; similar; to be or become the same; together with

同學
同学 **tóngxué** 402, 123
classmate

"same"/"together with" + "study"
- people that study together

—不是，我是学生。你找谁啊？
- Bú shì, wǒ shì xuésheng. Nǐ zhǎo shéi a?
- No am, I am student. You look for who a?
- No, I am a student. Who are you looking for?

—我找齐老师。他在不在？
- Wǒ zhǎo Qí lǎoshī. Tā zài bú zài?
- I look for Qi teacher. He present no present?
- I am looking for teacher Qi. Is he here?

—齐老师不在。
- Qí lǎoshī bú zài.
- Qi teacher no present.
- Teacher Qi is not here.

—哦。那是谁呢？
- O. Nà shì shéi ne?
- O. That is who [and what about]?
- Oh. And who is that?

认 **rèn** 403
认 to recognize; to admit; to accept

Originally means "to admit guilt", so "words" 讠 yán (言) are needed; the traditional form has "heart" element 心 xīn (implies sincerity), and phonetic element 刃 rèn (interesting in its own right: represents a knife 刀 dāo cutting into something 刃, so it means "a blade"). Simplified form has 人 rén for pronunciation.

識 **shí** 404
识 to know

The simplified form has 只 zhǐ for pronunciation.

認識 **rènshi**
认识 to be acquainted with; to know someone

"admit" + "to know" = to know a person; see grammar notes

先 **xiān** 405
first

先生 **xiānsheng** 126
mister; sir; master

"first" + "suffix for person"= the one who comes before me, my superior; the first one; this is an honorific title used to refer to our superiors; it originally means "master," could be used to address both men and women, and is still used today for teachers and masters of kungfu etc., but it also means "husband."

找 **zhǎo** 406
to look for

Almost the same as 我, consists of the same elements: hand 扌 shǒu and dagger 戈 gē; up to us to guess why in Chinese we look for people with a dagger in our hand …

啊 **a** 407
exclamatory particle

Like in many particles, this one also has a 口 kǒu "mouth" radical; we may need it when we want to exclaim; 阿 a is phonetic and it is usually used on its own to transcribe the Latin letter and sound "a" in Chinese.

在 **zài** 408
to be present; to be somewhere; to exist

This is the closest word Chinese has to the verb "to be."

哦 **o** 409
oh

Another particle, hence the 口 kǒu "mouth" radical. This character has no meaning, it only imitates the sound of "oh;" 我 wǒ sounds similar to "o."

那 **nà** 410
that

We saw this element in 哪 nǎ "which?"; 口 kǒu "mouth" radical turns it into a question word.

—那是我妈妈的朋友。
- **Nà shì wǒ māma de péngyou.**
- That is I mom's friend.
- That is my mom's friend.

—他很老。
- **Tā hěn lǎo.**
- He very old.
- He is old.

—他是北京大学的老师。
- **Tā shì Běijīng Dàxué de lǎoshī.**
- He is Beijing University's teacher.
- He is a teacher from Beijing University.

—是吗? 你是北京大学的学生吗?
- **Shì ma? Nǐ shì Běijīng Dàxué de xuésheng ma?**
- Is [question]? You are Beijing University's student [question]?
- Is he? Are you a Beijing University student?

—我是。可是他不是我的老师,
- **Wǒ shì. Kěshì tā bú shì wǒ de lǎoshī,**
- I am. But he no is I's teacher,
- I am. But he is not my teacher,

也不是我的朋友。
yě bú shì wǒ de péngyou.
also no is I's friend.
and he is not my friend.

突然, 齐老师骑 Jerry 来上课。
Tūrán, Qí lǎoshī qí Jerry lái shàng kè.
Suddenly, Qi teacher ride Jerry come attend class.
Suddenly, teacher Qi comes to class riding on top of Jerry.

—这是什么呢?
- **Zhè shì shénme ne?**
- This is what and [what about]?
- And what is this?

朋 **péng** 411
friend

Two moon 月 yuè radicals together represent a close relationship; the moon often symbolises friends or lovers staying apart – they look at the same moon thinking of each other.

友 **yǒu** 412
friend; companion

朋友 **péngyou**
friend

Modern Chinese likes two syllable words to avoid confusuion (too many single syllable words have the same pronunciation and mean different things); often, we put together two syllables that mean similar thing in order to emphasise the meaning, e.g. "friend" + "companion."

北 **běi** 413
North

京 **jīng** 414
capital

北京 **Běijīng**
Beijing

"Northern Capital"→ Beijing, a.k.a. Peking, built by Kublai Khan, capital of China since Yuan dynasty (1271-1368), then called 大都 dà dū "The Great Capital."

大學 **dàxué** 101, 123
university
大学

big + study = university

突然，齐老师骑 Jerry 来上课。

—这不是"什么"，这是"谁"！
- **Zhè bú shì "shénme," zhè shì "shéi"!**
- This no is "what," this is "who"!
- This is not "what," this is "who"!

这是我们大学的马。 他叫 Jerry。
Zhè shì wǒmen dàxué de mǎ. Tā jiào Jerry.
This is we university's horse. He call Jerry.
This is the horse from our university. His name is Jerry.

他是我的朋友。
Tā shì wǒ de péngyou.
He is I's friend.
He is my friend.

—他很帅！
- **Tā hěn shuài!**
- He very handsome!
- He is handsome!

突　**tū** 415
sudden; to break through

Radical 穴 xuè on top means "cave"/"hole;" the lower part 犬 quǎn means "dog," typically a really fierce one; a cur in a cave may give the idea of something sudden and the unexpected.

然　**rán** 416
so; thus; such; in such a way

突然　**tūrán**
suddenly

sudden + in such a way = suddenly

騎
骑　**qí** 2
to ride (a horse; a bike)

马 mǎ radical suggests the meaning; 奇 qí "weird" for pronunciation.

這
这　**zhè** 417
this

Radical 辶 chuò means "road." 言 yán "words" in the traditional form has been replaced with 文 wén "language" in order to reduce the number of strokes.

帥
帅　**shuài** 418
handsome; cute

Note that 帅 is only one stroke away from 师 shī "master".

57

Little great particle 的 de

The little character 的 **de** happens to be one of the most important and frequently used function particles in Chinese. One of the main functions of 的 **de** is expressing possession and the closest English equivalent is *'s*. For example, let's see how to say *Jerry's high heels* (高 **gāo** *tall* + 跟 **gēn** *heel* + 鞋 **xié** *shoe(s)*):

    Jerry 的高跟鞋 **Jerry de gāogēnxié** *Jerry's high heels*

gāo 421
tall; high

gēn 422
heel

xié 423
shoe

gāogēnxié
high heels

Do not get this confused with *of* (or with the Spanish/French *de*)! In English we can say *high heels of Jerry* in that order, but in Chinese we can only say *Jerry's high heels*: ~~高跟鞋的 Jerry~~ ~~**gāogēnxié de Jerry**~~ is incorrect! This sentence says *high heels' Jerry* (*Jerry of high heels*).

We also use 的 **de** to express that someone or something is associated with an institution or place:

    我是北京大学的老师 **Wǒ shì Běijīng dàxué de lǎoshī**
Literally: *I am Peking University's teacher. (I am a teacher at/from Peking University.)*

的 **de** can create some distance between the owner and the possession. Therefore, when we talk about our closest family members, we usually do not use 的 **de** and simply say:

    我妈妈 **wǒ māma** *I mom (my mom)*
    你爸爸 **nǐ bàba** *you dad (your dad)*
    他大姐 **tā dàjiě** *he big sister (his big sister)*

But in other cases, it is useful to remember this list:

我的	**wǒ de**	*my* (literally: *I's*)
你的	**nǐ de**	*your* (literally: *you's*)
他的	**tā de**	*his* (literally: *he's*)
她的	**tā de**	*her* (literally: *she's*)
我们的	**wǒmen de**	*our* (literally: *we's*)
你们的	**nǐmen de**	*your* (plural) (literally: *you all's*)
他们的	**tāmen de**	*their* (literally: *they's*)
她们的	**tāmen de**	*their* (female) (literally: *female they's*)

Jerry 的高跟鞋

For example:
> 我的朋友 **wǒ de péngyou** *my friend*
> 他们的马 **tāmen de mǎ** *their horse*

However sometimes we just drop 的 **de** because it is easier, quicker, and less formal, so it may be ok to say 我朋友 **wǒ péngyou** literally: *I friend*.

We also use 的 **de** in descriptions.
We can describe things in Chinese by simply putting one word in front of another, e.g. 好人 **hǎo rén** *good person*; however, this works only when the description consists of one syllable; if the description is longer, we must separate it from the object we want to describe by means of 的 **de**.

For example 很好的人 **hěn hǎo de rén** *very good person/people* we must use 的 **de**, because now our description consists of two syllables.
Similarly:
> 新学生 **xīn xuésheng** *new student*, but:
> 新来的学生 **xīn lái de xuésheng** *the new coming (new arrival) student*.

Or in any more complex description:
> 北京大学的老师 **Běijīng dàxué de lǎoshī**
> *Beijing University's teacher* (*teacher from Peking University*)

> 我妈妈的朋友 **wǒ māma de péngyou**
> *I mom's friend (my mom's friend)*

And lastly, we have seen 的 **de** in short expressions, such as 真的 **zhēn de** and 是的 **shì de**. It is best to simply learn them by heart, meaning *really* and *yes*, but if we want to look at the grammar, then what 的 **de** is doing here is turning these words into adjectives; it means something is *of the kind*: 真的 **zhēn de** *something of the real kind (something that is real)*; 是的 **shì de** *something that is so*. We can create more words like that:
> 好的 **hǎo de** *one that is good; something good; a good one; OK*
> 贵的 **guì de** *one that is expensive; the expensive one*

You will learn more about this in chapter 11.

在 zài *to be present*

Strictly speaking 在 **zài** means *to be at*, *to be in*, or *to be present*. Many learners of Chinese think of 在 **zài** as a preposition like *in* or *at*; however 在 **zài** is actually a verb. In many contexts it means *to be somewhere*, such as 我在中国 **wǒ zài Zhōngguó** *I'm [present] in China*. In this sentence, 在 **zài** does not mean *in*, but *am in*. Look at these examples:

> Jerry 在北京 **Jerry zài Běijīng** *Jerry is in Beijing*.
> Jerry 不在家 **Jerry bú zài jiā** *Jerry is not at home*.

在 **zài** really means *to be present* or *to exist*. When your Chinese teacher gives roll call he might say Jerry 在吗? **Jerry zài ma?** *Is Jerry present?* If he is present, then an appropriate response would be 在 **zài** *[he] is*.

Fortune cookie:

cíqì
porcelain

cí 419
porcelain; china

qì 420
utensil; ware

cíqì
chinaware; porcelain

Particle 啊 a

The particle 啊 **a** is quite versatile. It can be used to express enthusiasm and stronger emotions. It is very informal and it can express an aggressive, imposing or intimate manner of speaking.

> 你找谁啊? **Nǐ zhǎo shéi a?**
> *You look for who a?*
> (Yo! Who are you looking for?/Come on! Who are you looking for, eh?)

> 好吃啊! **hǎo chī a!**
> *Good eat a* (It tastes pretty good alright!/It's tasty huh!)

We can think of it as something approximating *eh*, *uh* or *huh* in English.

Using 啊 **a** is not a grammatical requirement, it's just a way of speaking – it adds some "flavor" to the sentence.

The verb 骑 qí

骑 **qí** means to mount something. When riding animals or vehicles that you mount on, we would use this verb. The most common animal that we can 骑 **qí** is a horse, hence the horse 马 **mǎ** radical in the character. But nowadays, we will more likely 骑 **qí** vehicles, such as:

自行车 **zìxíngchē** bicycle (*self + move + vehicle*)
摩托车 **mótuō chē** motorcycle (*motor + vehicle*)
滑板车 **huábǎn chē** scooter (*skate + board + vehicle*)

齐老师骑Jerry来上课 **Qí lǎoshī qí Jerry lái shàng kè**
Qi Teacher ride Jerry come to class. (Teacher Qi comes to class riding Jerry.)

我骑自行车去上课 **Wǒ qí zìxíngchē qù shàng kè**
I ride [my] bicycle to go to class.

自	**zì** 424 self; personal
行	**xíng** 425 to move
车	**chē** 426 car; vehicle
摩	**mó** 427 to rub; to scrape
托	**tuō** 428 to support by hand
滑	**huá** 429 to skate
板	**bǎn** 430 board; plank

1. Convert the following pinyin phrases into Chinese characters.
a) nǐ shì bú shì lǎoshī?
b) tā hěn lǎo
c) tā shì běijīng dàxué de lǎoshī
d) nǐ zhǎo shéi
e) nà shì shénme rén
f) tā xué shénme
g) tā hěn shuài
h) tā shì wǒ māma de péngyou

2. Convert the following Chinese phrases into pinyin, then translate into English.
a) 你找谁?
b) 齐老师不在。
c) 你为什么学中文?
d) 他骑马来上课。
e) 这是我们大学的马。
f) 他很帅!
g) 你是我妈妈的朋友吗?
h) 马和老虎不同。

3. Translation 翻译 fānyì
Translate the following English sentences to Chinese, then transcribe them into pinyin.
a) Your mom's friends are not my friends
b) Is teacher Wang here?
c) My teacher is really handsome.
d) My mother is a teacher from Beijing University
e) He is the friend of my older brother's teacher.
f) I am your teacher's mother's older brother.
g) The psychology of cats is not easy to study.
h) Humans and horses have different hobbies.

4. Fix the errors and rewrite the sentences in proper Chinese.
a) 我姐姐是美。
b) 我的妈妈看书。
c) 你是不是老师吗?
d) 都我的朋友爱我的女朋友。
e) 她是朋友的我哥哥。

5. Answer the questions from the text in Chinese.
a) 马先生找谁？
b) 王小猫妈妈的朋友是什么大学的老师？
c) 马先生是新的学生吗？
d) 齐老师骑自行车来上课吗？
e) Jerry是谁的朋友？

6. Put the words in the right order to make sentences:
a) 的 / 也 / 马 / 美 / 你 / 很 (Your horse is beautiful, too)
b) 中文 / 好 / 你 / 很 / 的 (Your Chinese is good)
c) 骑 / 谁 / 马 / 她 / 的 (Whose horse does she ride?)
d) 书 / 大学 / 中文 / 好看 / 北京 / 的 / 很 (Peking University's Chinese books are interesting)
e) 啤酒 / 中国 / 的 / 贵 / 不 (Chinese beer is not expensive)

老师来了!
Teacher has arrived!

Part 1

王小猫：老师，你来了！
Wáng Xiǎomāo: Lǎoshī, nǐ lái le!
Wang Little Cat: Teacher, you come [complete]!
Wang Xiaomao: Teacher! You have arrived!

老师：我来了、我来了！
Lǎoshī: Wǒ lái le, wǒ lái le!
Teacher: I come [complete], I come [complete]!
Teacher: I have, I have!

王小猫：马先生，你看，这就是齐老师！
Wáng Xiǎomāo: Mǎ xiānsheng, nǐ kàn, zhè jiù shì Qí lǎoshī!
Wang Little Cat: Ma Mister, you look, this just is Qi teacher!
Wang Xiaomao: Look, Mr. Ma, and here is teacher Qi!

马先生：不可思议！
Mǎ xiānsheng: Bù kě sī yì!
Ma mister: No can comprehend!
Mr. Ma: Unfathomable!

老师：什么"不可思议"？
Lǎoshī: Shénme "bù kě sī yì"?
Teacher: What "no can comprehend"?
Teacher: What "unfathomable"?

就 **jiù** 501
just; see grammar explanations

思 **sī** 502
thoughts; to think; to ponder, to cosider

"Heart" radical at the bottom; here it appears in its full form 心 xīn instead of the short form 忄. The upper part 田 tián means "field;" in early agricultural society, the fields was what had to be primarily on peoples' minds, a matter of constant thoughts and concerns.

議 议 **yì** 503
to comment; to discuss; to suggest

Speech 讠(言) yán radical on the left; 義 yì, "beautifully" simplified to 义, is the classical Chinese virtue of "righteousess" and serves here as the phonetic element.

思議 思议 **sī yì**
to consider; to comprehend; to imagine

可 **kě** 322
may; can; be able to

We've seen this character before in chapter 3, it has multiple meanings and uses.

你才不可思议！你是哪位？
Nǐ cái bù kě sī yì! Nǐ shì nǎ wèi?
You only no can comprehend! You are which [honorable] one?
You "unfathomable"! Who are you even?

马先生：对不起，对不起，
Mǎ xiānsheng: Duì bù qǐ, duì bù qǐ,
Ma mister: Sorry, sorry,
Mr. Ma: Sorry, sorry,

我是新来的同学，叫马王。
wǒ shì xīn lái de tóngxué, jiào Mǎ Wáng.
I am new-come's classmate, called Ma [Horse] King.
I am a new student, my name is Ma Wang.

不可
bù kě
not able to; cannot; unable

不可思議
不可思议
bù kě sī yì
121, 322, 502, 503
incomprehensible; unfathomable; beyond comprehension

纔/才
才
cái 504
not until; only when; *see grammar explanations*

The traditional form is almost never used anymore, even in traditional publications from Hong Kong or Taiwan; Pay attention to the simplified form: it looks almost the same as the "hand" 扌 shǒu radical; the bottom stroke in both characters goes in different directions; please see writing instructions and do not confuse!

位
wèi 505
position; rank; polite measure word for people

哪位
nǎ wèi 318, 505
Politely "who are you?"

Literally "which honorable one [are you]?"

對
对
duì 506
to face; to address; to treat; correct; often used as "yes" or "that's right"

起
qǐ 507
to rise; to get up; to stand up

對不起
对不起
duì bù qǐ
to be sorry, Literally, "I treat you not up to it" – "I fail you"

How to complete things

If we want to say that we completed an action, we put the particle 了 **le** after the verb or at the end of the sentence:

老师来 **lǎoshī lái** *the teacher comes/is coming*
→ 老师来了 **lǎoshī lái le** *Teacher come [complete]*
→ *the teacher came/has come*

我吃饭 **wǒ chī fàn** *I eat/I am eating*
→ 我吃饭了／我吃了饭 **wǒ chī fàn le/wǒ chī le fàn**
I eat rice [complete] / I eat [complete] rice → *I ate/I have eaten*

Jerry 看我 **Jerry kàn wǒ** *Jerry is looking at me*
→ Jerry 看了我／Jerry看我了 **Jerry kàn le wǒ/Jerry kàn wǒ le**
Jerry look [complete] I / Jerry look I [complete] → *Jerry looked at me*

As there are no tenses in Chinese, 了 **le** does not express the past tense, but only the completion of a particular action, so we don't use it every time we talk about past events. We can only use it with actions that we can actually complete and finish, such as eating, cooking, going somewhere or making something, but not "liking", "wanting" or "thinking". After all, those verbs are not real actions and therefore cannot be completed.

To negate 了 **le** we use 没(有) **méi** (**yǒu**):

我吃饭了 **wǒ chī fàn le** *I eat rice [complete]* (*I ate/I have eaten*)
→ 我没(有)吃饭 **wǒ méi (yǒu) chī fàn** *I not (have) eat rice*
→ *I didn't eat/have not eaten*

Compare: 我不吃饭 **wǒ bù chī fàn** *I not eat rice* (*I don't eat*)

Since 没 **méi** is a negation inseparably associated with 有 **yǒu**, we can use it alone and skip the 有 **yǒu**.
And since 了 **le** indicates completion of an action, when we negate it (when we say we did not complete something), we naturally don't use 了 **le**, i.e. it is incorrect to say 我没(有)吃饭了 ~~wǒ méi (yǒu) chī fàn le~~ *I not (have) eat rice[complete]*.

我们没吃饭

To ask a question, we can use 吗 **ma**:
> 老师来了吗? **lǎoshī lái le ma?**
> Teacher come [complete] [question]? (Has the teacher come?)

Or alternate questions with 没(有) **méi** (**yǒu**):
> 老师有没有来? **lǎoshī yǒu méi yǒu lái?**
> Literally: *Teacher has not has come?*
> (*Teacher has or has not come? / Did the teacher come?*)

A common way of asking a question with the help of 没(有) **méi** (**yǒu**) is to skip the repetition and just use it as a pseudo question particle:
> 老师来了没(有)? **lǎoshī lái le méi (yǒu)?**
> Literally: *Teacher come [complete] has not?*
> (*Has the teacher come or hasn't he?*)

了 **le** has many other functions and meanings. We will learn much more about it in chapters 7, 8, and 9.

就 jiù and 才 cái: Two opposite things that mean almost exactly the same …

English does not have anything quite like 就 **jiù** and 才 **cái**.

就 **jiù** means *just*, and we must always put it before a verb:
> 我就有一个男朋友 **wǒ jiù yǒu yí gè nánpéngyou**
> *I just have one [quantity of] boyfriend* (*I have just one boyfriend.*)

But most of the time, we use 就 **jiù** when something happens sooner than expected. E. g. Wang Xiaomao and Mr. Ma are talking about teacher Qi, whom Mr. Ma has never met before. Suddenly, teacher Qi appears. That's when Wang Xiaomao says:
> 这就是齐老师! **zhè jiù shì Qí lǎoshī**
> Literally: *This just is teacher Qi!* (*And here he is: Teacher Qi precisely!*)

Wang Xiaomao could simply have said: 这是齐老师 **zhè shì qí lǎoshī** *This is teacher Qi* without using the 就 **jiù**, but then the statement would not be as strong. 就 **jiù** adds an element of surprise and revelation. Mr. Ma was looking forward to meeting teacher Qi, and here he is!

Since teacher Qi arrives before we expected him to, we can say:

齐老师就来了 **Qí lǎoshī jiù lái le** *Teacher Qi just come [complete]*
(*Teacher Qi has just arrived. / And here he is!*)

Somebody does not know Mr. Ma and is looking for him:

A: 马先生是谁？ **Mǎ xiānsheng shì shéi?**
Ma Mr. is who? (*Who is Mr. Ma?*)
B: 我就是！ **wǒ jiù shì!** Literally: *I just am!* (*This is me!*)

Speaker A was not expecting Speaker B to be Mr. Ma, so there is a surprise.

才 **cái** is the direct opposite of 就 **jiù**. It means *only*, but we use it when things happen later than expected:

老师才来 **lǎoshī cái lái** *Teacher only come*
(*Only now the teacher arrived* [He was expected earlier])

Mr. Ma calls teacher Qi *unfathomable*. Mr. Qi does not accept that and turns it around; he uses 才 **cái** to declare that it is not he who is unfathomable, but on the contrary, it is Mr. Ma!

你才不可思议！ **nǐ cái bù kě sīyì!**
You're the one that's unfathomable! (Literally: *You only are unfathomable!*)

老师才来

Same as 就 **jiù**, 才 **cái** also must always come before a verb!

不可思议 **bù kě sīyì** and other descriptions (好 **hǎo**, 不好 **bù hǎo**, 贵 **guì**, etc.) act as verbs: something or someone "is unfathomable, good, expensive," etc.

就 **jiù** and 才 **cái** are extremely useful, but they may be a little hard to grasp at this stage in your study. However, you don't need to worry about them too much right now, it will be enough if you just understand what they mean. You will learn much more about them in part 3 of this chapter and in chapter 9.

Part 2

老师： 你是哪里的？
Lǎoshī: Nǐ shì nǎ lǐ de?
Teacher: You are where's?
Teacher: Where are you from?

马先生：我是法国的。
Mǎ xiānsheng: Wǒ shì Fǎguó de.
Ma Mister: I am France's.
Mr. Ma: I am from France.

王小猫：法国的呀！
Wáng Xiǎomāo: Fǎguó de ya!
Wang Little Cat: France's ya!
Wang Xiaomao: From France!

我听说法国男人都有很多女朋友。
Wǒ tīng shuō Fǎguó nánrén dōu yǒu hěn duō nǚpéngyou.
I hear say France male all have very many girlfriend.
I have heard all French men have many girlfriends.

你看，这就是我一个女朋友的照片。

裡 / 里 **lǐ** 508
in; inside

The traditional form has the "clothes" radical 衤(衣) yī, suggesting being "in" one's clothes; therefore, sometimes the traditional character is written 裏: you can see how 衣 is split into two parts and the phonetic 里 is placed literally inside of it! This suggestive and creative idea was abandoned, and the simplified version was reduced to the phonetic element alone, which is not only sad, but also confusing, because 里 can mean "hamlet", "Chinese mile", and now also "inside."

哪裡 / 哪里 **nǎlǐ** 318, 508
where?
Literally "in where?"

法 **fǎ** 344
law; French

法國 / 法国 **fǎguó** 344, 316
France

呀 **ya** 509
Particle expressing surprise, often used as an exclamation mark

口 kǒu "mouth" radical same as in other particles; 牙 yá means "tooth," but is here for pronunciation.

— 没错。
— **Méi cuò.**
— No [have] wrong.
— True.

— 你有没有?
— **Nǐ yǒu méi yǒu?**
— You have no have?
— Do you?

— 我当然有! 你看,
— **Wǒ dāngrán yǒu! Nǐ kàn,**
— I of course have! You look,
— Of course I do! Look,

这就是我一个女朋友的照片。
zhè jiù shì wǒ yí gè nǚpéngyou de zhàopiàn.
this just is I one [item] girlfriend's photograph.
here's a picture of one of them.

聽
听
tīng 510
to hear; to listen

You may be happy to see the simplified form so much easier: it has a 口 kǒu "mouth" radical, presumably because we listen to what comes out of peoples' mouths, but it is still illogical, and kingdom to whomever guesses why we see an "ax" 斤 jīn here; the traditional has an "ear" 耳 ěr radical, the rest is just madness.

聽說
听说
tīng shuō 321
to have heard; literally "hear say"

男
nán 511
male

田 tián means "field;" 力 lì means "power" or "strength;" in early agricultural society, men were the main force working in the fields.

男人
nánrén 511, 122
man
"male" + "person"

多
duō 512
many; much

Radical 夕 xī means "sunset; evening;" here we have two, which apparently is one too many.

很多
hěn duō 304
a lot; many

女
nǚ 513
woman; female

We've seen this character a lot as a radical in all sorts of characters indicating women or womenhood, e.g. 妈 mā, 她 tā, 姐 jiě, etc. The character itself is one of the oldest and most common radicals, and its form is supposed to resemble the shape of a woman.

女朋友
nǚpéngyou
513, 411, 412
girlfriend
"female" + "friend"

男朋友
nánpéngyou
511, 411, 412
boyfriend
"male" + "friend"

錯
错
cuò 514
wrong; mistake

Radical 金 jīn "metal" is one of the five phases (another one we have learned before is 水 shuǐ "water"). Its original form has been simplified to 钅. "Metal" is here because the original meaning of 错 cuò is "grindstone".

没错
没错
méi cuò 213
true; correct; "no mistake"

没(有) méi yǒu "there is not" + "mistake"

當
当
dāng 515
to work as; to serve as; to have to; must; just at

Where are you from, again?

We learned before that to ask *Where are you from?* we say 你是哪国人？ **nǐ shì nǎ guó rén?** *You are which country man?* (*You are from which country?*) However, this phrase is a little stiff and few people use it. It is much more common to use the question word 哪里 **nǎlǐ** *where*:

你是哪里的？ **nǐ shì nǎlǐ de?**
Literally: *You are where's?* (*You are of where?*)

他是哪里人？ **tā shì nǎlǐ rén?**
Literally: *He is where person?*

These questions do not necessarily ask about a country, but generally *from where*?

We answer replacing the question 哪里 **nǎlǐ** *where* with our answer, keeping the rest of the sentence structure intact, e.g.:

我是中国的 **wǒ shì Zhōngguó de**
Literally: *I am China's.* (*I'm from China.*)

他是北京人 **tā shì Běijīng rén**
Literally: *He is Beijing person.* (*He is from Beijing.*)

The most common way to ask specifically about the country of origin is:
你是哪个国家的？
nǐ shì nǎ gè guójiā de?
Literally: *You are which country's?*

Again, to answer we replace the question with the answer:
我是美国的
wǒ shì Měiguó de
Literally: *I am America's.* (*I'm from America.*)

她是哪里的？

當然 / 当然 **dāngrán** 416
of course

"must be/work as" + "thus" = of course

一 **yī** 516
one

個 / 个 **gè** 517
measure word for general objects and people

The traditional form has the 亻 rén "human" radical, because this measure word is primarily used for counting people; 固 gù is for pronunciation; however, you surely much more appreciate the made up simplified!

照 **zhào** 518
to shine upon; to flash; to photograph; to reflect

灬 is "fire" (火 huǒ), one of the five phases, an appropriate radical for the "flash;" 日 rì is "the sun;" 刀 dāo is "knife," together with 口 kǒu "mouth" it becomes 召 zhào and serves as the phonetic element.

片 **piàn** 519
a piece; a slice; a chip

照片 **zhàopiàn**
photograph

"to photograph" + "a piece"

國 / 国家 **guójiā**
316, 102
country

Numbers

For the most part, Chinese numbers are easy:

零 **líng** (533) 0 (also ○ **líng** (534), but only in serial numbers, e.g. years)

一 **yī** 1	(516)	六 **liù** 6	(539)
二 **èr** 2	(535)	七 **qī** 7	(540)
三 **sān** 3	(536)	八 **bā** 8	(541)
四 **sì** 4	(537)	九 **jiǔ** 9	(542)
五 **wǔ** 5	(538)	十 **shí** 10	(543)

> You can listen to the numbers at www.skapago.eu/jerry/bonus. The numbers in brackets indicate the videos where the writing is explained..

Other numbers are pretty straightforward; 11-19 are formed using 十 **shí** (10) + unit:

十一 **shí yī** 11   十三 **shí sān** 13
十二 **shí èr** 12   十四 **shí sì** 14 ...

Numbers 20-90 are formed using unit + 十 **shí** (10):

二十 **èr shí** 20   五十 **wǔ shí** 50
三十 **sān shí** 30   六十 **liù shí** 60
四十 **sì shí** 40   ...

Numbers between 21-29, 31-39 etc., are formed in a regular way *unit* + 十 **shí** (10) + *unit*:

二十一 **èr shí yī** 21   七十四 **qī shí sì** 74
二十二 **èr shí èr** 22   八十九 **bā shí jiǔ** 89

In numbers from 100 upwards we need to pay attention to a few particularities:

一百 **yì bǎi** 100   (544)

We must always indicate the number of hundreds, therefore we always say 一百 **yì bǎi** for *one hundred*.

二／两百 **èr bǎi/liǎng bǎi** 200
(most speakers prefer 两百 **liǎng bǎi**, but 二百 **èr bǎi** is the "correct" one)
三百 **sān bǎi** 300 etc.

In numbers with "zero" tens (101-09; 201-09; 301-09; etc.) we must always read the *zero*:

一百零五 **yì bǎi líng wǔ** 105 (*one hundred zero five*)
七百零七 **qī bǎi líng qī** 707 (*seven hundred zero seven*)

> **Pronunciation note:**
> 一 **yī** will always change the tone depending on the word coming after it:
>
>
>
> - Before 1st, 2nd, and 3rd tones, we will say **yì**, e.g 一千 **yì qiān** (1,000); 一百一十 **yì bǎi yì shí** (110)
> - Before 4th tone, we will say **yí**, e.g. 一个 **yí gè** (one item).
> - If 一 **yī** is part of a serial number (e.g. a phone number), the tone does not change.

In numbers 110-119, 210-219, 310-319, etc., we need to add 一 **yī** in front of 十 **shí**. Think of it as e.g. one hundred and one ten.

一百一十 **yì bǎi yī shí** 110
二百一十一 **èr bǎi yì shí yī** 211
三百一十二 **sān bǎi yì shí èr** 312)

It is incorrect to say 一百十二 **yì bǎi shí èr** 112!

In numbers 110-190, 210-290, 310-390, etc., we can drop the final 十 **shí**:

一百一十 **yì bǎi yì shí**   or   一百一 **yì bǎi yī**

(The pronunciation on yī remains intact because it is not followed by any other syllable)

七百六十 **qī bǎi liù (shí)**   or   七百六 **qī bǎi liù**

Compare:

一百零五 **yì bǎi líng wǔ** 105

but

一百五 **yì bǎi wǔ** 150

Numbers 1000-9000 are formed regularly, except 2,000, which is always 两千: **liǎng qiān**:

一千 **yì qiān** 1,000   (545)
三千 **sān qiān** 3,000
九千 **jiǔ qiān** 9,000

In numbers 1001-1009, 2001-2009, etc., it is ok to say only one *zero*:

一千零五 **yì qiān líng wǔ** 1005 (pronounced **yì qiān líng wǔ**)

In numbers 1010-1019; 2010-2019, 3010-3019, etc., the *one ten* rule applies:

一千零一十五 **yì qiān líng yī shí wǔ** 1015

In numbers 1020-1090, 2020-2090, 3020-3090, etc., we may not drop the final 十 **shí**, because if we did, then 1002 and 1020 would sound the same:

一千零二 **yì qiān líng èr** 1002
一千零二十 **yì qiān líng èr shí** 1020

But we can drop the final 百 **bǎi** in numbers 1100-1900, 2100-2900, 3100-3900, etc.:

一千五(百) **yì qiān wǔ (bǎi)** 1500

The rest is regular:

一千一百 **yì qiān yì bǎi**   or 一千一 **yì qiān yī** 1,100
一千一百一十 **yì qiān yì bǎi yì shí**   or 一千一百一 **yì qiān yì bǎi yī** 1,110
一千一百一十一：**yì qiān yì bǎi yì shí yī** 1,111

The pattern remains the same all the way up to 9,000 九千 **jiǔ qiān**.

The nightmare begins after 10,000, but we will deal with that in the second book.

"Three pieces of person"?
Counting and indicating with measure words

When we count people or things in English, we usually just say *one person* or *two cars*.
In Chinese, we must always use the so called **counter** or **measure word** that we put between the number and the item that we are counting. Measure words exist in English, too, e.g. we say *one cup of tea* or *three pieces of furniture*, but we only use them to indicate a measurable quantity, such as cups, packets, plates, etc. In Chinese, we must use a measure word every time we say the number of things, and for different things, we will use different measure words (in English, also, we can measure tea in cups, but not shirts or dogs).

The most common measure word in Chinese is 个 **gè**. We usually use it to count people, but also various other objects. If you don't remember the specific measure word for a particular thing, you can always try 个 **gè**, even if it will not always be correct. For example:

一个人 **yí gè rén** *one [measure of] person*
两个人 **liǎng gè rén** *two [measures of] person* (= *two people*)
三个朋友 **sān gè péngyou** *three [measures of] friend* (= *three friends*)

But for horses, we have the specific measure word 匹 **pǐ**.

五匹马 **wǔ pǐ mǎ** *five [measures of] horses* (= *five horses*)

If we use 个 **gè** instead, people will still understand, but it will sound incorrect; however, if we skip the measure word altogether, people will have a hard time understanding what we want to say.

One measure word other than 个 **gè** that we learned in chapter 5 is 位 **wèi**. It is a more respectful way of referring to a person; we would usually use it with words such as e.g. *teacher* or *Mister*.

一位老师 **yī wèi lǎoshī** *one [honorific measure] teacher* (= *one teacher*)
五位先生 **wǔ wèi xiānsheng** *five [honorific measure] gentleman*

In each case, we could just as well use 一个 **yí gè**; 位 **wèi** just makes our speech more polite.

> We use 二 **èr** only in numbers. When we count people or things, we always have to use 两 **liǎng**. See also page 85.

一个 **yí gè** is often used in spoken Chinese as the article *a* in English, e.g.
   他有一个男朋友吗？**tā yǒu yí gè nán péngyou ma?**
   Does he have a boyfriend? (literally *one*)

In this particular sentence, we do not actually need to use 一个 **yí gè** at all, but if we do, then we would not translate it literally as *does he have one boyfriend*.

And lastly, we must use measure words not only with numbers, but also after 这 **zhè** *this*, 那 **nà** *that*, and 哪 **nǎ** *which*:
   这个人 **zhè gè rén** *this [measure] person* (*this person*)
   那个女人 **nà gè nǔrén** *that [measure] woman* (*that woman*)
   那位先生 **nà wèi xiānsheng** *that [honorific measure] gentleman*
      (*that gentleman [respectfully]*)
   哪位老师？**nǎ wèi lǎoshī** *which [honorific measure] teacher?*
      (*which teacher?*)

这个 **zhè gè** and 那个 **nà gè** 哪个 **nǎ gè** are usually pronounced 这（一）个 **zhèi ge**, 那（一）个 **nèi ge**, 哪（一）个 **něi ge**; only the Taiwanese and some extreme Southerners stick to the "original" pronunciation.

How to say *a lot*

To say *a lot* we always have to say 很多 **hěn duō** *very + a lot/much*:
   我有很多中国朋友 **wǒ yǒu hěn duō Zhōngguó péngyou**
   I have very many China friends (*I have a lot of/many Chinese friends.*)

   Jerry 喝了很多啤酒 **Jerry hē le hěn duō píjiǔ**
   Jerry drink [complete] very much beer (*Jerry drank a lot of beer.*)

   王小猫问很多问题 **Wáng Xiǎomāo wèn hěn duō wèntí**
   Wang Xiaomao asks very many questions
   (*Wang Xiaomao asks a lot of/many questions.*)

Fortune cookie:

茶 **chá** tea

531

Part 3

王小猫和齐老师都看照片。
Wáng Xiǎomāo hé Qí lǎoshī dōu kàn zhàopiàn.
Wang Little Cat and Qi Teacher both look picture.
Wang Xiaomao and teacher Qi both look at the picture.

—这个女的就是你的女朋友吗?
- **Zhè gè nǚ de jiù shì nǐ de nǚpéngyou ma?**
- This [item] woman just is you's girlfriend [question]?
- Is this woman your girlfriend?

—不是,这是我妈妈。
- **Bú shì, zhè shì wǒ māma.**
- No is, this is I mom.
- No, this is my mom.

—这个吗? 那个女的呢? 她是谁?
- **Zhè gè ma? Nà gè nǚ de ne? Tā shì shéi?**
- This [item] [question]? That [item] woman [and how about]? She is who?
- This one? How about that woman? Who is she?

—那个女的不是我妈妈! 她就是我的女朋友!
- **Nà gè nǚ de bú shì wǒ māma! Tā jiù shì wǒ de nǚpéngyou!**
- That [item] woman no is I mom! She just is I's girlfriend!
- That woman is not my mom! She is my girlfriend!

—她很老… 这个人呢? 他是你爸爸吗?
- **Tā hěn lǎo … Zhè gè rén ne? Tā shì nǐ bàba ma?**
- She very old … This [item] person [and how about]? He is you dad [question]?
- She's old … How about this person? Is he your father?

—哪个? 这个吗? 不是! 这不是一个男人!
- **Nǎ gè? Zhè gè ma? Bú shì! Zhè bú shì yí gè nánrén!**
- Which [item]? This [item] [question]? No is! This no is one [item] male person!
- Which one? This one? He is not! This is not a man!

女的 **nǚ de** 513, 310
woman

"female" + "'s" = "female's [sort]" → woman; we can do the same with 男的 nán de "man"

她 **tā** 118
she

Indicates a female, hence the "woman" 女 nǚ radical, as opposed to the male pronoun 他 tā, which has the same pronunciation, but is written with the "human" radical 亻(人) rén.

这个人是我爸爸的姐姐！
Zhè gè rén shì wǒ bàba de jiějie!
This [item] person is I dad's elder sister!
This person is my dad's elder sister!

— 哦，很有意思！
— **O, hěn yǒu yìsi!**
— Oh, very interesting!
— Oh, very interesting!

就 jiù again

We see 就 **jiù** again in 这个女的就是你的女朋友吗？ **zhè gè nǚ de jiù shì nǐ de nǚpéngyou ma?**, which we can translate as *And this woman here is your girlfriend?* Wang Xiaomao and Mr. Ma have been talking about Mr. Ma's girlfriend. By asking a question with 就 **jiù**, Wang Xiaomao conveys a sense of urgency: she is looking for an answer to a question she's just asked and expects an immediate result; she is looking for a confirmation to her guess. We can understand 就 **jiù** as *exactly* or *precisely* – *exactly this woman (and not another one) right here?* or *Isn't it this one right here?*

We see the same situation in Mr. Ma's response when Wang Xiaomao confuses his mom with his girl-friend:

那个女的不是我妈妈！她就是我的女朋友！
nà gè nǚ de bú shì wǒ māma! tā jiù shì wǒ de nǚpéngyou
That woman is not my mom! She's exactly the girl-friend [that we've talked about before].

Here, 就 **jiù** helps express Mr. Ma's frustration and an immediate response to it: *Not this one; this one right here!*

姐	**jiě** 337 elder sister

"Woman" radical 女 nǚ to imply the meaning. The element on the right implies the sound: 且 qiě → jiě.

姐姐	**jiějie** elder sister
意	**yì** 157 idea; intention

"heart" 心 xīn radical as usual in characters implying thoughts and emotions

意思	**yìsi** 157, 502 meaning; sense; interest

"ideas" + "thoughts"

有意思	**yǒu yìsi** 214, 157, 502 interesting

literally "there is sense/interest"

覺 觉	**jué** 520 to perceive; to feel

The traditional form has been simplified in the same way as 學→学 (the upper part); the lower part 见 (覺) jiàn means "to see" or "to sense" – one of the main sensory words in Chinese. Do not confuse this with "cowry shell" 贝 (貝) bèi that we have seen earlier; almost the same, but very different!

Part 4

马先生： 你不觉得我女朋友美吗？
Mǎ xiānsheng: Nǐ bù jué de wǒ nǚpéngyou měi ma?
Ma Mister: You no think I girlfriend beautiful [question]?
Mister Ma: You don't think my girlfriend is beautiful?

王小猫: 不觉得。
Wáng Xiǎomāo: Bù jué de.
Wang Little Cat: No think.
Wang Xiaomao: I don't.

马先生： 老师，你也不觉得吗？
Mǎ xiānsheng: Lǎoshī, nǐ yě bù jué de ma?
Ma Mister: Teacher, you also no think [question]?
Mister Ma: You too, teacher?

老师： 马马虎虎。
Lǎoshī: Mǎmǎ hūhū.
Teacher: Horse Horse Tiger Tiger.
Teacher: Meh.

马先生： 我真丢脸！
Mǎ xiānsheng: Wǒ zhēn diū liǎn!
Ma Mister: I really lose face.
Mister Ma: Shame on me!

王小猫: 老师当然不觉得。
Wáng Xiǎomāo: Lǎoshī dāngrán bù jué de.
Wang Little Cat: Teacher of course no think.
Wang Xiaomao: Of course [the] teacher does not think your girlfriend is beautiful.

他老说 Jerry 很美。
Tā lǎo shuō Jerry hěn měi.
He constantly say Jerry very beautiful.
He keeps saying Jerry is beautiful.

得 **dé** 521
to get; to achieve; to be able to; to the degree of

We will learn much more about this character in chapter 12.

覺得 / 觉得 **juéde**
to feel; to think; to be of an opinion

"feeling" + "get"; "feel to the degree of"

丢 **diū** 522
to lose; to miss; to go missing; to be missing

臉 / 脸 **liǎn** 523
face

月 (肉) ròu radical means "meat; flesh" and is usually applied in characters indicating body parts; 僉 (佥) qiān is often used as a phonetic element in words pronounced lian, qian, or jian.

丢臉 / 丢脸 **diū liǎn**
to lose face; to be disgraced; to be ashamed

老 **lǎo** 108
here: constantly

see grammar notes

马先生：我也说Jerry很美。
Mǎ xiānsheng: Wǒ yě shuō Jerry hěn měi.
Ma Mister: I also say Jerry very beautiful.
Mr. Ma: I also say Jerry is beautiful.

他是中国马吗？
Tā shì Zhōngguó mǎ ma?
He is China horse [question]?
Is he a Chinese horse?

王小猫：是的，他是西安的。
Wáng Xiǎomāo: Shì de, tā shì Xī'ān de.
Wang Little Cat: Yes, he is Xi'an's.
Wang Xiaomao: Yes, he is from Xi'an.

马先生：他有男朋友吗？
Mǎ xiānsheng: Tā yǒu nánpéngyou ma?
Ma Mister: He has boyfriend [question]?
Mr. Ma: Does he have a boyfriend?

王小猫：你问齐老师！
Wáng Xiǎomāo: Nǐ wèn Qí lǎoshī!
Wang Little Cat: You ask Qi teacher!
Wang Xiaomao: You ask teacher Qi!

西 **xī** 524
west

安 **ān** 525
peace; safe; safety

A woman 女 nǚ under the roof 宀 mián means peaceful and safe.

西安 **Xī'ān**
Xi'an City

We write Xi'an with an apostrophe (') to separate the two syllables xi and an, otherwise we would get one syllable "xian" pronounced differently (see pronunciation videos on the web: www.skapago.eu/jerry/bonus).

西安 Xi'an

Xi'an **Xī'ān** is China's former capital and one of the main tourist attractions. It is the home of the famous Terracotta Army, excellent historical museums, and ancient temples and pagodas, such as the iconic Great Goose Pagoda. Xi'an is located in the West, hence the name *Western Peace*, but originally it was called 长安 **Cháng'ān** *Chéng'ān Perpetual Peace*. During the Tang Dynasty (618-907), Chang'an was the greatest and most cosmopolitan metropolis in the world, the starting point of the Silk Route. Xi'an today has a vast Muslim population with a famous Muslim quarter and an ancient mosque built in the Chinese style. In facht, 马 **mǎ** is also a common Muslim name in China, short for Mohammed, but written with the character for *horse*.

西安 **Xi'an** is also famous for the Terracotta Warriors or in Chinese **Bīngmǎyǒng** 兵马俑。兵 **Bīng** means soldier and 马 **mǎ** means *horse*, like our friend Jerry. 俑 **yǒng** is a type of sculpture that was often buried with the dead in ancient times. The Emperor **Qínshǐhuáng** 秦始皇 was the first emperor of imperial China and the only emperor of the Qin dynasty. When he died, many statues of soldiers and horses were buried with him in order to accompany him in the afterlife.

The curious incident of 老 lǎo

As we have learned earlier, 老 **lǎo** means *old*. It is also used to express awe and respect in words such as 老师 **lǎoshī** *teacher* or 老虎 **lǎohǔ** *tiger* – here, 老 **lǎo** functions as a description (**adjective***) to the noun. However, when we put 老 **lǎo** in front of a verb, it functions as an **adverb**** and means *constantly* or *all the time*. It is usually used this way to describe an annoyingly repetitive action, until it becomes *old*:

> * An **ajective** is a word that describes things or persons: *green, old, lazy*... these are all adjectives.
>
> ** An **adverb** is similar to an adjective, but it describes a verb, not a person or thing. For example: She walks quickly. *Quickly* describes how she walks, not what she is like. Therefore *quickly* is an adverb.

你老喝啤酒! **nǐ lǎo hē píjiǔ!** *You constantly drink beer!*

我老学马的爱好 **wǒ lǎo xué mǎ de àihào**
I constantly study horses' hobbies (I study the hobbies of horses all the time)
(= like I do nothing else, and who in the world studies horses' hobbies, anyway?)

她老看 Jerry **tā lǎo kàn Jerry**
She constantly watches Jerry (She keeps watching Jerry.)

他老说 Jerry很美 **tā lǎo shuō Jerry hěn měi**
He constantly says Jerry very beautiful (He keeps saying Jerry is beautiful.)

Note again that in order to get this meaning, we must put 老 **lǎo** in front of a verb: I am doing something "in a 老 **lǎo** way."

It is interesting to look at 老 **lǎo** in 老外 **lǎowài**, the informal, slightly condescending term for *foreigner*. 老 **lǎo** here is both an expression of attention and respect (as Chinese speakers often insist) – the "old foreigner;" but it also refers to someone who is "always out of it," who does not understand anything around her – the "permanent outsider." In fact, 老外 **lǎowài** does not need to be a foreigner, but anyone who lacks expertise in something, a "greenhorn."

失 **shī** 526
to lose

败 **bài** 527
to defeat; to be defeated

失败 **shībài**
a defeat; a failure; to fail

功 **gōng** 528
a merit; an achievement; a practice; a skill

成功 **chénggōng** 333
success

之 **zhī** 546
possessive particle; "of"

母 **mǔ** 530
mother

失败是成功之母
shībài shì chénggōng zhī mǔ
Failure is the mother of success

1. 绕口令 *rào kǒu lìng:* Read the tongue twister out loud.

牛郎恋刘娘
刘娘念牛郎
牛郎年年恋刘娘
刘娘连连念牛郎

niúláng liàn liúniáng
liúniáng niàn niúláng
niúláng niánnián liàn liúniáng
liúniáng liánlián niàn niúláng.

"A cow boy fell in love with a girl called Liu,
The girl Liu misses the cow boy,
The cow boy loved Girl Liu every year
Girl Liu continuously loved the cow boy"

2. Translation 翻译 *fānyì:* Translate from English to Chinese.
a) I heard that your mother and father both study Chinese.
b) My girlfriend is not beautiful.
c) Does her mother have a boyfriend?
d) She keeps on saying that I am not handsome!
e) My father drinks a lot of tea.
f) Wang Xiaomao and teacher Qi are both reading.
g) Forget it, students always curse teachers.
h) Of course I love you, you are my love and no other! You are the one who does not love me!
i) That's really a shame.

3. Fix the errors and rewrite them in proper Chinese.
a) 中国的啤酒不是贵。
b) 我妈妈有五好朋友。
c) 我不有筷子。
d) 我的老师是高。
e) 老师没来了。

4. Rearrange words into sentences.
a) 啤酒／爸爸／我／喝／老
b) 我／老师／是／也
c) 上课／来／骑马／他
d) 的／男朋友／你／是／的／哪里
e) 的／新／老师／她／是

5. Questions from the text.
a) 马先生是哪国人？
b) 马先生叫什么名字？
c) 马先生有没有女朋友？
d) 王小猫觉得马先生的女朋友美吗？
e) 齐老师觉得马先生的女朋友美吗？
f) 谁才不可思议？

6. Fill in the blanks using vocabulary from the list:

个	才	就	没	了	位
一	都	有	那	饭	

a) 这___很帅的老师___是我们的中文老师。
b) 哪___同学不爱Jerry？
c) 他下午___来上课。
d) 大家___说马先生爱吃豆腐。
e) 你错 ___ ！
f) 你吃___了吗？我___吃饭。我很饿。
g) ___个法国学生也上中文课。
h) 我有___个中国的男朋友。
i) 老师不是好人；他没___一个好朋友。

7. Write the text in pinyin, mark the tones, and translate:
我姓文，名字叫美女。我是韩国人 (hánguórén)。我的家不大。我有一个弟弟，他也姓文，可是他不叫美女，他叫帅哥。我弟弟学日文。他的日文很好。他是一个好弟弟。

美女 **měi nǚ** 319, 513
beautiful woman; a beauty

This word originally means "a beauty" (like in a fairy tale), but in recent years it has become a widely used form of address, same as "miss" or "madam;" we can address any female stranger in the street by calling her 美女. It seems awkward, but somehow it works.

韓
韩
hán 529
South Korea

韓國
韩国
hánguó 529, 316
South Korea

韓國人
韩国人
hánguórén 529, 316, 122
South Korean person

帥哥
帅哥
shuài gē 418, 335
handsome bro; handsome dude; hot guy;

Same as 美女, this has become a regular form of address for men.

6

Part 1

马先生： 老师，你家有几口人？
Mǎ xiānsheng: Lǎoshī,   nǐ jiā yǒu jǐ kǒu rén?
Ma Mister: Teacher, you family has how many [mouth] people?
Mr. Ma: Teacher, how many people are there in your family?

齐老师： 我的家很小，只有我姐姐和我。
Qí lǎoshī: Wǒ de jiā hěn xiǎo,   zhǐ yǒu wǒ jiějie hé wǒ.
Qi Teacher: I's   family very small, only have I elder sister and I.
Teacher Qi: My family is small, only my elder sister and I.

— 你姐姐做什么工作呢？
— **Nǐ   jiějie zuò shénme gōngzuò ne?**
— You elder sister do what job [and what about]?
— What job does your elder sister do?

— 她是马医。她有两个孩子，
— **Tā shì mǎ yī.   Tā yǒu liǎng gè háizi,**
— She is horse doctor. She has two [item] child,
— She is a horse doctor. She has two kids,

一个儿子和一个女儿。
yí gè érzi   hé yí gè nǚ'ér.
one [item] son   and one [item] daughter.
one son and one daughter.

我们都爱马！
We all love horses!

幾
几
jǐ 601
how many? (for numbers less than 10)

The simplified form is originally pronounced jī and means "table;" it was borrowed to substitute the much more complicated traditional form.

口
kǒu 602
mouth; measure word for family members

Family members are counted by the number of mouths to feed.

只
zhǐ 603
only

工
gōng 604
work; craft

作
zuò 605
to do; to compose

做 and 作 are both pronounced the same way and essentially mean the same thing; for a while, they were interchangable. Nowadays, conventionally it is agreed that 做 is more general, while 作 is reserved for more creative "doings," such as composing poems, music, writing essays and novels, etc.

工作
gōngzuò
job; work; to work

醫
医 **yī** 606
medical science; medicine; here: (medical) doctor

The traditional character has the wine vessel 酉 yǒu for mixing concoctions, but the simplified form keeps only one of the original three radicals.

馬醫
马医 **mǎ yī** 3, 606
horse doctor

If you understand this combination, then you can surely guess how to say "dentist"? (牙医 yá yī "tooth doctor")

兩
两 **liǎng** 607
two of

Used only when counting people or things (see chapter 5). Note the slight but significant difference between the tradtional and simplified forms. In the simplified, we see two 人 rén "walking man" figures, but the elements in the traditional form are 入 rù "to enter" written differently.

孩 **hái** 608
child

子 zǐ "son" indicating the meaning; 亥 hài (Chinese zodiac sign meaning "pig") is phonetic.

子 **zǐ** 132
(male) child; son

We've seen it as a part of 好 hǎo "good" – a woman with a child; the character is supposed to look like a baby.

孩子 **háizi**
child

子 zǐ here does not actually mean "son" but instead serves as a suffix; when it is added to another character, it emphasizes that the character is a noun - an object or a person; it is similar to the suffix "-er" in English (work-er; blend-er; fly-er; etc.); the word pronounced "hái" can have many meanings; when we add 子 zǐ to it, it becomes clear that we mean the noun "child;" in this way, we avoid confusion.

兒
儿 **ér** 609
son; child

兒子
儿子 **érzi** 609, 132
son

子 zǐ means "son" in classical (literary) Chinese and is no longer used in modern speech; to say "son" in Mandarin, we must use 儿子 érzi – the modern word for "son" 儿 ér + the noun suffix 子 zi

女兒
女儿 **nǚér** 513, 609
daughter

"woman" + "child" = "female child"

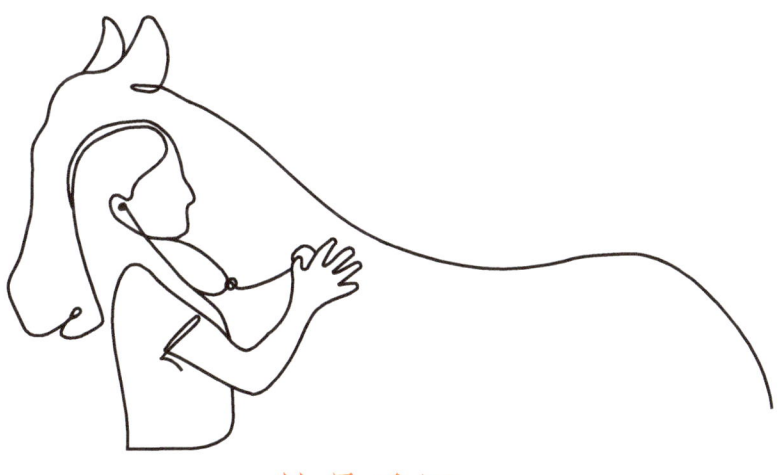

她是马医。

但是她不爱她的孩子，她只爱她的马。
Dànshì tā bú ài tā de háizi, tā zhǐ ài tā de mǎ.
But she no love she's child, she only love she's horse.
But, she does not love her kids, she only loves her horses.

王小猫：我也爱马！
Wáng Xiǎomāo: Wǒ yě ài mǎ!
Wang Little Cat: I also love horse!
Wang Xiaomao: I also love horses!

马先生：老师，你有爱人吗？
Mǎ xiānsheng: Lǎoshī, nǐ yǒu àirén ma?
Ma Mister: Teacher, you have spouse [question]?
Mr. Ma: Teacher, do you have a spouse?

— 没有啊！但是那没有关系，
— **Méi yǒu a! Dànshì nà méi yǒu guānxi,**
— No have a! But that no have relationship,
— Oh no! But that does not matter.

因为我有 Jerry。 Jerry 和我是好朋友。
yīnwèi wǒ yǒu Jerry. Jerry hé wǒ shì hǎo péngyou.
because I have Jerry. Jerry and I are good friends.
I have Jerry. Jerry and I are good friends.

愛人
爱人
àirén 313, 122
spouse

"to love" + "a person" = "a loved person." This is a word that was introduced into Chinese somewhat artificially and it does not mean "lover"! Quite the contrary, it sounds pretty unromantic in Chinese and can refer to both a male and a female spouse.

但
但是
dàn 610
but; yet
dànshi 610, 107
but
interchangeable with 可是 kěshì

關
关
guān 611
related; relationship; to involve; to negotiate; to go between

"Gate" 門 mén radical in the traditional form, because originally the character meant a checkpoint / border pass. At checkpoint people connect and form relationships with each other.

係
系
xì 612
to bind; to attach; to connect with

Traditionally, 係 had the 亻rén "human" radical to distinguish it from 系 ("system"); the simplified form has 系 for all the meanings.

關係
关系
guānxi
connection(s); bonds; relationship

沒(有)關係
没(有)关系
méi (yǒu) guānxi
it does not matter; nevermind; "there is no connection"

How many? Question word 几 jǐ

几 **jǐ** is a question word meaning *how many*, but only for numbers lower than 10. Since we are counting, we must always use a measure word after 几 **jǐ** – *how many* measures of something?

Mr. Ma asks teacher Qi:

> 你家有几口人？ **nǐ jiā yǒu jǐ kǒu rén?**
>
> Your family has how many mouths [of] people?
>
> (How many people are in your family?)

The measure word is 口 **kǒu** as in *mouth*. Think of it as: *How many mouths to feed?* Mr. Ma is assuming that teacher Qi's family has less than 10 people.

> 几个人？ **jǐ gè rén?**
>
> How many [measures of] people (expected to be less than 10 or around)

> 几个学生不爱齐老师？ **jǐ gè xuésheng bú ài Qí lǎoshī?**
>
> How many [measures of] students not love Qi Teacher?
>
> (How many students do not love teacher Qi?)

(generously assuming they are not countless)

> 几位老师骑马？ **jǐ wèi lǎoshī qí mǎ?**
>
> How many teachers (polite measure word) ride horses?

(assuming there are less than 10 or so, i.e. we are not asking about all teachers in the world)

> 几匹马上中文课？ **jǐ pǐ mǎ shàng zhōngwén kè?**
>
> How many [measures of] horses go to Chinese class?

(assuming not too many ...)

Only 只 zhǐ

只 **zhǐ** means *only*. Unlike in English, it must always come before a verb:

我姐姐只有一个女朋友 **wǒ jiějie zhǐ yǒu yí gè nǚpéngyou**
My elder sister only has one [measure of] girl-friend.
(My elder sister has only one girlfriend.)

我只爱Jerry **wǒ zhǐ ài Jerry** *I only love Jerry*

Jerry 不只吃草 **Jerry bù zhǐ chī cǎo**
Jerry not only eats grass
(Jerry does not only eat grass / Jerry eats not only grass)

In English, we can put *only* in different places. Try this: *She said that she loved him*. We can put *only* in any place in that sentence, sometimes more than once. But not so in Chinese!

没关系 méi guānxi *it doesn't matter*

关系 **guānxi** is the Chinese word for *relationship* or *connections*. It actually officially entered the English language and, according to Oxford dictionary, it indicates *the system of social networks and influential relationships that facilitate business and other dealings*. The general idea is that in China, you need **guānxi** – friends and relationships – to get around.

没关系

关系 **guānxi** may be an intense, politically and culturally charged word, but 没关系 **méi guānxi** is just an innocent and polite phrase to use in response to an apology: *It does not matter; It's ok*. Literally, it means *there is no connection/relationship*. No strings attached.

Part 2

马先生： Jerry 有没有家？
Mǎ xiānsheng: Jerry yǒu méi yǒu jiā?
Ma Mister:　　 Jerry　　 have no have family?
Mr. Ma:　　　　Does Jerry have a family?

— Jerry 没有家，他只有一个老朋友，
- **Jerry méi yǒu jiā, tā zhǐ yǒu yí gè lǎo péngyou,**
- Jerry　 no have family, he only have one [item] old friend,
- Jerry has no family, he only has an old friend,

但是他不在北京。
dànshì tā bú zài Běijīng.
but　　 he no present Beijing.
but he is not in Beijing.

— 他老朋友做什么工作？
- **Tā lǎo péngyou zuò shénme gōngzuò?**
- He old friend do what job?
- What job does his old friend do?

— 他没有工作；他画画儿。
- **Tā méi yǒu gōngzuò; tā huà huà'er.**
- He no have job;　　 he paint paintings.
- He doesn't have a job, he paints.

畫
画
huà 613
to paint; painting

Notice how the traditional form is similar to 書 shū "book" and also contains a pen 聿 yù element; Chinese characters, like paintings, were originally written using a brush. We can also see a "field" 田 tián, because originally paintings represented landscapes. The simplified form is a rather curious invention; kind of looks like a … picture?

兒
儿
ér 609
the sound "r" added after a noun; diminutive

see grammar explanations

畫兒
画儿
huà'er
painting

畫畫兒
画画儿
huà huà'er
to paint

verb + default object: "to paint" + "paintings"

89

Let's get professional

To ask people about their jobs, we say:
> 你做什么工作? **nǐ zuò shénme gōngzuò?** *You do what work/job?*

To answer this, we can simply say:
> 我是 ... **wǒ shì** ... *I am* ... + the name of the profession or occupation

工作 **gōngzuò** is both a noun (*work; job*) and a verb (*to work*), so if not working, we can simply say 爸爸不工作 **bàba bù gōngzuò** *dad does not work / is not working*.

Here are some professions you may consider for your career:
> 医生 **yīshēng** 606, 124 *doctor*
> 律师 **lǜshī** 629, 109 *lawyer*
> 调酒师 **tiáo jiǔ shī** 632, 212, 109 *bartender*
> 画家 **huàjiā** 613, 102 *painter*
> 司机 **sījī** 619, 620 *driver*

Notice that these words often end with characters 师 **shī**, 家 **jiā**, 生 **shēng**. 生 **shēng** can be *an adept* of some skill; we saw it earlier in 学生 **xuésheng** *an adept of learning → student*; 医 **yī** means *medicine* or *medical science* (医学 **yīxué** *medical studies*), hence 医生 **yīshēng** is *someone who practices medicine*. 师 **shī** means *teacher* or *master*, so 律师 **lǜshī** means *master of the law*. We know from earlier that 家 **jiā** means *family* or *house*. By extension, 家 **jiā** can also mean *a specialist* – someone familiar with a particular discipline. 画 **huà** means *to draw* or *to paint*, so 画家 **huàjiā** means *someone specialising in painting*. 司 **sī** means *to be in charge of* or *to handle something*, so 司机 **sījī** is *a person who is in charge of a machine*.

There are more words that are commonly used in professions:
> 商人 633, 122 **shāngrén** *commerce + person = businessman*
> 官员 634, 635 **guānyuán** *office + member = official; bureaucrat*
> (a useful word in China)
> 服务员 636, 637, 635 **fúwùyuán** *to serve/to wait on + member = waiter; attendant*

The story of a little sound: 儿 er

儿 **er** was originally used in Beijing dialect as a *diminutive* – that means, it was added to the word to make it sound small and cute, e.g. 猫儿 **māo'er** *kitten*, 狗儿 **gǒu'er** (638) *doggy*, etc. (儿 **er** can only occur at the end of the word). Beijing people love to use it a lot and add it to all kinds of words. Nowadays, 儿 **er** became standard also in Mandarin.

In this chapter, we learn the verb 画画儿 **huà huà'er** *to paint [paintings]*. 儿 **er** after the second 画 **huà** indicates that it is a noun, and so it helps us distinguish it from the first 画 **huà**, which is a verb (we cannot use 儿 **er** with verbs). Literally, 画儿 **huà'er** means *little painting*. However, we don't have to use 儿 **er** if we don't like to, and it is absolutely fine to say 画画 **huà huà**, with the meaning unchanged. That's what people from the South of China prefer to do when they speak Mandarin.

Part 3

王小猫： Jerry 的老朋友是画家吗?
Wáng Xiǎomāo: Jerry de lǎo péngyou shì huàjiā ma?
Wang Little Cat: Jerry's old friend is painter [question]?
Wang Xiaomao: Jerry's old friend is a painter?

那他一定很帅，也很有钱！
Nà tā yídìng hěn shuài, yě hěn yǒu qián!
Then he certainly very handsome, also very have money!
Then he must be good looking and rich!

马先生：哪里呀！我爸爸也是画家，
Mǎ xiānsheng: Nǎ lǐ ya! Wǒ bàba yě shì huàjiā,
Ma Mister: Where ya! I dad also is painter,
Mr. Ma: Not at all! My dad is a painter, too.

他不但很难看，而且没有钱。
tā bú dàn hěn nán kàn, érqiě méi yǒu qián.
he not only very difficult look, but also no have money.
Not only is he ugly, but also poor.

– 他有名吗?
– **Tā yǒu míng ma?**
– He have name [question]?
– Is he famous?

– 他没有名。他是司机。
– **Tā méi yǒu míng. Tā shì sījī.**
– He no have name. He is driver.
– Nope. He works as a driver.

– 我听说画家都有很多情人。老师，对不对?
– **Wǒ tīng shuō huàjiā dōu yǒu hěn duō qíngrén. Lǎoshī, duì bú duì?**
– I hear say painters all have very many lovers. Teacher, correct no correct?
– I have heard that all painters have lots of lovers! Teacher, is that correct?

那　**nà** 410
then; in that case
see grammar explanations

定　**dìng** 614
to decide; to fix; to settle

一定　**yídìng**
certainly; surely
一 yī here = "all/whole": "all is set."

錢
钱　**qián** 615
money

钅(金) jīn "metal" radical for coins; 戋 jiān is for pronunciation.

有錢
有钱　**yǒu qián** 214, 605
rich ("to have" + "money")

哪裡
哪里　**nǎlǐ** 318, 508
where on earth, not at all

see grammar explanations

而　**ér** 616
and; also; nevertheless; and yet

且　**qiě** 617
moreover; besides

We saw 且 as a phonetic element in 姐 jiě 337.

而且　**érqiě**
and; besides; and also

不但
–而且　**bú dàn – érqiě**
not only – but also

齐老师：我不认识Jerry 的老朋友，
Qí lǎoshī: Wǒ bú rènshi Jerry de lǎo péngyou,
Qi Teacher: I no know Jerry's old friend,
Teacher Qi: I don't know Jerry's old friend

不知道他帅不帅、有没有钱。
bù zhīdào tā shuài bú shuài, yǒu méi yǒu qián.
no know he handsome no handsome, have no have money.
and I don't know if he is handsome or rich,

我只听说他不是人，可是也不是马。
Wǒ zhǐ tīng shuō tā bú shì rén, kěshì yě bú shì mǎ.
I only hear say he no is person, but also no is horse.
but I have heard he is not a person and not a horse, either.

非常奇怪！
Fēicháng qíguài!
Extremely strange!
Extremely weird!

難/难 **nán** 618
difficult

Do you see my favorite radical 隹 zhuī "bird with a short tail"? Why here? Because it's cute? We don't know.

難看/难看 **nán kàn** 618, 208
ugly ("hard to look at")

有名 **yǒu míng**
famous
"to have" + "name"

司 **sī** 619
to be in charge of; preside over

機/机 **jī** 620
machine

Machinery and mechanisms were made of wood 木 mù; we know 幾 (几) jǐ – serves here as the phonetic element.

司機/司机 **sījī**
driver
"machine operator"

情 **qíng** 621
feelings; emotions

"Heart" 忄(心) xīn radical: we are talking about feelings; phonetic element 青 qīng that we have seen in 请 qǐng.

情人 **qíng rén**
lover
"feelings" + "person;" not to confuse with 爱人!

對/对 **duì** 436
correct; that's right!; yes

We saw this character in 对不起; most often, it is used as "yes".

知 **zhī** 622
to know

道 **dào** 623
road; way; method; doctrine

Ancient Chinese concept of Tao – (in Taoism); "the way things are"/"way of doing something;" note the 辶 chuò "road" radical.

知道 **zhīdào**
to know (how; something)
"to know" + "the way"

非 **fēi** 624
negation particle

Only used in fixed expressions now. Means same as 不是 bú shì.

常 **cháng** 625
ordinary

非常 **fēicháng**
extremely; extraordinarily
"is not" + "ordinary"

奇 **qí** 626
strange; wondrous; bizarre

怪 **guài** 627
strange; odd; monstrous; freak; monster

忄 xīn "heart" radical

奇怪 **qíguài**
strange; weird

93

Where on earth, or how to use 哪儿／哪里 nǎ'er/ nǎlǐ?

哪儿 **nǎ'er** or 哪里 **nǎlǐ** mean *where*. There is no difference in meaning between these two; it is just a matter of pronunciation and different accents that people in China are using. In Southern China, Taiwan, Malaysia, and Singapore, it is more common for people to use 哪里 **nǎlǐ**. However, in Northern China, especially Beijing, it is more common for people to use 哪儿 **nǎ'er**. 儿 er has no meaning; the character only represents the sound "r," which southern dialects don't have and that Southerners find hard to pronounce; therefore, they prefer to stick with 里 **lǐ**, which means *inside* and is the original component of the word. But you can use either one you like anywhere you go without being misunderstood.
The same rule applies to:

> 这儿 **zhè'er** / 这里 **zhèli** *here*
> 那儿 **nà'er** / 那里 **nàli** *there*

Regardless of the regional preferences, 哪儿 **nǎ'er**, 这儿 **zhè'er** and 那儿 **nà'er** are considered standard Mandarin.

When asking *where?*, remember to put 哪儿 **nǎ'er** / 哪里 **nǎlǐ** at the end of the sentence:

> Jerry在哪儿/哪里？ **Jerry zài nǎ'er / nǎlǐ?**
> *Jerry is where?* (*Where is Jerry?*)

In response, we replace the question word with the answer:

> Jerry在酒吧。 **Jerry zài jiǔbā.**
> *Jerry is in a drink bar.* (酒吧 **jiǔbā** *alcohol bar; drink bar*).

Special use

哪里 **nǎlǐ** (but not 哪儿 **nǎ'er**!) can also be used figuratively. Literally, it still means *Where?*, but we use it when we want to deny or protest a statement and say that the opposite is true; it is better understood as *where on Earth?*, *not at all!*, or *absolutely not!* Let's see some examples:

> —马先生是好学生吗？ **Mǎ xiānsheng shì hǎo xuésheng ma?**
> *Is Mr. Ma a good student?*
> —哪里！（他不是好学生） **Nǎlǐ! (Tā bú shì hǎo xuésheng)**

Where (on Earth)! (He is not a good student.)

—齐老师好看吗？
Qí lǎoshī hǎo kàn ma? *Is teacher Qi good-looking?*
—哪里！（他难看）
Nǎlǐ! (tā nánkàn) *Where! (Absolutely not!) (He is ugly.)*

—齐老师的姐姐爱她的孩子吗？
Qí lǎoshī de jiějie ài tā de háizi ma?
Does teacher Qi's elder sister love her kids?

—哪里！（她只爱她的马） **Nǎlǐ ! (tā zhǐ ài tā de mǎ)**
Where! (Not at all!) (She only loves her horses.)

Most often, we use this kind of 哪里！ **nǎlǐ** to politely decline a compliment and to feign modesty, even when we may feel otherwise:

—你的中文很好！ **nǐ de zhōngwén hěn hǎo** *Your Chinese is good.*
—哪里，哪里！ **Nǎlǐ, Nǎlǐ!** Literally: *Where, where! (Oh, not at all!)*

—你很美！ **nǐ hěn měi** *You are beautiful.*
—哪里，哪里！ **Nǎlǐ, Nǎlǐ!** *Where, where! (Oh I'm not at all!)*

—你男朋友很帅！ **nǐ nánpéngyou hěn shuài!** *Your boyfriend is cute.*
—哪里，哪里！ **Nǎlǐ, Nǎlǐ!** *Where, where! (Oh no no!)*

Fortune cookie:

jiǎo 628
dumpling

jiǎozi 628, 132
dumpling

Why do we use "that"?

We said in chapter 4 that 那 **nà** means *that*. By extension, it also means *in that case* or *then*. If we see 那 **nà** in a sentence and it does not point to any person or thing (and is not followed by a measure word), then it means *then*:

> 那他一定很帅 **nà tā yídìng hěn shuài**
> *Then/In that case he must be cute.*

The opposite of 好 hǎo

In chapter 2, we learned that putting 好 **hǎo** in front of a verb means something is good or easy to do; e.g. 好吃 **hǎo chī** *good to eat = tasty*.
We also said that to say the opposite, we may simply use 不 **bù**:

> 不好吃 **bù hǎo chī** *not tasty*

But in order to make our objection even more straightforward, we can use the word 难 **nán** *difficult; hard* by also putting it in front of the verb:

> 难吃 **nán chī** *hard to eat = disgusting; untasty*
> 难看 **nán kàn** *hard to look at = ugly, boring (about a book or a movie)*
> 难学 **nán xué** *hard to study = difficult (to learn)*
> 难做 **nán zuò** *hard to do*
> 难说 **nán shuō** *hard to say*

"To know" something or somebody?

In most languages, but curiously not in English, there are two different verbs that mean *to know*. In chapter 4, we have learned 认识 **rènshi** *to know somebody*; and now, we also know the much more common verb 知道 **zhīdao** *to know something*. The difference between these two verbs is exactly what the extended English translation suggests. We use 认识 **rènshi** only to indicate that we know a person – that we are acquainted with somebody:

> 我认识齐老师 **wǒ rènshi Qí lǎoshī**
> *I know teacher Qi. (I am acquainted with him and can recognize him.)*

But:

> 我知道齐老师没有爱人，因为他爱Jerry
> **wǒ zhīdào Qí lǎoshī méi yǒu àirén, yīnwèi tā ài Jerry**
> *I know that teacher Qi has no spouse, because he loves Jerry.*

知道 **zhīdào** expresses any kind of knowledge:

> 我知道你认识Jerry
> **wǒ zhīdao nǐ rènshi Jerry**
> *I know that you know Jerry.*

1. 绕口令 rào kǒu lìng – read the tongue twister out loud.

桌上有个盆　　zhuō shàng yǒu gè pén,
盆里有个瓶　　pén lǐ yǒu gè píng,
碰碰碰　　　　pèng pèng pèng,
是瓶碰盆　　　shì píng pèng pén,
还是盆碰瓶　　hái shì pén pèng píng.

"On the table there is a basin,
In the basin there is a bottle,
thump! thump! thump!
Was it the bottle that bumped into the basin,
Or was it the basin that bumped into the bottle?"

2. Translation 翻译 fānyì: Translate these phrases from English to Chinese.
a) She has 42 kids. Unfathomable!

b) My family is large, there are 8 people in it: mom, dad, two younger sisters, one elder brother, grandpa and grandma, and me; there also are two little cats (只 **zhī** 639 *measure word for cats*), and an old horse (匹 **pǐ** 547 *measure word for horses*).

c) Not only is he weird, but also he doesn't work.

d) My father is a businessman.

e) I don't have a boyfriend. But that doesn't matter, I have lots of good friends!

f) What does your father do for work?

3. Write a simple description of your family. These questions can help:
How many people are in your family?
What does your mother/father do for work?
Do you have any sisters/brothers? How many?

4. Fix the errors and rewrite the sentences in proper mandarin.
a) 我有二个孩子。
b) 我爱你也！
c) 我弟弟是画人！
d) 你有几兄弟姐妹？
e) 我不知道齐老师的好朋友。

5. Rearrange the words. Then write the sentences out in pinyin and English.
a) 有名／他／爱人／的／很
b) 很／他／有钱／而且／不但／有／女朋友／三／个

c) 医生／爸爸／我／的／老朋友／是
d) 情人／画家／都／有／很多

6. Questions from the text:
a) 齐老师的家有几口人？
b) 齐老师的姐姐做什么工作？
c) Jerry的老朋友在哪里？
d) 马先生的爸爸难不难看？
e) Jerry有没有家？

7. Rewrite the sentences using adverbs from the list. Choose one that fits best for each sentence:

才　　老　　也　　真　　都　　就　　一定　　只

a) 齐老师和Jerry的关系有意思。
b) 这个帅哥是齐老师。
c) 中文课的同学说Jerry很帅。
d) 你姓王吗？
e) 有名的画家很有钱。
f) 我们大学有一匹马。
g) 马先生上午不忙，因为他下午去上中文课。
h) 老师问我这个问题。

8. Ask questions about the underlined phrases:
a) 这个同学是法国的。
b) 她是中国人。
c) 我女朋友有两个孩子。
d) 王小猫是司机。
e) 那个帅哥是齐老师。
f) 我哥哥爱吃豆腐。

9. Write these sentences in pinyin with tones and translate:
a) 我爱人不爱工作。
b) 我爱我爱人，可是他不爱我。
c) 我哥哥很帅，可是他的女朋友不多。
d) 我男朋友的爱好就是啤酒。
e) 你上哪个大学？
f) 我姐姐上北大。

中文课
zhōngwén kè
314, 315, 218
Chinese language class

上大學 / 上大学
shàng dàxué
217, 101, 123
go to university/college; attend university

北大
Běidà
413, 101
Beijing University

This is an abbreviation of 北京大学 and that's how Beijing University is known in China.

7 七

老师怎么不管?
How come the teacher does not care?

Part 1

齐老师在他的办公室里看Jerry的照片。
Qí lǎoshī zài tā de bàngōngshì li kàn Jerry de zhàopiàn.
Qi Teacher present he's office inside look at Jerry's picture.
Teacher Qi is in his office looking at Jerry's pictures.

突然有人敲门。
Tūrán yǒu rén qiāo mén.
Suddenly have person knock door.
Suddenly, somebody knocks on the door.

— 谁啊?
— **Shéi a?**
— Who a?
— Who is it?

— 是我。
— **Shì wǒ.**
— Is I.
— It's me.

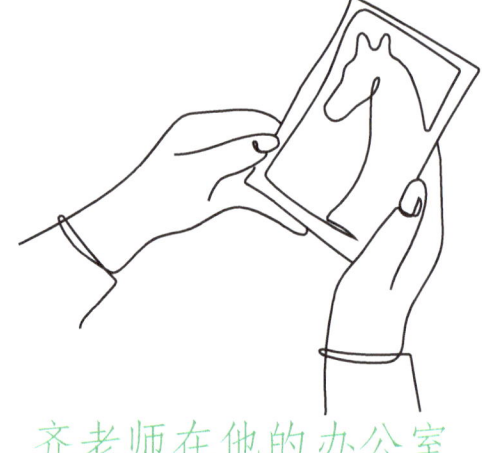

齐老师在他的办公室里看Jerry的照片。

辦 / 办 **bàn** 701
to manage; to handle; to deal with; to solve

辛 xīn "laborious; painful; hard work" on both sides of 力 lì "strength; power" in the traditional form (辦), which suggested the meaning of "double work and business," was reduced to mere dots in the simplified 办: much less work required to manage nowadays.

公 **gōng** 342
public; official duties

室 **shì** 702
room

A roof 宀 and 至 zhì for pronunciation (zhi → shi)

辦公室 / 办公室 **bàngōngshì**
office

"room where official business is handled"

— 马先生，是你呀？请进！
- **Mǎ xiānsheng, shì nǐ ya?　Qǐng jìn!**
- Ma Mister, is you ya?　Please enter!
- Oh, it's you, Mr. Ma?　Please come in!

— 老师早！
- **Lǎoshī zǎo!**
- Teacher morning!
- Good Morning teacher!

— 早上好！请坐！你有什么事？
- **Zǎoshang hǎo! Qǐng zuò!　Nǐ yǒu shénme shì?**
- Morning good! Please sit!　You have what matter?
- Good morning! Please sit down! What's the matter? (How can I help?)

— 今天是王小猫的生日。
- **Jīntiān shì Wáng Xiǎomāo de shēngrì.**
- Today　is Wang Little Cat's　birthday.
- Today is Wang Xiaomao's birthday.

— 是吗？你怎么知道？
- **Shì ma?　Nǐ zěnme zhīdao?**
- Is [question]? You how know?
- Is it?　How do you know?

— 她告诉我了。
- **Tā gàosu wǒ le.**
- She　tell　I [complete].
- She told me.

敲　**qiāo** 703
　　 to knock

門　**mén** 704
门　 door; gate

often a radical, e.g. 们, 问

敲門　**qiāo mén**
敲门　to knock on the
　　　door

進　**jìn** 705
进　 to enter

辶 chuò "road" radical indicates the meaning (movement); simplified forms uses 井 jǐng "a well" to indicate the pronunciation.

坐　**zuò** 706
　　 to sit

two people 人 rén sitting on the ground 土 tǔ

事　**shì** 707
　　 matter; agenda;
　　 business; thing

今　**jīn** 708
　　 present; now

天　**tiān** 709
　　 day; heaven; sky

今天　**jīntiān**
　　　today

日　**rì** 710
　　 day; sun

supposedly looks like the sun: a circle with a dot inside

生日　**shēngrì** 124
　　　birthday

"to give birth" + "day"

怎　**zěn** 711
　　 how; what; why

怎麼　**zěnme** 711, 128
怎么　how; why; how
　　　come

告　**gào** 712
　　 to report; to tell;
　　 to inform

"mouth" 口 kǒu radical for the meaning; otherwise, 告 by itself can serve as a phonetic element in characters, e.g. 酷 kù "cool".

訴　**sù** 713
诉　 to tell; to
　　 accuse; to file
　　 a suit

言 yán "speech" radical for the meaning; 斥 chì also means "to reprimand; to denounce".

告訴　**gàosu**
告诉　to tell (a per-
　　　son); to let know

—今天是几月几号?
- **Jīntiān shì jǐ yuè jǐ hào?**
- Today is how many month how many number?
- What day is today?

—四月一号。
- **Sì yuè yí hào.**
- Four month (April) one number.
- April 1.

—她今年多大了?
- **Tā jīnnián duō dà le?**
- She this year how much big [have become]?
- How old is she turning this year?

—21岁了。
- **21 suì le.**
- 21 year of age [have become].
- 21.

—她还小。
- **Tā hái xiǎo.**
- She still small.
- She's still young.

—不小了。可以喝酒了。
- **Bù xiǎo le.   Kěyǐ   hē jiǔ le.**
- No small [complete-change]. Can drink alcohol [complete-change].
- Not anymore.   She can drink alcohol now.

—那太好了!
- **Nà tài hǎo le!**
- That too good [emphasis]!
- That's great!

月   **yuè** 714
     month; moon

another ancient character, supposedly resembling a crescent moon

號
号   **hào** 715
     number

You may feel relieved to see this simplification; did you recognize 虎 hǔ "tiger"? The character originally meant "to roar" (like a tiger); 号 was for pronunciation.

年   **nián** 716
     year

Originally meant "harvest;" you still come across this meaning during the New Year's celebration, when people are wishing each other 好年 - "good bounty."

今年 **jīnnián** 708, 716
     this year

多   **duó** 512
     How? How much?

We saw 多 duō "a lot" before, pronounced in the 1st tone. Here the same character pronounced in the 2nd tone is a question word. Many speakers nowadays do not distinguish this pronunciation and always say 多 duō.

多大 **duó dà** 101
     How old?

"How much" + "big" = "How big" Usually used to ask about age.

Inside

Perhaps you have already noticed that to say *inside*, we put 里 **lǐ** not before, but after the place to which it refers, e.g.

齐老师在办公室里 **Qí lǎoshī zài bàngōngshì lǐ.**
Teacher Qi is office in (Teacher Qi is in the office.)

Such a function is called **postposition** (unlike the English *in* or *at*, which are prepositions). We don't always have to use 里 **lǐ**, but only when we want to emphasize that some action takes place inside a place; in fact, we can almost always skip it. E.g. in English, we say *in China*, but in Chinese we just say 在中国 **zài zhōng guó**, where 在 **zài** is a verb indicating being present somewhere.
Similarly, we could say:

齐老师在办公室 **Qí lǎoshī zài bàngōngshì**
Teacher Qi is [present] in the office. (dropping the *in*, i.e. 里 lǐ).

But if we want to emphasize that the teacher is inside the office doing something, we can say:

齐老师在办公室里 **Qí lǎoshī zài bàngōngshì lǐ**

We use 里 **lǐ** only for constricted places, such as houses or offices, but not for large and open entities, such as countries. Similarly:

Jerry在公园里吃草 **Jerry zài gōngyuán lǐ chī cǎo**
Jerry is park inside eating grass. (Jerry is inside the park eating grass.)

王小猫在家里喝酒 **Wáng Xiǎomāo zài jiā lǐ hē jiǔ**
Wang Little Cat is home inside drinking alcohol.
Wang Xiaomao is at home drinking.

Jerry在公园里吃草

suì 717
measure word for years of age

This character actually originally meant "year;" the simplification strategy is unclear: we see a mountain 山 **shān** over an evening 夕 **xī** - the passing time?

hái 718
still

Everybody is happy to see this character simplifed; again, the method applied here is unclear, except maybe the simplified form is supposed to look like the original character written very fast by hand. We see the "road" 辶 **chuò** radical here, because the same character also means "to return" and is pronounced **huán**.

以

yǐ 719
by means of; because of; to take

可以

kěyǐ 322, 719
can; be able to

"able to" + "have the means"

太

tài 720
too (much)

We can see the character 大 **dà** with the little dot, which represents the excess.

太 ... 了 **tài ... le**
extremely ...

Person Place Action

This is an important word order rule in Chinese! We always say where we do something before we say what we do. Think about it logically: Before we do something, we need a place to do it. I could not eat dinner at a restaurant if the restaurant didn't already exist.

> In our beautiful train analogy the place takes a seat in the adverb coach. Think of the place as a description of the action.

English: *I study Chinese in China.*
    subject – action – place

齐老师在北京工作 **Qí lǎoshī zài Běijīng gōngzuò**
Qi teacher present Beijing work
                place   action
English: *Teacher Qi works in Beijing.*

王小猫和Jerry在公园 吃草
Wáng Xiǎomāo hé Jerry zài gōngyuán chī cǎo
Wang Little Cat and Jerry present park eat grass
                          place   action
English: *Wang Xiaomao and Jerry eat grass in the park.*

马先生在法国有两个女朋友
Mǎ xiānsheng zài Fǎguó yǒu liǎng gè nǚpéngyou
Ma mister present France have two [item] girlfriend
           place   action
English: *Mr. Ma has two girlfriends in France.*

Jerry的老朋友在云南画画儿
Jerry de lǎo péngyou zài Yúnnán huà huà'er
Jerry's old friend present Yunnan paint paintings
                place   action
English: *Jerry's old friend paints in Yunnan.*

園 园 **yuán** 746
garden

公園 公园 **gōngyuán** 342, 746
park
"public" + "garden"

雲 云 **yún** 750
cloud

The beautiful traditional form has "rain" 雨 yǔ over the phonetic element 云, which originally means "to speak"; in the simplified form the logical "rain" radical has been heartlessly aborted.

南 **nán** 751
South

雲南 云南 **Yúnnán**
Yunnan

"South of Clouds" – Yunnan Province located in Southwest China

How to say "how?"

How in Chinese is 怎么 **zěnme**; we always put it before the verb:

你怎么知道？ **nǐ zěnme zhīdào?** *You how know?* (*How do you know?*)

中文怎么说 "I love you?"
Zhōngwén zěnme shuō "I love you?"
Chinese how say "I love you?"
How to say "I love you" in Chinese?

怎么做中国饭？ **zěnme zuò Zhōngguó fàn?**
How to make/cook Chinese food?

怎么 **zěnme** can also be used to indicate a surprise or annoyance; we can translate it as *why* or *how come*:

你怎么不认识 Jerry？ **nǐ zěnme bù rènshi Jerry?**
How come you don't know Jerry?

他怎么不吃饭呢？ **tā zěnme bù chī fàn ne?**
Why/how come he is not eating?

怎么办 **zěnme bàn** is a very useful expression. Literally, it means *how to deal [with something]*; we use it when we wonder what to do:

—家里没有酒 **jiāli méi yǒu jiǔ** *There is no booze in the house*
—那怎么办？ **nà zěnme bàn?** *What to do?*
—去买 **qù mǎi** *Go buy.*
—没有钱 **méi yǒu qián** *No money*
—那怎么办呢？ **nà zěnme bàn ne?** *Then what to do?*
—喝水 **hē shuǐ** *Drink water*
—哎呀妈呀 **aya maya** *Ay wey*

買
买
mǎi 726
to buy

Traditional form has the "cowry shell" 贝 **bèi** radical, pointing to purchases and valuables.

水 **shuǐ** 1363
water

哎 **āi** 919
an interjection of surprise mixed with regret

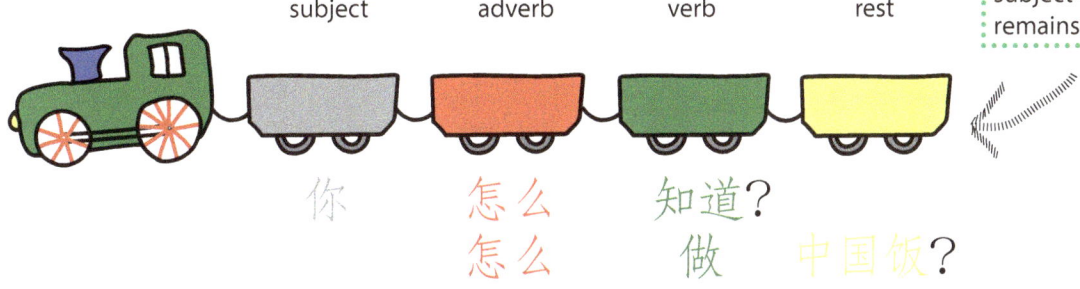

Look how the train analogy works also in this case. 怎么 **zěnme** as an adverb comes before the verb. When we don't have a subject the subject coach remains empty.

105

How to tell the date

Years

A year in Chinese is called 年 **nián**. We tell the year by simply saying each digit and finishing with the word for *year* 年 **nián**:

一九七三年 **yī jiǔ qī sān nián** *One Nine Seven Three Year* (1973)

二〇一八年 **èr líng yāo/yī bā nián** *Two Zero One Eight Year* (2018)

There is a pronunciation detail: 一 is often pronounced **yāo** instead of **yī**, particularly in the North of China. But this is not mandatory. We also say **yāo** in telephone or room numbers.

年 **nián** serves as its own measure word, so when we count the number of years, we say 一年 **yì nián** *one year*, 两年 **liǎng nián** *two years*, 一百年 **yì bǎi nián** *one hundred years*, etc. It is incorrect to add 个 **gè** and say 三个年 **sān gè nián**.

Months

月 **yuè** means *moon*, but also *month*. Clever, huh? Chinese months have no names, only numbers. We simply put the number in front of the word for month 月 **yuè**:

一月 **yī yuè** *January* (Month 1)
二月 **èr yuè** *February* (Month 2)
十一月 **shí yī yuè** *November* (Month 11)

Pay attention: 一月 **yī yuè** never means *one month*! If we want to count the number of months, we need to use a measure word: 一个月 **yí gè yuè** *one [measure of] month*, 两个月 **liǎng gè yuè** *two [measures of] months*, 十五个月 **shíwǔ gè yuè** *fifteen [measures of] months*, etc.

Days

There are two different ways to refer to a day. 日 **rì** means *sun* and it also means *day* in Classical Chinese. 日 is an old and formal way to refer to a day. 天 **tiān** means *sky* or *heaven*, but it also means *day* in modern Chinese. 天 **tiān** is the most common way to talk about days in general. We may use 天 **tiān** as a measure word to count days, e.g. 一天 **yì tiān** *one day*, 两天 **liǎng tiān** *two days*, etc.

To indicate the day in the month, we use the word 号 **hào**, which simply means *number*. We may also use the word 日 **rì**. These two are interchangeable, except that 日 **rì** is more often used in written language.

When telling the date in Chinese, we always start from the largest unit and finish with the smallest, in the sequence of year, month, and day:

二〇一八年一月十四号(日)
èr líng yāo/yī bā nián yī yuè shí sì hào (rì)
Two Zero One Eight Year First Month Fourteen Day
= January 14th, 2018

As we can see, English word order is completely different; but it is the Chinese one that is more logical! A year needs to exist before we can have a month; and the month exists before the day within it.

To ask about the date, we use the question word 几 **jǐ**. We just replace it with the number:

今天是几月几号(日)? **jīntiān shì jǐ yuè jǐ hào (rì)?**
Today is what number month what number day?

今天是一月十四号(日) **jīntiān shì yī yuè shí sì hào (rì)**
Today is First Month Fourteen Day.

The (not so) delicate matter of asking about age ...

Chinese people are not shy at all about asking and being asked about age. Actually, being older is perceived as an honorable thing. So, don't be shy, just ask!
Still, the way of asking depends on whom we want to ask.
First of all, there is a special word for the *year(s) of age*: 岁 **suì**. Think of it as a measure word. To tell the age, in Chinese we don't use the verb *am* (*I am 20 years old*); instead, we say 我 [number]岁 **wǒ [number] suì** *I [number] years of age*.
To ask the question, we can use the question word for numbers 几 **jǐ**:

你几岁? **nǐ jǐ suì?** *You how many years of age?* (*How old are you?*)

But there is a trick. Remember that we use 几 **jǐ** to ask about numbers less than, or around, 10; so, it is appropriate to use the question 你几岁? **nǐ jǐ suì?** only when we are talking to a child; using it with an adult would sound weird and inappropriate. In Taiwan, and increasingly in mainland China, people use it anyway, but still, it seems rather awkward, so be polite and do not do it.

Instead, use the phrase 你多大? **nǐ duó dà?** Literally: *You how much big?*

We learned the word 多 **duō** *how much* before; note that in this question it should be pronounced **duó** (in the second tone). This is the original and correct pronunciation; however, many people nowadays just say **duō**, so you don't need to be hyper careful about it.

你多大?

How to change things

We talked about the particle 了 **le** in chapter 5. Here we see it again, in one of its most common uses.

When we put 了 **le** at the end of the sentence, it often means that the situation we are describing has changed and is now the opposite to what it was before:

我是学生 **wǒ shì xuésheng** *I am a student*
我是学生了 **wǒ shì xuésheng le** *I am a student (but I was not before)*
= *I've become a student*

马先生是爸爸了 **Mǎ xiānsheng shì bàba le**
Mr. Ma is a father (but he was not before)
= *Mr. Ma has become a father*

我不是学生 **wǒ bú shì xuésheng** *I am not a student*
我不是学生了 **wǒ bú shì xuésheng le**
I am not a student (but I was before) = *I am not a student anymore"*

我有钱 **wǒ yǒu qián** *I am rich*
我有钱了 **wǒ yǒu qián le** *I am rich (but I was not before)*
= *I've become rich*

我没有钱 **wǒ méi yǒu qián** *I am not rich*

我没有钱了 **wǒ méi yǒu qián le**
I am not rich (but I was before) = I've become poor

We typically use it when we ask about time:
现在几点了？ **xiànzài jǐ diǎn le?** Literally: *What time has it become?*

Just a moment before, it was a different hour, and now, when we are asking, it has changed, so we need to update.

Same when we ask someone about their age:
他多大了 **tā duó dà le?** *How old has he turned?*
(before, he was a different age)

他21 岁了 **tā 21 suì le** *He's turned 21*

王小猫不小了。 **Wáng Xiǎomāo bù xiǎo le.**
Wang Xiaomao is not little anymore.

她可以喝酒了 **tā kěyǐ hē jiǔ le** *She can drink alcohol [now]*
(before, she could not, because she was not yet 21)

We can use 了 **le** like this very liberally, any time we want to emphasize that something has changed.

Too good

太 **tài** means *too* (in excess):
马先生有太多女朋友 **Mǎ xiānsheng yǒu tài duō nǚpéngyou**
Mr. Ma has too many girlfriends

中国人口太多 **Zhōngguó rénkǒu tài duō**
China's population is too large

Here, 了 **le** at the end intensifies the statement, so it will mean *extremely*:
啤酒太贵了 **píjiǔ tài guì le** *The beer is extremely expensive*

Jerry 太帅了 **Jerry tài shuài le** *Jerry is extremely handsome*

人口 **rénkǒu**
population
people + mouths = population

Part 2

— 我们怎么办?
- **Wǒmen zěnme bàn?**
- We how [to] deal?
- What should we do?

— 什么意思?
- **Shénme yìsi?**
- What meaning?
- What do you mean?

— 我们送她什么礼物?
- **Wǒmen sòng tā shénme lǐwù?**
- We present she what gift?
- What present should we give her?

— 我不管。
- **Wǒ bù guǎn.**
- I no care.
- I don't care.

— 我们可以给她买很多很多啤酒。
- **Wǒmen kěyǐ gěi tā mǎi hěn duō hěn duō píjiǔ.**
- We can give she buy very much very much beer.
- We can buy her lots and lots of beer.

— 我没有钱，也没有时间。
- **Wǒ méi yǒu qián, yě méi yǒu shíjiān.**
- I no have money, also no have time.
- I have no money and no time.

— 花呢? 我们送她花怎么样?
- **Huā ne? Wǒmen sòng tā huā zěnme yàng?**
- Flowers [and what about]? We present she flowers how about?
- How about flowers? What if we give her flowers?

怎麼辦
怎么办
zěnme bàn
what to do?
how to deal?
(with something)

送
sòng 721
to present a gift

Often means "to see/send someone off," hence the 辶 chuò "road" radical for the meaning.

禮
礼
lǐ 722
rites; ceremony; etiquette

Confucian ritual: a set of rules to be observed by any civilized human being; radical 示 (礻) shì looks almost exactly like 衤(衣) yī that we learned in traditional 裡 lǐ "inside". Do not confuse them!

物
wù 723
object; material thing

All things and objects except humans: animals, plants, material things, etc. Also referred to sacrificial objects. Radical 牜(牛) niú "ox" is found in other characters indicating beasts; 勿 wù is for pronunciation.

禮物
礼物
lǐwù
gift; present

"ceremony" + "object"

管
guǎn 724
to heed; to pay attention to; to care

Has multiple meanings, originally a bamboo pipe, hence the ⺮ (竹) zhú "bamboo" radical; 官 guān "official" for pronunciation.

給
给
gěi 725
to give

買
买
mǎi 726
to buy

Traditional form has the "cowry shell" 貝 bèi radical, pointing to purchases and valuables.

時
时
shí 727
time; season

Radical 日 rì "sun," for measuring time; in the traditional form, 寺 sì "temple" for pronunciation; the simplified makes no sense.

— 花儿好。可以给Jerry 吃！
- **Huā'er hǎo. Kěyǐ gěi Jerry chī!**
- Flowers good. Can give Jerry eat!
- Flowers are good. We can give them to Jerry to eat!

— 我有一个好主意！
- **Wǒ yǒu yí gè hǎo zhǔyì!**
- I have one [item] good idea!
- I have a good idea!

她可以骑Jerry！
Tā kěyǐ qí Jerry!
She can ride Jerry!
She can ride Jerry!

— 那不行！Jerry很累！
- **Nà bù xíng! Jerry hěn lèi!**
- That no go! Jerry very tired!
- No way! Jerry is tired!

— 那怎么办呢。
- **Nà zěnme bàn ne?**
- Then how [to] deal [and what about]?
- What to do then?

— 现在几点了？
- **Xiànzài jǐ diǎn le?**
- Now how many digits [time] [have become]?
- What time is it now?

— 两点半了。
- **Liǎng diǎn bàn le.**
- Two digits [of time] half [have become]
- 2:30.

— 算了吧。
- **Suàn le ba.**
- Count [complete] [suggestion].
- Let's just forget it.

間 / 间 **jiān** 728
space; room

门 (門) mén "door" radical

時間 / 时间 **shíjiān**
time (the concept); time (the duration)

"time" + "space"

花 **huā** 729
flower

艹 cǎo radical for plants; 化 huà "to transform" for pronunciation

樣 / 样 **yàng** 730
style, mode, form, appearance

木 mù "wood" radical – models and patterns were often made of wood; the simplified form is lovely and thoughtful: it uses 羊 yáng "lamb" for pronunciation.

怎麼樣 / 怎么样 **zěnmeyàng**
711, 128, 730
how? how about? in what way?

"how" + "mode"; often used to ask "how is it going?"

主 **zhǔ** 731
main; principal; master; leader

主意 **zhǔyì** 731, 157
idea

"main" + "idea"

累 **lèi** 732
tired

田 tián "field" and 糸 mì "silk"

現 / 现 **xiàn** 733
to appear; present

见 (見) jiàn (as in 觉 jué "to feel") means "to see" or "to be seen".

在 **zài** 408
(to be/exist) here and now; at the present moment

現在 / 现在 **xiànzài** 733, 408
now

點 / 点 **diǎn** 734
a dot; a point; unit of time (hours)

幾點 / 几点 **jǐ diǎn** 601, 734
What time is it?

"How many" + "units of time"

半 **bàn** 735
half

行 **xíng** 425
to move; to go; alright; to be OK

How is it?

怎么样 **zěnme yàng** literally means *in what fashion?*, *in what way?*, *how about?*, *what is it like?* It always comes at the end of the sentence.

If we want to ask someone how they are doing, we ask
  你怎么样? **nǐ zěnme yàng?** *you [are] in what way?* (How are you?)

Or just, 怎么样? **zěnme yàng?** *How is it going?*

We can use it to ask opinions about things, what things are like, good or bad:
  中国饭怎么样? **Zhōngguó fàn zěnme yàng?**
  China food is what like? (How is Chinese food?)

We can make suggestions and ask how people feel about them:
  我给你吃草，怎么样? **wǒ gěi nǐ chī cǎo, zěnme yàng?**
  I give you eat grass, how about it? (How about I feed you grass?)

  我们去骑马，怎么样? **wǒmen qù qí mǎ, zěnme yàng?**
  We go ride horses, how about? (How about we go horse riding?)

It is the most common way to ask about peoples' feelings and opinions.

The verb "to give" 给 **gěi**

给 **gěi** means *to give*:
  妈妈给爸爸很多钱 **māma gěi bàba hěn duō qián**
  Mom gives dad lots of money.

But 给 **gěi** often serves as an auxiliary verb, i.e. it introduces another action; then, we can translate it as *for* or *to*:
  我给你做饭 **wǒ gěi nǐ zuò fàn** *I give you make food = I cook for you*

  Jerry给王小猫吃草 **Jerry gěi Wáng Xiǎomāo chī cǎo**
  Jerry give Wang Little Cat eat grass.
  Jerry gives grass for Wang Xiaomao to eat.

  我不给你看Jerry 的照片 **wǒ bù gěi nǐ kàn Jerry de zhào piàn**
  I don't give you look at Jerry's picture. = I don't show Jerry's picture to you.

Very very

As we said earlier, 很 **hěn** does not really mean *very*. E.g. 很大 **hěn dà** simply translates as *big*, not *very big*. A special case 很多 **hěn duō** always means *a lot*, and we can't use 多 **duō** just by itself to express that meaning.
So, what do we do when we actually want to say *very*? As you will see, there are many ways. One of them is repetition, which adds emphasis to what we want to say:

很多很多 **hěn duō hěn duō**
a lot a lot (very much; lots and lots)

We can do that with any adjective at all:

很小很小 **hěn xiǎo hěn xiǎo**
very small very small (very, very small)

很贵很贵 **hěn guì hěn guì**
very expensive very expensive (very, very expensive)

很高很高 **hěn gāo hěn gāo**
very tall very tall (very, very tall)

Telling the time

To tell the hour in Chinese, we use the word 点 **diǎn**, which literally means *dot* or *point*, but it is also a measure word for the hours of the day. For instance:
>现在八点 **xiànzài bā diǎn** *It is 8:00, or it is 8 dots!*

The rest is easy:
>一点 **yì diǎn** *one hour*
>两点 **liǎng diǎn** *two hours*
>三点 **sān diǎn** *three hours*

For AM/PM, we use 早上 **zǎoshàng** *morning* / 晚上 **wǎnshàng** (749) *evening* put before (!) the hour .
>早上八点 **zǎoshàng bā diǎn** *8AM*
>晚上八点 **wǎnshàng bā diǎn** *8PM*

We say *morning/evening* before the hour, because those are larger time units that include the smaller ones, such as hours.
To ask what time it is, we use the question word 几 **jǐ**:
>现在几点 **xiànzài jǐ diǎn** *Now how many dots? (What time is it?)*

The easiest way to tell time is simply to say the number of 点 **diǎn** and then the number of minutes 分 **fēn** (747):
>早上八点二十五分 **zǎoshàng bā diǎn èrshíwǔ fēn** *8:25AM*

For multiple of five minutes, the word 分 **fēn** is optional.
If it is 8:01 (02, 03 ... 09), we must say *eight zero one (zero two... zero nine)*:
>八点〇一 **bā diǎn líng yī**

In Chinese, we can say 刻 **kè** (748) instead of "15 minutes":
>晚上八点三刻 **wǎnshàng bā diǎn sān kè** *8:45PM (eight and ³⁄₄)*

Instead of saying *30 minutes*, it is more common to use the word 半 **bàn** *half*:
>八点半 **bā diǎn bàn** *8 hours and a half (half past eight)*

Finally, to indicate the time before a certain hour, we often use 点 **diǎn** followed by the word 差 **chà** *to lack*, and then the number of minutes:
>九点差十分 **jiǔ diǎn chà shí fēn**
>*9 hours are lacking 10 minutes = 10 minutes to 9 (8:50)*

Part 3

— 请问老师，你的生日是几月几号？
— **Qǐng wèn lǎoshī, nǐ de shēngrì shì jǐ yuè jǐ hào?**
— May I ask teacher, you's birthday is how many month how many number?
— Teacher, may I ask what day is your birthday?

— 七月四号。
— **Qī yuè sì hào.**
— Seven month four number.
— July 4.

— 你今年多大了？
— **Nǐ jīnnián duó dà le?**
— You this year how much big [have become]?
— How old are you?

— 你怎么敢？
— **Nǐ zěnme gǎn?**
— You how dare?
— How dare you?

— 真不好意思。我没有文化。
— **Zhēn bù hǎo yìsi. Wǒ méi yǒu wénhuà.**
— Really no good sense.   I no have culture.
— Sorry.   I have no culture.

— 好了、好了，我44岁了。
— **Hǎo le, hǎo le, wǒ 44 suì le.**
— Good [have become], good [have become], I 44 years of age [have become].
— OK, OK, I'm 44.

— 我不相信！你不年轻了。
— **Wǒ bù xiāngxìn! Nǐ bù niánqīng le.**
— I no believe.   You no young [have become].
— I don't believe it!   You are no longer young! (You are old; you've aged)

敢 **gǎn** 736
to dare

不好意思 **bù hǎo yìsi** 121, 103, 157, 502
sorry; my bad; excuse me

"no good" + "sense"

化 **huà** 737
to transform; to change; to influence; to civilize

文化 **wén huà** 315,737
culture

transformation through letters and learning

没有文化 **méi yǒu wén huà** 213, 214, 315, 737
rude; uncivilized ("to have no culture", "to be uneducated/uncivilized")

没有文化

usually used to describe a rude behavior

相 **xiāng** 738
mutual; reciprical; each other; towards another person

信 **xìn** 739
honesty; trust; to believe; to trust; to rely upon

the person 亻rén and his word 言 yán

— 那没办法。
- Nà méi bànfǎ.
- That no [have] solution.
- Can't do anything about that. (That can't be helped; there's no solution to it.)

— 可是你还很帅！
- Kěshì nǐ hái hěn shuài!
- But you still very handsome.
- But you are still handsome.

— 谢谢。我希望 Jerry 也这样想！
- Xièxie. Wǒ xīwàng Jerry yě zhè yàng xiǎng!
- Thank you. I hope Jerry also so think!
- Thanks. I hope Jerry also thinks so!

相信 **xiāngxìn** to believe

"mutual" + "faith"

輕 / 轻 **qīng** 740 light

车 (車) chē "car" radical, for carrying things; 巠 jīng is for pronunciation.

年輕 / 年轻 **niánqīng** 716, 740 young

"years" + "light"

法 **fǎ** 344 rule; method; way of doing something

originally means "law;" see chapter 3

辦法 / 办法 **bànfǎ** 701, 344 solution; way of dealing with something

"to handle" + "method/way" = "the way to handle"

沒(有)辦法 / 没(有)办法 **méi (yǒu) bànfǎ** 213, 214, 701, 344

"there is nothing I can do about it"; "what to do?"; "there is no way"

希 **xī** 741 to hope; to expect; to wish

望 **wàng** 742 to gaze into the distance

希望 **xīwàng** to hope

這樣 / 这样 **zhè yàng** 417, 730 this way; in this fashion; so

this + style; pattern = this way

想 **xiǎng** 743 to think

心 xīn "heart" radical for thoughts, desires, and longings that are on the mind; we saw 相 xiāng in 相信 xiāngxìn. Here it suggests the pronunciation.

How to exaggerate a little bit

We said in chapter 3 that 很 **hěn** doesn't really mean *very*. So how to say we like something very much or something is very expensive?
We can still use 很 **hěn**. When put in front of a verb, 很 **hěn** always means *very*:

我很爱Jerry **wǒ hěn ài Jerry** *I very love Jerry = I love Jerry a lot*

It is only when we describe things that 很 **hěn** loses its original meaning. However, things change when we simply repeat the statement:

Jerry 很美 **Jerry hěn měi** *Jerry is beautiful* (not *very*!)
Jerry 很美很美 **Jerry hěn měi hěn měi** *Jerry is really/very beautiful*

(the repetition indicates we think Jerry is really beautiful)

We can use the word 真 **zhēn** *really* that we have learned in chapter 3:

Jerry 真美 **Jerry zhēn měi** *Jerry is really beautiful*

Or we can use the clause 太 ... 了 **tài ... le**:

Jerry 太美了 **Jerry tài měi le** *Jerry is extremely beautiful*

Lastly, we can use the word 非常 **fēicháng** *extremely* that we've just learned; remember to always put it in front of a verb!

草非常好吃 **cǎo fēicháng hǎo chī** *Grass is extremely delicious.*
我非常爱吃草 **wǒ fēicháng ài chī cǎo** *I extremely love to eat grass*

Of course, there are many more ways of intensifying our statements, so keep looking out for them! 太好了! **tài hǎo le!** *GREAT*!

Fortune cookie:

长城 **chángchéng** The Great Wall

長
长
城
城
長
城
长 城

cháng 744
long

chéng 745
wall

cháng chéng
the Great Wall of China

The Rule

法 **fǎ** is an interesting little word. We saw it in 法国 **fǎguó** *France* and we said that literally, it means *the country of law*. 法 **fǎ** means *law* or *rule*, and by extension *method* or *the way of doing something*. We can add it to many verbs and create new words. Here are a few examples using the verbs we have studied:

办法 **bànfǎ** = 办 *to deal* + 法 = *way of dealing with something; solution*
做法 **zuòfǎ** = 做 *to do/to make* + 法 = *the way to do/make something*
吃法 **chīfǎ** = 吃 *to eat* + 法 = *the way of eating something*
看法 **kànfǎ** = 看 *to look* + 法 = *the way of looking at something; opinion*
说法 **shuōfǎ** 说 *to speak* + 法 = *the way of speaking/saying; expression*
想法 **xiǎngfǎ** 想 *to think* + 法 = *the way of thinking, thought, idea*

And a less obvious, but a very useful one:

书法 **shūfǎ** = 书 *book; to write (in ancient Chinese)* + 法 = *calligraphy*

This way

In English, we say *do it this way*, *don't think this way*, etc. In Chinese, the word order will be the exact opposite, i.e. we will say *this way do*, *this way think*, etc.
This is because the Chinese *this way* 这样 **zhè yàng** (literally: *this model*) is an adverb and, as any Chinese adverb, it must come before the verb.
Hence:

这样说 **zhè yàng shuō** *this way speak* → *to say so; to speak this way*
这样做 **zhè yàng zuò** *this way do* → *to do so; to do this way*
这样吃 **zhè yàng chī** *this way eat* → *to eat so; to eat in this way*
这样想 **zhè yàng xiǎng** *this way think* → *to think so; to think this way*

1. 绕口令 *rào kǒu lìng* **Read the tongue twister aloud!**

一个庙里两个判官	yí gè miào lǐ liǎng gè pànguān,
一个姓潘，一个姓管	yí gè xìng pān, yí gè xìng guǎn.
是潘判官管管判官	shì pān pànguān guǎn guǎn pànguān,
还是管判官管潘判官	háishì guǎn pànguān guǎn pān pànguān.

"There are two magistrates in a temple
One is surnamed Pan, the other is surnamed Guan
Is magistrate Pan in charge of magistrate Guan
Or is magistrate Guan in charge of magistrate Pan?"

2. Translate 翻译 *fānyì* **the following sentences from English to Chinese:**
a) What presents do I send to my doctor?   d) When is your grandma's birthday?
b) You drank my beer! How dare you!   e) How old are you?
c) My little brother is hungry!

3. Fix the errors and write them in proper mandarin.
a) 我是23岁。   d) 我爸爸不有钱也！
b) 你今年多老了？   e) 我不认识他叫什么名字。
c) 现在二点半了。   f) 老师也说这样。

4. Practice telling time in Chinese.
a) 2:30 pm   e) 7:00 am   h) 5 minutes to 8 (pm)
b) 1:05 pm   f) 3:15 pm   i) 6:15 pm
c) 3:00 am   g) 10 minutes to 9 (pm)   j) 12:00 noon
d) 5:20 pm

5. Questions from the text
a) 王小猫今年多大了？   d) 谁来找齐老师？
b) 齐老师今年多大了？   e) 齐老师在哪儿？
c) 王小猫的生日几月几号？   f) 齐老师的生日几月几号？

6. Practice saying the date.
a) April 15th   h) January 5th 2017   o) February 10th 1988
b) 2001   i) July 30th 1972   p) March 2nd
c) 1997   j) February 14th 2042   q) September 9th 2007
d) 1653   k) October 20th 3101   r) June 30th 2004
e) 1711   l) December 31st 1999   s) March 28th 2018
f) 1868   m) November 6th 1993   t) August 31st 2012
g) May 26th 2005   n) 1853

7. Person Place Action
Translate to Chinese:
Wang Xiaomao is drinking beer at the teacher's office.
Teacher Qi is riding a bicycle in Beijing.
Mr. Ma is climbing the Great Wall in China.
Jerry is in the park eating flowers
Mr. Ma studies painting at the university.

8. Transcribe into pinyin, mark the tones, and translate:
a) 我不管她想什么。
b) 老师错了。
c) 马先生在北京上了大学。
d) 齐老师太奇怪了，学生都不敢去找他。
e) Jerry做了好吃的饭，你怎么不吃呢?
f) 妈妈不爱爸爸了。
g) 这个问题我要问谁?
h) 齐老师不相信王小猫会看中文书。

9. Fill in the blanks using vocabulary from the list:
Vocabulary:
了　　听说　吧　　好　　办法　行累　怎么
这样　不管　主意

a) Jerry ___ 了
b) 我不忙 ___
c) 你的 ___ 不错
d) 你 ___ 不认识我?
e) 我 ___ Jerry在家里骑齐老师。
f) 没 ___ ，我们要听老师。
g) 我们吃饺子 ___ 。
h) 这个看法不 ___ 。
i) 你怎么会 ___ 说?
j) 我 ___ 她是谁。
k) 你觉得中文好不 ___ 学?

10. Put words in the right order:
a) 意思/很/文化/中国/有
b) 了/吃/谁/的/饭/我?
c) 个/很/这/奇怪/说法
d) 中文/你/学/为什么/了/不?
e) 呢/有/你/我男朋友/的/怎么/照片?

8 八

我们都那么爱Jerry!
We all love Jerry so much!

Part 1

昨天王小猫没有来上课。
Zuótiān Wáng Xiǎomāo méi yǒu lái shàng kè.
Yesterday Wang Little Cat no have come attend class.
Yesterday, Wang Xiaomao did not come to class.

齐老师以为她生病了,
Qí lǎoshī yǐwéi tā shēng bìng le,
Qi Teacher assume [mistakenly] she get sick [complete],
Teacher Qi thought she got sick,

因为平常她每天都来上课。
yīnwèi píng cháng tā měi tiān dōu lái shàng kè.
because usually she every day all come attend class.
because usually she comes to class every day.

不是因为她那么爱学习,而是因为她爱看Jerry。
Bú shì yīnwèi tā nàme ài xuéxí, ér shì yīnwèi tā ài kàn Jerry.
No is because she so love [to] study, but is because she love watch Jerry.
Not because she loves to study so much, but because she loves to look at Jerry.

昨 **zuó** 801
yesterday; past

日 rì "sun" radical, seen in characters indicating time periods

昨天 **zuótiān** 709
yesterday

以为/以为 **yǐwéi** 719, 308
to have assumed mistakenly

"to take" + "to be;" used when we thought something that turned out to be different.

病 **bìng** 802
sick; ill; illness; disease

Radical 疒 chuáng always appears in characters about sickness; 丙 bǐng for pronunciation.

生病 **shēng bìng** 124
to get sick

"to give birth" + "disease"

平 **píng** 803
flat; level; even; equal

平常 **píng cháng** 625
usually

"even" + "ordinary"

每 **měi** 804
every; each

习 **xí** 805
to learn; to practice

老师想问她还会休息多久，
Lǎoshī xiǎng wèn tā hái huì xiūxi duō jiǔ,
Teacher wish ask she still may rest how long,
The teacher wanted to ask how much longer she was going to rest,

所以给她打了一个电话。
suǒyǐ gěi tā dǎ le yí gè diànhuà.
therefore give she hit [complete] one [item] telephone.
so he just gave her a phone call.

學習 / 学习 **xuéxi** 123, 805
to study; to learn

see grammar explanations

而 / 而 **ér shì** 616, 107
是 / 是 but rather

不 / 不 **bú shì A, ér shì B**
A, / A, not A, but rather B
而 / 而
是 / 是
B / B

想 / 想 **xiǎng** 743
to wish; to want to; would like to

還 / 还 **hái** 718
here: also; in additon to; on top of

Originally: "still," often used as a conjunction: "still (more);" always before verb/predicate; see grammar explanations.

會 / 会 **huì** 320
to be likely to; will

Here indicates the future. See grammar explanations.

休 / 休 **xiū** 806
to rest; to take a break; to cease

man 亻 rén resting by tree 木 mù

息 / 息 **xī** 807
breath; to breathe; to rest; to pause

心 xīn "heart" radical for calming down

休息 / 休息 **xiūxi**
to rest; to take a break

"to rest" + "a breath"

久 / 久 **jiǔ** 808
long time

多久 / 多久 **duō jiǔ** 512, 808
how long?

所 / 所 **suǒ** 809
a place; that which

所以 / 所以 **suǒyǐ** 809, 719
therefore

"the reason for which"

打 / 打 **dǎ** 810
to hit

Hand 扌(手) shǒu is necessary for hitting; 丁 dīng is phonetic; it looks like a nail and it means "nail" when written with a metal 钅(金) jīn radical (钉/釘 dīng).

電 / 电 **diàn** 811
electricity; electronic

originally meant "lightening," hence the 雨 yǔ "rain" radical

話 / 话 **huà** 812
words; spoken language

讠 yán "speech" + 舌 shé "tongue"

電話 / 电话 **diànhuà**
telephone

"electricity" + "words"

打電話 / 打电话 **dǎ diànhuà**
to make a phone call

"to hit" + "telephone"

給A打電話 / 给A打电话 **gěi A dǎ diànhuà** 725
to give A a phone call

Some useful time expressions

昨天 **zuótiān** yesterday　　今天 **jīntiān** today　　明天 **míngtiān** tomorrow
去年 **qùnián** (330, 716) last year　　今年 **jīnnián** this year　　明年 **míngnián** (827) next year
现在 **xiànzài** now　　平常 **píngcháng** usually　　常常 **chángcháng** often

To say *every day* or *every year*, we can just repeat the word for *day* and *year*:
　　天天 **tiān tiān** daily　年年 **nián nián** annually

But it is much more common to use the word 每 **měi** *every*:
　　每天 **měi tiān** every day, 每年 **měi nián** every year

每 **měi** always requires a measure word (天 **tiān** *day* and 年 **nián** *year* are measure words in their own right):
　　每个月 **měi gè yuè** every month
　　每个人 **měi gè rén** every person (everybody)

In a sentence, 每 **měi** usually comes together with 都 **dōu** *all*, which must always be placed before the verb:
　　我每天都喝酒 **wǒ měi tiān dōu hē jiǔ**
　　I every day all drink alcohol (I drink alcohol every day)

　　每个学生都爱 Jerry **měi gè xuésheng dōu ài Jerry**
　　Every student all love Jerry. (All students love Jerry.)

天天

In these sentences we can theoretically drop 都 **dōu**, but it sounds like something is missing.

But I thought ...

We use 以为 **yǐwéi** when we thought something, but it turned out to be wrong:
　　我以为你生病了 **wǒ yǐwéi nǐ shēngbìng le**
　　I thought you were sick (but you were not)
　　她以为 Jerry 是人 **tā yǐwéi Jerry shì rén**
　　She thought Jerry was a human being (but Jerry is a horse)
　　爸爸以为妈妈爱他 **bàba yǐwéi māma ài tā**
　　Dad thought mom loved him (she does not)

Lonely verbs

We talked about verbs in chapter 2 and we said they don't like to stand alone and need company; most of them have a default object, e.g. 吃饭 **chī fàn** *to eat (cooked rice)*. However, some verbs don't have a default object, but they still don't like to stand alone in the world, so they look for another verb that means almost exactly the same thing as the "original" lonely verb, thus becoming a two-syllable and no longer lonely. The most common example is 学习 **xuéxí** *to study*, literally *to study* and *to practice/to learn*. If we don't want to specify what we study, but just say that we like to study or have to study, or will study in general, then we use 学习 **xuéxí** instead of just 学 **xué** alone:

> 我爱学习 **wǒ ài xuéxí** *I love to study (and practice)*
> (nothing specific, just in general)

To compare, if we want to say *I love to eat*, we still need to add the object:

> 我爱吃饭 **wǒ ài chī fàn** *I love to eat (cooked rice)*
> (even though I love to eat in general, not necessarily only rice).

We could not say ~~我爱学~~ **wǒ ài xué** or ~~我爱吃~~ **wǒ ài chī**, because these sentences sound incomplete; these verbs are begging for objects.

Another example of such a two-syllable verb that we just learned in this chapter is 休息 **xiūxi** *to rest*.

Two syllable verbs can still take objects, e.g.

> 我爱学习中文 **wǒ ài xuéxí zhōngwén**
> *I love to study (and practice) Chinese.*

We love Jerry SO much

这么 **zhème**, 那么 **nàme** and 多么 **duōme** all mean *so* and we always use them before the verb or adjective we want to intensify:

> 齐老师多么爱 Jerry **Qí lǎoshī duōme ài Jerry**
> *Teacher Qi so much loves Jerry. (Teacher Qi loves Jerry so much.)*
> Jerry 那么好看 **Jerry nàme hǎo kàn** *Jerry is so good looking.*
> 王小猫这么想看 Jerry **Wáng Xiǎomāo zhème xiǎng kàn Jerry**
> *Wang Xiaomao so wants to see/visit Jerry.*

What will the future bring?

We learned in chapter 3 that 会 **huì** means *can* or *to know how*. We can use it to describe a skill:

Jerry 会说中文 **Jerry huì shuō zhōngwén** *Jerry can speak Chinese.*

王小猫会骑马 **Wáng Xiǎomāo huì qí mǎ**
Wang Xiaomao can (knows how to) ride horses.

我不会做饭 **wǒ bú huì zuò fàn**
I can't (don't know how to) cook.

会 **huì** also indicates that something can, may, or is likely to happen, so we can use it as a future marker and translate as *will (likely)*:

我明年会去中国 **wǒ míngnián huì qù Zhōngguó**
Next year I may/I will (likely) go to China.

Jerry不会吃你的花 **Jerry bú huì chī nǐ de huā**
Jerry will not/is not likely to eat your flowers.

王小猫，你会休息多久？ **Wáng Xiǎomāo, nǐ huì xiūxi duō jiǔ?**
Wang Xiaomao, how long are you likely to/will you rest?

你明天会不会来上课？ **nǐ míngtiān huì bú huì lái shàng kè?**
May you/will you come to class tomorrow?"

你会休息多久？

Fortune cookie:

韭菜
韭菜
韭菜

jiǔ 825
green garlic

cài 826
vegetable

jiǔcài
green garlic
chives

Part 2

— 喂，王小猫！ 我是齐老师。 你昨天
— **Wéi, Wáng Xiǎomāo! Wǒ shì Qí lǎoshī. Nǐ zuótiān**
— Hello, Wang Little Cat! I am Qi Teacher. You yesterday
— Hello, Wang Xiaomao! This is teacher Qi. Why were you

为什么没有来上课？ 你不舒服吗？
wèishénme méi yǒu lái shàng kè? Nǐ bù shūfu ma?
why no have come attend class? You no comfortable [question]?
not in class yesterday? Are you not feeling well?

— 老师，你太客气了， 谢谢你，
— **Lǎoshī, nǐ tài kèqi le, xiè xie nǐ,**
— Teacher, you too polite [emphasis], thank you,
— Teacher, you are really kind! Thank you,

我去商店买花了。

喂	**wèi** 813 hello

口 kǒu "mouth" radical for the meaning; 畏 wèi "to fear" is for pronunciation.

舒	**shū** 814 to relax; to make oneself comfortable
服	**fú** 636 to obey; to accept; to acclimatize
不舒服	**bù shūfu** 121, 814, 636 uncomfortable; feeling unwell; sick; under the weather
客	**kè** 815 guest

Roof 宀 mián under which the guest is received; 各 gè is for pronunciation.

氣 气	**qì** 816 air; ether; gas; vapor; the atmosphere

Radical 米 mǐ in the traditional form means "uncooked rice." This is an ancient word meaning the primeval energy, the ether that the whole world consist of, the vital energy, the breath of life.

客氣 客气	**kèqi** kind; polite

"guest" + "air" = to treat others like guests

我没事，我很舒服！
wǒ méi shì,　　wǒ hěn shūfu!
I have no matter,　I very comfortable!
I'm fine, I am well relaxed!

— 怎么了？你没有生病吗？
— **Zěnme le?　　Nǐ méi yǒu shēng bìng ma?**
— How [have become]? You no have get sick [question]?
— What's going on? Didn't you get sick?

— 没有！
— **Méi yǒu!**
— No have.
— No I didn't.

— 我以为你去看病了，
— **Wǒ yǐwéi nǐ qù kàn bìng le,**
— I assume [mistakenly] you go look [at] illness [complete],
— I thought you went to see a doctor,

所以没来上课。
suǒyǐ méi lái shàng kè.
therefore no [have] come attend class.
therefore you didn't come to class.

— 看什么病？我没有病。昨天没去上课，
— **Kàn shénme bìng?　Wǒ méi yǒu bìng.　　Zuótiān méi qù shàng kè,**
— Look [at] what illness? I no have illness. Yesterday no [have] go attend class,
— Check what?　　　　I'm not sick.　　　　I didn't go to class yesterday,

是因为我去商店买花了。
shì yīnwèi wǒ qù shāngdiàn mǎi huā le.
is because I go store buy flowers [complete].
because I went to buy flowers.

没事　**méi shì** 213, 707
everything is alright

"There is no issue/matter". Colloquial and casual way of saying "no problem; It's alright."

舒服　**shūfu** 814, 636
comfortable; feeling good; relaxed

This word may have a double meaning; often, it describes a state of gleeful satisfaction. The teacher asks Wang Xiaomao whether she is "unwell," meaning "sick;" her emphasis on being 很舒服 may be related to other circumstances, not necessarily her not being sick.

看病　**kàn bìng**
208, 802
to see a doctor; to get checked up (for an illness)

"to look at" + "illness"

怎麼了 / 怎么了　**zěnme le**
711, 128, 329
how now? what's up? what's going on? (*a slightly agressive and rude way of asking "what's going on?"*)

How to be more expressive

To make a strong statement in Chinese, we often use the negative, e.g. 没错 **méi cuò** *there is no mistake* actually means *absolutely correct*. Similarly, 不错 **bú cuò** *not bad* actually means *really quite good*. We can find more examples as we go, 不高 **bù gāo** *not tall* means *quite short*, 不舒服 **bù shūfu** *not well* means *unwell*, 不好看 **bù hǎo kàn** *not handsome* means *quite ugly*, 不小 **bù xiǎo** *not little* means *huge*, etc.

Completing things (part 2)

In chapter 5 we met the wonderful particle 了 **le** that allows us to complete actions. We can put it in different places in the sentence, depending on what aspect we want to emphasize, but the meaning will not change much:

我吃饭了 **wǒ chī fàn le** *I ate/I have eaten* (in general)
我吃了饭 **wǒ chī le fàn** *I ate* (emphasis on the verb)
我吃了饭了 **wǒ chī le fàn le** *I ate already*
(emphasis on fact that the situation has changed compared to before)

*This might seem a bit confusing, but the point is: it is not so important where you put the 了 **le**, so don't worry about it.*

Generally speaking, the particle 了 **le** indicates a completion of an action, e.g.

我去看Jerry了 **wǒ qù kàn Jerry le** *I went to see Jerry*
(the action is completed, I did it, it's over).

Thus, 了 **le** allows us to talk about some past events, but it does not indicate a past tense! In other words, we do not always use 了 **le** to talk about the past, but only to emphasize that we completed something. For example if we used to do something often and there was no point at which we completed the action and stopped doing it, we don't need to use 了 **le**:

去年我常常去看Jerry **qùnián wǒ chángcháng qù kàn Jerry**
Last year I often went to see Jerry.

We also learned that to say we did not do something, we use 没(有) **méi (yǒu)** *have not*. We use it more generally when we want to say we did not/have not/would not do something in the past, whether we completed the action or not:

王小猫没(有)来上课 **Wáng xiǎomāo méi (yǒu) lái shàng kè**
Wang Xiaomao did not come to class.

她没(有)生病 **tā méi (yǒu) shēng bìng** She did not get sick.

去年王小猫没(有)常常吃草
Qùnián Wáng xiǎomāo méi (yǒu) chángcháng chī cǎo
Last year Wang Xiaomao did not often eat grass.

Jerry常常也没(有)吃草 **Jerry chángcháng yě méi (yǒu) chī cǎo**
Jerry often also didn't eat grass.

But we can never use it with actions that cannot be completed, such as verbs expressing feelings, existence, or states of mind, just because they occurred in the past. We can never say:

~~去年我没(有)是学生~~ ~~**qùnián wǒ méi (yǒu) shì xuésheng**~~

Instead we have to say:

去年我不是学生 **qùnián wǒ bú shì xuésheng**
Last year I no be student (Last year I was not a student.)

We know this took place in the past only from the context – using 去年 **qùnián**.

It is incorrect to say:

~~去年我还没(有)会说中文~~
~~**qùnián wǒ hái méi (yǒu) huì shuō zhōngwén**~~

Instead we have to say:

去年我还不会说中文 **qùnián wǒ hái bú huì shuō zhōngwén**
Last year I still no can speak Chinese
(Last year I still could not speak Chinese.)

Also incorrect:

~~昨天我没(有)在中国~~ ~~**zuótiān wǒ méi (yǒu) zài Zhōngguó**~~

Instead we have to say:

昨天我不在中国 **zuótiān wǒ bú zài Zhōngguó**
Yesterday I no be present China (I was not in China yesterday).

Part 3

— 你买花干什么?
— **Nǐ mǎi huā gàn shénme?**
— You buy flowers do what?
— What did you buy flowers for?

— 因为我觉得一个人
— **Yīnwèi wǒ jué de yí gè rén**
— Because I think one [item] person (alone)
— Because I thought it is extremely sad to

过生日太难过,
guò shēngrì tài nán guò,
spend birthday too hard [to] spend (sad),
spend my birthday all by myself,

所以我去买了很多花。
suǒyǐ wǒ qù mǎi le hěn duō huā.
therefore I go buy [complete] very many flowers.
therefore I just went and bought lots of flowers.

過生日
过生日
guò shēngrì
818, 124, 710
to celebrate birthday ("to spend birthday")

難過
难过
nánguò
618, 818
sad
"difficult" + "to pass"

商
shāng 633
trade; commerce; business
originally means "to negotiate"

店
diàn 819
shop; store

商店
shāngdiàn
shop; store
"business" + "shop"

因為…
所以…
因为…
所以…
yīnwèi … suǒyǐ …
308, 309, 808, 719
because …, therefore …

幹
干
幹什麼
干什么
gàn 817
to do (very colloquial)

gàn shénme
817, 127, 128
what are you doing? what for? (very colloquial slang, may sound rude at times)

一個
一个
yí gè rén
516, 517, 122
alone; by oneself ("one person")

人

過
过
guò 818
to cross; to pass; to spend (time)

辶 chuò "road" radical to indicate the meaning

129

— 我的天啊，你花了多少钱？
- **Wǒ dē tiān a,　　nǐ　huā le duōshao qián?**
- I's heaven a, you spend [complete] how much money?
- Oh my God, how much money did you spend?

— 花很贵，我花了七百四十块钱。
- **Huā hěn guì,　　wǒ huā le　qī bǎi sì shí kuài qián.**
- Flowers very expensive, I spend [complete] 740 pieces [of] money.
- Flowers are expensive, I spent 740 yuan.

— 七百四十块！那太贵了！
- **Qī bǎi sì shí kuài!　　Nà tài guì le!**
- 740 pieces!　　That too expensive [emphasis]!
- 740!　　That's extremely expensive!

你干吗买那么多花？它们很快会死！
Nǐ gàn ma mǎi nàme duō huā?　　Tāmen hěn kuài huì sǐ!
You do [question] (what for) buy so many flowers? They very quick can die!
What for did you buy so many? They will soon die!

— 不会死、不会死！ 我给 Jerry 吃了。
- **Bú huì sǐ,　bú huì sǐ!**　　**Wǒ gěi Jerry chī le.**
- No can die,　no can die!　　I give Jerry eat [complete].
- They won't, they won't!　　I gave them to Jerry to eat.

天 tiān 709
heaven; God

我的天 wǒ de tiān
104, 310, 709
oh my God

花 huā 729
to spend

Yes. Exactly the same as 花 "flower." I don't know why, either ...

少 shǎo 820
few

looks / sounds like 小 xiǎo "little"

多少 duōshao 512
how much/ many? (numbers over 10)

"lots" + "few"= "a lot or a little?"

块 kuài 821
a piece; *measure word for money*

Radical 土 tǔ "earth" for the meaning (a piece of land). 鬼 guǐ in the traditional form is for pronunciation, means "ghost; devil;" the simplified form imitates the character 快 kuài "fast; quick" with the same pronunciation.

幹嗎 gàn ma
817, 125
why? what for?

very colloquial, often rude

牠/它 tā 822
it

This is the same 3rd person pronoun as 他/她 tā "he/she", but it is written this way when it does not refer to a man or a woman, but instead indicates animals (牠) or material objects (它); in traditional script, "he/she" for animals is always written 牠, where radical 牛 niú "cow; ox" is used instead. Simplified texts never use 牠, but always 它 for both animals and objects.

牠/它們 tāmen
它们 822, 133
they (objects or animals)

快 kuài 823
fast; quick; soon

忄(心) "heart" radical, because this character originally means "sharp" and "happy;" also, to convey the sense of urgency; notice that the simplified form of the character 块 kuài "piece" has the same phonetic element, but a different radical; when used before a verb, 快 kuài is an adverb and means "quickly; soon;" see grammar explanations.

死 sǐ 824
to die

Alone

Alone in Chinese is 一个人 **yí gè rén**, literally *one person*. It is an adverb, which means it describes how the action is performed, in this case "*singly*". Therefore, in Chinese it must always come before the verb it describes:

我一个人在家 **wǒ yí gè rén zài jiā**
I alone am at home. (I'm at home alone.)

她一个人过生日 **tā yí gè rén guò shēngrì**
She alone spends birthday. (She is spending birthday alone.)

王小猫一个人喝酒 **Wáng Xiǎomāo yí gè rén hē jiǔ**
Wang Xiaomao alone drinks alcohol. (Wang Xiaomao is drinking alone.)

The same is true about other adverbs, e.g. 快 **kuài** *quick*, which means *soon; quickly* when followed by a verb:

我快死了 **wǒ kuài sǐ le** *I quick die complete. (I'm going to die soon.)*

我们快吃饭了！ **wǒmen kuài chī fàn le**
We quick eat [change]. (We are eating soon!)

了 **le** here is used for emphasis; it indicates the change that is about to occur.

你们很快知道了！ **nǐmen hěn kuài zhīdao le!**
You all very quick know [change]! ("You all will know soon!")

王小猫很快会过生日 **Wáng Xiǎomāo hěn kuài huì guò shēngrì**
Wang Xiaomao very quick will pass birthday.
(Very soon it's going to be Wang Xiaomao's birthday.)

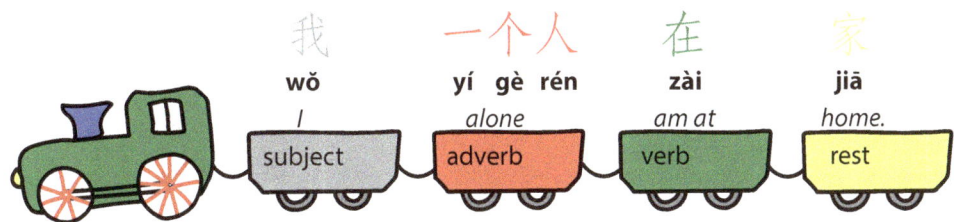

Let's talk about money

We've learned how to say the numbers, now let's learn how to count money! To ask how much something costs, we use the question phrase: 多少钱 **duōshao qián**, literally *how much money?* Another extremely common and colloquial way of asking the same question is 怎么卖 **zěnme mài** (1225), literally *How [do you] sell [it]?*

To count money, we use the measure word 块 **kuài** (821) *piece*:
    一块（钱）**yí kuài (qián)** *one piece (of money)*

Saying *money* at the end is optional and in fact redundant, so people usually don't say it; therefore, many people assume the name of the Chinese currency is **kuai** (just as we would say *one dollar* in English, we say 一块 **yī kuài** *one kuai* in Chinese). In fact, the Chinese monetary unit is named 元 **yuán** (828). It is used in official speech and in written language, and it serves as a measure word, so when we say it, we don't use 块 **kuài**:
    一元 **yì yuán** *one yuan*

Another, even more "official" and most formal name of the Chinese money is the RBM 人民币 **rénmínbì** (128, 829, 830) *people's currency*, which is actually often used in everyday speech. We need the measure word 块 **kuài** to count it, e.g. 两块人民币 **liǎng kuài rénmínbì** *two pieces of People's Currency (two RMB)*.

We use 块 **kuài** to count any kind of currency, e.g. American dollars.

The official name for USD in Chinese is 美元 **měi yuán** (319, 828), literally *American yuan*.

1. Fix the errors.
a) 一个年
b) 一个月三号二〇〇八年
c) 昨年
d) 下个年
e) 二个天

2. Translation 翻译 **fānyì (use** 会**):**
a) Jerry will likely go to the United States.
b) Wang Xiaomao will not study French.
c) Teacher Qi will likely call Jerry on the phone.
d) Jerry will not call teacher Qi.
e) Mister Ma will likely go to the store to buy high heels and beer.
f) We are all likely to die.

3. Questions about the text (true 对 **or false** 不对**).**
a) ( ) 王小猫平常不上课。
b) ( ) 王小猫去商店买啤酒。
c) ( ) 王小猫花了很多钱。
d) ( ) 王小猫买的花不贵。
e) ( ) 齐老师以为王小猫会死。
f) ( ) 王小猫昨天很舒服。

4. Transcribe from pinyin to characters.
Wǒ bù zhīdào wǒ gēge wèishénme nàme ài chī cǎo. Wǒ wèn le tā, dànshì tā méi gàosu wǒ. Tā shuō wǒ tài xiǎo. Tā měi tiān dōu chī. Jīntiān tā bú dàn chī cǎo, érqiě yě chī huā le. Wǒ yǐwéi tā huì sǐ, kěshì tā méi yǒu. Wǒ xiǎng tā yídìng huì shēngbìng. Wǒ bù guǎn, yīnwèi wǒ bú ài tā, kěshì wǒ juéde hěn qíguài. Wǒ gēge shì bú shì yì pǐ mǎ?

5. Fill in the blanks.
以为　这么　会　一个人　　所以　休息

a) 我今天不忙，不去上课，就在家里 ____ 。
b) ____ 过生日很难过。
c) 我没有 ____ 多钱。
d) 我 ____ 他会画画儿。
e) 你 ____ 给她什么礼物？
f) 因为我爱人做的饭不好吃，____ 我不在家吃饭。

6. Rewrite the sentences adding the time expression in the parentheses:
a) 妈妈打爸爸 （平常）
b) 马先生去商店买豆腐 （每天都）
c) 我才可以去中国 （明年）
d) 我爱人老说她就会死 （今天）
e) 老师上中文课 （九点；上午）
f) 那个帅哥请我女朋友喝茶了，所以我明天去他家打他。(今天下午)

7. What is the price of these items? Write it down in Chinese.
a) cat (I give it to you as a present)
b) high heels (105)
c) dumplings (11)
d) bicycle (1040)
e) motorcycle (2117)
f) Mr. Ma's ugly painting (250)
g) Chinese meal (14)
h) book (42)
i) flowers (116)
j) tea (2)
k) chopsticks (22)

9 九

老师明白了
The teacher got it

Part 1

齐老师不明白王小猫的意思。他问：
Qí lǎoshī bù míngbai Wáng Xiǎomāo de yìsi. Tā wèn:
Qi Teacher no understand Wang Little Cat's meaning. He ask:
Teacher Qi does not understand what Wang Xiaomao meant. He asked:

—你什么时候、在哪儿给Jerry吃了花？
— **Nǐ shénme shíhou, zài nǎ'er gěi Jerry chī le huā?**
— You what time (when), where give Jerry eat [complete] flowers?
— When and where did you give Jerry flowers to eat?

你没来学校啊。
Nǐ méi lái xuéxiào a.
You no [have] come school a.
You were not at school.

—我请他来我家了。他昨天在我家吃花了。
— **Wǒ qǐng tā lái wǒ jiā le. Tā zuótiān zài wǒ jiā chī huā le.**
— I invite he come I house [complete]. He yesterday present I house eat flowers [complete].
— I invited him to my house. He ate flowers yesterday at my house.

明 **míng** 710, 714
bright

sun 日 + moon 月 = brightness.

白 **bái** 901
white

We've seen 白 as part of 的 de, (originally also means "white").

明白 **míngbai**
to understand; comprehend; get (a meaning)

"Bright" + "clear" = to have a clear understanding/ a bright and white/clear idea of something

候 **hòu** 902
to wait; time; season

This character originally means "to wait (for a period of time)".

時候
时候 **shíhou**
(a point in) time; time (when); at the time (when)

not to be confused with 时间 shíjiān (chapter 7); see grammar explanations

什麽
时候
什么
时候 **shénme shíhou**
when? ("What time?")

—你说什么？他怎么知道你家里有花呢？
- **Nǐ shuō shénme?　Tā zěnme zhīdào nǐ jiā li yǒu huā ne?**
- You say what? He how know you house inside have flowers [and how about]?
- What are you talking about? And how did he know you had flowers at home?

—Jerry 有手机。我打电话告诉他了。
- **Jerry yǒu shǒujī.　Wǒ dǎ diànhuà gàosu tā le.**
- Jerry have cell phone.　I hit phone tell he [complete].
- Jerry has a cell phone, I gave him a phone call and told him.

—我不相信！你知道他的手机号码吗？
- **Wǒ bù xiāngxìn!　Nǐ zhīdào tā de shǒujī hàomǎ ma?**
- I no believe!　You know he's cell phone number [question]?
- I can't believe it!　You know his cell phone number?

—当然啊！他上个星期就给我了。
- **Dāngrán a!　Tā shàng gè xīngqī jiù gěi wǒ le.**
- Of course a!　He previous [item] week just give I [complete].
- But of course, he gave it to me already last week.

我们常常打电话。
Wǒmen cháng cháng dǎ diànhuà.
We　often　hit　phone.
We call each other often.

校 **xiào** 903
schoolhouse
木 mù "wood" radical, one of the Five Agents; schools used to be built with wood; 交 jiāo is for pronunciation (jiao → xiao).

學校
学校 **xuéxiào** 123, 903
school
"to study" + "schoolhouse"

手 **shǒu** 904
hand
We've seen this character often before as a radical, e.g. in 我, 打, 找, 看, etc.

手機
手机 **shǒujī** 904, 620
cellphone
"hand" + "machine"

碼
码 **mǎ** 905
a code; a sign or symbol indicating number
石 shí radical means "stone;" 马, of course, is for pronunciation

號碼
号码 **hàomǎ** 715, 905
number
"number" + "code"

星 **xīng** 906
star; heavenly body; planet
combination of 日 rì "the sun" and 生 shēng "to be born" → any heavenly body that shines

期 **qī** 907
period of time; designated time; time limit
其 qí for pronunciation, 月 yuè "moon" can mean "time" or "age"

星期 **xīngqī**
week
"star" + "time period" = cycle of the stars

上个星期 **shàng gè xīngqī** 217, 517, 906, 907
last week

常常 **cháng cháng** 625
often
"ordinary" + "ordinary"

就 **jiù** 501
just; only

— 你就请了Jerry一个人吗?
— Nǐ jiù qǐng le Jerry yí gè rén ma?
— You just invite [complete] Jerry one [item] person (alone) [question]?
— You just invited Jerry alone?

— 对！Jerry来我家给我过生日。
— Duì! Jerry lái wǒ jiā gěi wǒ guò shēngrì.
— Correct! Jerry come I house give I spend birthday.
— That's right! Jerry came to my house to celebrate my birthday.

他还带了一个蛋糕！
Tā hái dài le yí gè dàngāo!
He still bring [complete] one [item] cake!
He even brought a cake!

給 Jerry 過生日 给 Jerry 过生日	**gěi Jerry guò shēngrì** 725, 818, 124, 710 to organize a party for Jerry
帶 带	**dài** 908 to carry; to bring
蛋	**dàn** 909 egg

Radical 虫 chóng means "worm;" probably refers to the embrio inside an egg.

糕	**gāo** 910 cake

A cake made of rice is meant here, hense the 米 mǐ "rice" radical; 羔 gāo is for pronunciation.

蛋糕	**dàngāo** Western style cake

"egg" + "cake;" traditionally, 糕 gāo is a rice cake and would not contain eggs (and other traditional Western ingredients, such as milk, sugar, flour, etc.); therefore, an "egg (rice) cake" is a Western style thing.

Time: 时间 shíjiān versus 时候 shíhou

There are two ways to say *time* in Chinese and they are not the same.

时间 **shíjiān** means *time* as a concept; we can have it or not, we can waste or spend it, or we can measure it:

我没有时间 **wǒ méi yǒu shíjiān** *I don't have time*

老师花太多时间学马的心理 **lǎoshī huā tài duō shíjiān xué mǎ de xīnlǐ**
Teacher spends too much time studying horses' psychology

多长时间？ **duō cháng shíjiān?** *How long time? (How long?)*

时候 **shíhou** refers to a point in time when something happens. We will learn more about it in chapter 13. For now, just remember we use it to ask *when*?

什么时候？ **shénme shíhou?** *what time? (When?)*
你什么时候会去中国？ **nǐ shénme shíhou huì qù Zhōngguó?**
You what time can go China? (When will you go to China?)

王小猫什么时候吃花了？
Wáng Xiǎomāo shénme shíhou chī huā le?
Wang Xiaomao what time eat flowers [complete]?
(When did Wang Xiaomao eat flowers?)

那时候我还不认识Jerry **nà shíhou wǒ hái bú rènshi Jerry**
That time I still no know Jerry. (At that time I still didn't know Jerry.)

Time Place Action

In chapter 7, we saw that in Chinese place always comes before action: we first say where we do something, and only then what we do. e.g. 我在中国学中文 **wǒ zài Zhōngguó xué zhōngwén** *I study Chinese in China*. Now, we will see that time comes even before.

English: I study Chinese in China this year.

Again, the word order in English is exactly the opposite; but in Chinese, we may never change it! The time of an action ALWAYS comes first:

我早上八点吃饭 **wǒ zǎoshàng bā diǎn chī fàn**
I morning eight o'clock eat rice (I eat at eight in the morning)

他今天没来上课 **tā jīntiān méi lái shàng kè**
He today no have come attend class (He didn't come to class today)

Jerry昨天在我家吃花了 **Jerry zuótiān zài wǒ jiā chī huā le**
Jerry yesterday present my house eat flowers [complete]
(Yesterday Jerry ate flowers at my house)

你什么时候去中国？ **nǐ shénme shíhou qù Zhōngguó?**
You when go China? (When are you going to China?)

More time expressions

We've learned a few time expressions in chapter 8. Let's learn some more! 星期 **xīngqī** is only one of three ways to say *week* in Chinese. We count weeks with a measure word, just like months 月 **yuè**:

一个星期 **yí gè xīngqī** *one week*
两个月 **liǎng gè yuè** *two months*

Days of the week don't have names, only numbers:

星期一 **xīngqī yī** 906, 907, 516 *Monday*
星期二 **xīngqī èr** 535 *Tuesday*
星期三 **xīngqī sān** 536 *Wednesday*
星期四 **xīngqī sì** 537 *Thursday*
星期五 **xīngqī wǔ** 538 *Friday*
星期六 **xīngqī liù** 539 *Saturday*
星期天 / 星期日 **xīngqī tiān** 709 / **xīngqī rì** 710 *Sunday*

> This is an exception; instead of a number, we use 天 **tiān** *Heaven/God* or 日 **rì** *the Sun*, which makes it a perfect translation from European languages.

Also, remember these:

上个星期 **shàng gè xīngqī** *last week*
下个星期 **xià gè xīngqī** *next week*
上个月 **shàng gè yuè** *last month*
下个月 **xià gè yuè** *next month*

Still on top

还 **hái** means *still*.
We must always use it before a verb:
他还没有来 **tā hái méi yǒu lái** *He still has not come*

我	还	爱	你
wǒ	**hái**	**ài**	**nǐ**
I	still	love	you
subject	adverb	action	rest

It also means *and also*, *in addition to* or *on top of*:

我有一个女朋友，还有两个男朋友
wǒ yǒu yí gè nǚpéngyou, hái yǒu liǎng gè nánpéngyou
I have one girlfriend and (on top of that) two boyfriends.

Jerry还带了一个蛋糕给王小猫吃
Jerry hái dài le yí gè dàngāo gěi Wáng Xiǎomāo chī.
Jerry still bring [complete] a cake give Wang Xiaomao eat.
(In addition, Jerry also brought a cake for Wang Xiaomao.)

Part 2

— 你买的花他都吃了吗?
- **Nǐ mǎi de huā tā dōu chī le ma?**
- You-buy's flowers he all eat [complete] [question]?
- Did he eat all of the flowers you bought?

— 都吃了！ 他很高兴！
- **Dōu chī le! Tā hěn gāoxìng!**
- All eat [complete]! He very happy!
- He did! He was very happy!

他说我买的花不但很漂亮,而且非常香。
Tā shuō wǒ mǎi de huā bú dàn hěn piàoliang, érqiě fēicháng xiāng.
He say I buy's flowers not only very pretty, but also extremely delicious.
He said the flowers I bought were not only pretty, but also delicious.

我也吃了， 也觉得好吃。
Wǒ yě chī le, yě jué de hǎo chī.
I also eat [complete], also think good [to] eat (tasty).
I also ate them and also thought they were tasty.

— 王小猫， 我看你真的有病。 你得去
- **Wáng Xiǎomāo, wǒ kàn nǐ zhēn de yǒu bìng. Nǐ děi qù**
- Wang Little Cat, I see you really have illness. You must go
- Wang Xiaomao, the way I see it, you certainly are sick (crazy). You must go to

他说我买的花不但很
漂亮,而且非常香。

高 **gāo** 421
tall; high

兴 **xìng** 911
enthused; excited; stimulated; elated

高兴 **gāoxìng**
happy; glad; high-spirited

"high" + "stimulated"

漂 **piào** 912
pretty

originally "to float," hence the water 氵(水) shuǐ radical

亮 **liàng** 913
bright, light, shiny

漂亮 **piàoliang**
pretty

香 **xiāng** 914
fragrant; delicious; yummy

我看 **wǒ kàn**
104, 208
in my opinion; I think...; the way I see it

"I" + "look at"

有病 **yǒu bìng**
214, 802
double meaning of "sick"

"To have a disease"; this can mean "crazy"/"mentally ill".

得 **děi** 521
must; to have to

This is the same character as in 觉得 juéde. Here both pronunciation and meaning are different!

医院看心理医生。
yīyuàn kàn xīnlǐ yīshēng.
hospital see psychology doctor.
the hospital and see a psychologist.

院 **yuàn** 915
a yard; a courtyard; a designation for government offices or public places

When radical 阝 fù appears on the left side of a character, it is a short form of 阜 "a mound" and often refers to landmasses or constructions; 完 wán is here for pronunciation (wán → yuàn); however, when 阝 appears on the right side, as in 都 dōu that we have learned before, then it is a different radical pronounced yì, a short version of 邑 "city".

醫院 / 医院 **yīyuàn** 606, 915 hospital

"illness" + "yard" = "sickhouse"

Must

得 **děi** means *must; have to* and it is a modal verb – it requires another verb in a sentence:

我得去医院看病 **wǒ děi qù yīyuàn kàn bìng**
I must go hospital watch disease .
(I must go to the hospital to get checked by a doctor.)

學生每天都得上课 **xuésheng měi tiān dōu děi shàng kè**
Students every day must attend class
(Students must go to class every day)

學生得听老师的话 **xuésheng děi tīng lǎoshī de huà**
Students have to listen teacher's words.
(Students have to listen to what the teacher says.)

醫生 / 医生 **yīshēng** 606, 124 medical doctor

"medical science" + "adept"

心理醫生 / 心理医生 **xīnlǐ yīshēng** 311, 312, 606, 124 psychologist

"psychology" + "doctor"

Fortune cookie:

醋 **cù** vinegar

吃醋 **chī cù** 202, 929 *to eat vinegar* means *to be jealous*.

Part 3

— 你是中文老师，不是医生，怎么能说我
— **Nǐ shì zhōngwén lǎoshī, bú shì yīshēng, zěnme néng shuō wǒ**
— You are Chinese language teacher, no are doctor, how can say I
— You are a Chinese teacher, not a doctor, how can you say I

有病？如果Jerry给你吃花，你不会吃吗？
yǒu bìng? Rúguǒ Jerry gěi nǐ chī huā, nǐ bú huì chī ma?
have illness? If Jerry give you eat flowers, you no may eat [question]?
am sick? If Jerry gave you flowers to eat, you wouldn't eat them?

— 算了！我还想问你一个问题。
— **Suàn lē! Wǒ hái xiǎng wèn nǐ yí gè wèntí.**
— Count [complete]! I still wish ask you one [item] question.
— That's enough! I'd like to ask you one more question.

你有没有骑Jerry?
Nǐ yǒu méi yǒu qí Jerry?
You have no have ride Jerry?
Did you ride Jerry?

— 哎呀，没有！Jerry 吃了花就睡觉了...
— **āi yā, méi yǒu! Jerry chī le huā jiù shuì jiào le ...**
— Ai ya, no have! Jerry eat [complete] flowers just sleep [complete]...
— Aw, I didn't! Jerry slept as soon as he finished eating the flowers ...]

能 **néng** 916
can; be able to

如 **rú** 917
to be like; to be similar to; to be as good as

果 **guǒ** 918
fruit; result; outcome

sun 日 rì on top of a tree 木 mù; According to a Chinese myth, the sun was born like a fruit on a mulberry tree.

如果 **rúguǒ**
if

Literally: "like result/outcome" → "if the result is ..., then ...". See grammar explanations.

哎 **āi** 919
interjection of surprise mixed with regret

哎呀 **āi yā** 919, 509
exclamation of surprise, grief, exasperation; "oh well!"

口 kǒu "mouth" radical for exclaiming

睡 **shuì** 920
to sleep

目 mù "eye" radical; 垂 chuí is for pronunciation (shui~chui)

覺
觉 **jiào** 921
a sleep; a nap

Same as 覺 jué "to feel," but different pronunciation; both contain element 见 jiàn "to see".

睡覺
睡觉 **shuì jiào**
to sleep

"to sleep" + "a sleep"

— 什么？？ Jerry 昨晚在你那儿过夜了吗？
— **Shénme ?? Jerry zuówǎn zài nǐ nà'er guò yè le ma?**
— What?? Jerry last night present you there spend night [complete] [question]?
— What??   Last night Jerry spent a night at your place?

— 是啊，他睡了一夜，第二天早上才回去。
— **Shì a,   tā shuì le yí yè,   dì èr tiān zǎoshang cái huí qù.**
— Is [so] a, he sleep [complete] one night, second day morning only return go.
— Yeah, he slept all night and went back only the next morning.

齐老师很生气。 他想： "我真笨！
Qí lǎoshī hěn shēngqì. Tā xiǎng: "Wǒ zhēn bèn!
Qi Teacher very angry.   He think: "I really stupid!
Teacher Qi got pissed.   He thought: "I am really stupid!

昨天为什么没听马先生的话请王小猫
Zuótiān wèishénme méi tīng Mǎ xiānsheng de huà qǐng Wáng Xiǎomāo
Yesterday why no [have] listen Ma Mister's words invite Wang Little Cat
Why didn't I listen to Mr. Ma yesterday and invited Wang Xiaomao

喝啤酒？现在很后悔。"
hē píjiǔ?   Xiànzài hěn hòu huǐ."
drink beer?   Now very regret."
for a beer?   Now, I regret."

晚
晚
wǎn 922
late; evening

日 rì radical; traditional and simplified forms look similar, but the simplified has less strokes; see the writing instructions.

昨晚
昨晚
zuó wǎn 801, 922
yesterday night; last night

abbreviation of 昨天 zuótiān "yesterday" and 晚上 wǎnshàng "evening"

夜
夜
yè 923
night

那兒
那儿
nà'er 410, 609
there

你那兒
你那儿
nǐ nà'er
your place; at your place; at your house

literally "you there; there where you are"

過夜
过夜
guò yè 818, 923
spend the night; sleep over; stay overnight

"to pass" + "night"

一
yī 516
(one) whole

一夜
yí yè 516, 923
the whole night

第
dì 924
prefix for ordinal numbers; number in a sequence

Bamboo ⺮(竹) zhú radical as in other characters that have something to do with counting (e.g. 算 suàn "to count" that we have learned before); counting used to be done with bamboo slips.

第二
dì èr 924, 535
second (in a row)

第 dì + number

第二天
dì èr tiān 924, 535, 709
the next day

"second day"

回
huí 925
to return; go back; turn back

回去
huí qù 925, 330
to go back

去 qù indicates direction away from the speaker

生氣
生气
shēng qì 124, 816
to get upset

"to give birth" + "air/energy"

What if?

如果 **rúguǒ** means *if* and we use it when we want to say what would or would not happen *if*. We often use 如果 **rúguǒ** with 会 **huì** *can; may; will*:

如果我有钱，我会去中国
rúguǒ wǒ yǒu qián, wǒ huì qù Zhōngguó
If I have money, I will go to China

如果你下午有时间，我们去酒吧吧
rúguǒ nǐ xiàwǔ yǒu shíjiān, wǒmen qù jiǔbā ba
If you afternoon have time, we go bar [suggestion]
(If you have time in the afternoon, let's go to a bar)

如果妈妈真的爱爸爸，她不会打他
rúguǒ māma zhēnde ài bàba, tā bú huì dǎ tā
If mom really love dad, she no can beat he.
(If mom really loved dad, she would not beat him.)

Wishing and thinking

想 **xiǎng** means *to think* and we can say whatever we think right after it:
我想他不爱我 **wǒ xiǎng tā bú ài wǒ** *I think he does not love me*
我想他不好看 **wǒ xiǎng tā bù hǎo kàn** *I think he is not good-looking.*
王小猫想我不是好画家
Wáng Xiǎomāo xiǎng wǒ bú shì hǎo huàjiā
Wang Xiaomao thinks I am not a good painter.

When followed by another verb though, 想 **xiǎng** means *to wish [to do sth.]*:
我想吃草 **wǒ xiǎng chī cǎo** *I'd like to eat grass.*
我想去中国 **wǒ xiǎng qù Zhōngguó** *I'd like to go to China.*

And finally, when followed by an object or a person, 想 **xiǎng** means *to miss (someone or something)*:
我想我男朋友 **wǒ xiǎng wǒ nán péngyou** *I miss my boyfriend.*
我想家 **wǒ xiǎng jiā** *I miss home.*

笨 **bèn** 926
stupid; dumb

⺮(竹) zhú "bamboo" radical for being dumb like a stick; 本 běn "root; origin" is for pronunciation.

聽(誰的)話
听(谁的)话
tīng (shéi de) huà
510, 119, 310, 812
to listen (to somebody); to consider someone's opinion; to obey; to be obedient

"to listen to" + (somebody's) + words

後
后
hòu 927
behind; after

The traditional character has been replaced with 后, which originally means "empress" and is also pronounced hòu.

悔 **huǐ** 928
to regret; to repent; to remorse

忄(心) xīn radical suggests that emotions are involved.

後悔
后悔
hòu huǐ
to reget

"after" + "remorse"

Completing things (3)

When we use 了 **le** in the same sentence with 就 **jiù**, we emphasize that something happened immediately after another action had been completed; in such cases, 了 **le** must follow immediately after the verb it completes:

我吃了饭就睡觉
wǒ chī le fàn jiù shuìjiào
I ate complete rice immediately slept
→ *I slept as soon as I ate./
I slept right after I ate./
I ate and then I slept.*

老师下了课就去骑 Jerry
lǎoshī xià le kè jiù qù qí Jerry
Teacher finish class at once go ride Jerry.
→ *The teacher goes to ride Jerry right after class.*

1. 绕口令 *rào kǒu lìng* **Read the tongue twister aloud.**

村前有个颜圆眼　　cūn qián yǒu gè yán yuán yǎn
村后有个颜眼圆　　cūn hòu yǒu gè yán yǎn yuán
不知颜圆眼的眼圆　bù zhī yán yuán yǎn de yǎn yuán
还是颜眼圆的眼圆　hái shì yán yǎn yuán de yǎn yuán?

"In front of the village there is a Yan Round Eye
Behind the village there is a Yan Eye Round
I don't know if Yan Round Eye's eyes are round
Or if Yan Eye Round's eyes are round"

2. Ask questions about the the time:
Pattern:
齐老师<u>今天</u>不上课。 *Teacher Qi does not have class <u>today</u>.*
→ 齐老师<u>什么时候</u>不上课？ *When does teacher Qi not have class?*

我<u>十点</u>睡觉。 *I sleep <u>at 10</u>.*
→ 你<u>几点</u>睡觉？ *<u>At what time</u> do you sleep?*

a) 王小猫<u>昨天</u>买自行车了。
b) 学生每天早上<u>八点</u>上中文课。
c) 他们<u>星期五</u>晚上请我们吃饭。
d) 齐老师<u>三天</u>没有睡觉了。
e) 马先生<u>两个</u>星期没有来学校了。
f) 王小猫病了<u>三个月</u>。
g) 她<u>三月八号</u>过生日。

3. Guess where? Some words are missing. Fix the sentences using vocabulary from the list. One word is missing per sentence unless indicated otherwise:

还　　多　　那儿　　是　　时间　　以为　　可是　　没　　很　　事
个　　那　　得　　时候

a) 爸爸今天有很多：他给妈妈做饭，得去商店买酱油。
(3 words missing here)
b) 我爱人不爱我了，我还爱她。
c) 我Jerry没有男朋友。
d) – 王小猫病了久？
– 她有病。
– 真的吗？她为什么没来上课？

148

e) 我哥哥高，但是他没有很多女朋友。他一个男人，可是他找一男朋友。(3 words missing here)
f) 你什么会有给我打电话？(2 words missing here)
g) 我们去你喝酒吧！

4. Make meaningful sentences out of the following words.
a) 过 / 跟 / 想 / 我 / 夜 / 他
b) 下午 / 时间 / 今天 / 有没有 / 你？
c) 晚上 / 八点 / 事 / 有/我
d) 什么时候 / 你 / 美国 / 去？
e) 蛋糕 / 几 / 吃 / 个 / 了 / 她？
f) 早上 / 商店 / 啤酒 / 买 / Jerry / 里 / 六点 / 在
g) 明白 / 你 / 了 / 吗？
h) 外星人 / 相信 / 不 / 我 / 你 / 爸爸 / 是 / 一个

5. Fill in the gap using a suitable modal verb:
会　　能　　可以　　得　　想

a) 我明年才 ___ 去中国。
b) 我很 ___ 去中国，可是我没有钱。
c) 如果你老吃醋，你 ___ 生病。
d) 我觉得你 ___ 去看心理医生。
e) 他才13岁，还不 ___ 喝啤酒。

6. Make sentences using 如果 *if*; when necessary, use 会 *may*, 可以 *can*, or 得 *must*:
老虎吃草；死 *(tiger eats grass; to die)*
→ 如果老虎吃草，它会死。→ *If the tiger eats grass, he will die.*

a) 我有钱；我请大家喝酒
b) 我有时间；一定给你打电话
c) 我有事；我告诉你
d) 你累；休息
e) 你太忙；找新的工作
f) 你不会做蛋糕；去商店买
g) 你不舒服；你看医生
h) 你打我；你后悔

外星人 wàixīngrén
325, 906, 128
alien; extra-ter-restial

Outside-star-person

7. Which sentences belong together?

1) 我真笨。   a) 他的脸很奇怪。

2) 我爱你。   b) 他花太多钱。

3) 王小猫做什么呢？   c) 没错。

4) 我不爱我弟弟。   d) 是谁啊？

5) 我的猫不是老虎。   e) 他不能睡觉。

6) 我哥哥没有女朋友。   f) 小猫很不高兴。

7) 我吃的豆腐很好看。   g) 它太小了。

8) 姐姐做了一个蛋糕。   h) 我知道。

9) 我想我哥哥是一个外星人。   i) 也很香。

10) 老师想Jerry。   j) 她休息呢。

11) 老虎吃小猫。   k) 我常常打他。

12) 有人敲门。   l) 她给我过生日。

8. Reading exercise: try to read the following text aloud, transcribe to pinyin, and translate to English.

我家有四口人：爸爸，妈妈，哥哥和我。我爸爸今年55岁。他不高。爸爸是司机，可是他常常喝酒，所以他不能每天都工作。妈妈说喝酒的司机不是好司机。我妈妈也55岁，她是一个美女，因为她的脸很漂亮。妈妈是心理医生。她常常看爸爸的病，她也常常不高兴。我哥哥今年23岁，他很酷。他的名字叫明星，可是大家都叫他帅哥。帅哥说他是画家，但是我不相信，因为他不会画画儿。我看了他画的画儿，都非常难看。我不明白他为什么那么爱画小猫……帅哥不工作，可是他有两个女朋友，还有一个男朋友，所以他很忙。他们都给他钱，所以他能买饭。他男朋友是商人。他爱骑马。他不年轻了，今年68岁。帅哥说那没有关系，因为他很有钱，而且非常爱帅哥。他老说帅哥不但很高而且很帅。帅哥还有一个爱好，就是做中国饭。

我今年19岁。我是大学生，在北京学中文。帅哥常常打我，因为我不给他钱。昨天帅哥很生气，因为他男朋友给我送了新的手机。我想打帅哥，可是我不敢，因为他很大。

10

老师和 Jerry 在一起了
Teacher and Jerry are together now

Part 1

Jerry 有一个很大的麻烦。
Jerry yǒu yí gè hěn dà de máfan.
Jerry have one [item] very big['s] trouble.
Jerry has a big problem (is in big trouble).

因为他是一匹马, 而且没有家,
Yīnwèi tā shì yì pǐ mǎ, érqiě méi yǒu jiā,
Because he is one [measure word for horses] horse, and besides no have home,
Because he is a horse and he has no home;

所以他每天晚上都在公园里睡觉。
suǒyǐ tā měi tiān wǎnshang dōu zài gōngyuán li shuì jiào.
therefore he every day evening all present park inside sleep.
therefore, every night he sleeps in a park.

他也不能在那儿做饭,
Tā yě bù néng zài nà'er zuò fàn,
He also no can there make cooked rice,
He is not able to cook there, either;

所以天天一个人吃草。
suǒyǐ tiān tiān yí gè rén chī cǎo.
therefore daily one [item] person (alone) eat grass.
therefore, every day he eats grass there all by himself.

麻 **má** 1001
hemp; numb; to numb; to tingle

Two trees 木 mù (林 lín "forest") under 广 yǎn "house on a cliff" radical; we've seen it in the traditional form of 什麼 shénme, where it is a phonetic element. Here, the second meaning of "numbing and tingling" (after effects of hemp ...) is relevant.

煩 / 烦 **fán** 1002
irritated; anoyed; tired of; bothered; inconvenienced

火 huǒ "fire" radical for burning, irritating and inflaming.

麻煩 / 麻烦 **máfan**
troublesome; inconvenient; trouble; inconvenience; bother; to bother

"numbing" + "irritating" = big annoyance; very useful and common expression in Chinese.

匹 **pǐ** 547
measure word for horses

晚上 **wǎnshang**
749, 217
(in the) evening

现在已经是秋天了，天气越来越冷了，
Xiànzài yǐjīng shì qiūtiān le, tiānqì yuè lái yuè lěng le,
Now already is autumn [have become], weather more and more cold [have become],
Now, it's autumn already, the weather is getting colder and colder,

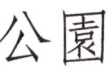 所以他每天晚上都在公园里睡觉。

公	**gōng** 342 public; communal
园	**yuán** 746 garden

Walled enclousure 囗 wéi with a phonetic element 袁 yuán; same rule applies in the simplified form, except the phonetic element is a much more common 元 yuán, which, among other things, also is the name of the Chinese currency Yuan.

公園 / 公园 **gōngyuán** park
"public" + "garden"

天天 **tiān tiān** 709 every day; day by day; daily
"day" + "day" = "every day"

秋 **qiū** 1003 autumn
秋天 **qiūtiān** autumn
"Autumn" + "sky; world; season; weather"; as we have seen, 天 tiān has many meanings, all of them related to Heaven and more generally Nature; here it's best to understand it as "season".

已 **yǐ** 1004 stop; cease; end; already (finished)

經 / 经 **jīng** 1005 to pass through; to undergo

This is an ancient character that originally means "warp" of textile, hence the 纟(糸) mì "silk" radical; it can be understood as a stack of written documents made of silk, hence the later meaning "scripture; classic".

已經 / 已经 **yǐjīng** already
"to cease" + "to go through" → to stop passing → already (passed)

天氣 / 天气 **tiānqì** 709, 816 weather
"sky; world" + "air"

越 **yuè** 1006 get over; exceed
越來越 / 越来越 **yuè lái yuè** more and more + adjective; exceedingly + adjective
"exceed" + "come" + "exceed"

冷 **lěng** 1007 cold
Radical 冫 bīng means "ice;" note that it is only one "dot" shorter than 氵 "water;" 令 lìng is for pronunciation.

越來越冷 / 越来越冷 **yuè lái yuè lěng** 1006, 216, 1007 colder and colder; more and more cold

而且常常下雨，草也少了。
érqiě cháng cháng xià yǔ, cǎo yě shǎo le.
and besides often fall rain, grass also few [have become].
and it often rains; the grass became scarce, too.

很快就会下雪了。
Hěn kuài jiù huì xià xuě le.
Very quick just can fall snow [have become].
Very soon it will snow.

公园也不能住了。
Gōngyuán yě bù néng zhù le.
Park also no can live [have become].
Living in a park has become impossible (can no longer live in the park).

齐老师觉得 Jerry 很可怜。
Qí lǎoshī jué de Jerry hěn kělián.
Qi Teacher think Jerry very pitiful.
Teacher Qi feels pity for Jerry (thinks Jerry is pitiable).

More and more

越 **yuè** means *to exceed* or *to pass*. 越来越 **yuè lái yuè** followed by an adjective means *to become more and more ...*, e.g.

    Jerry越来越帅 **Jerry yuè lái yuè shuài**
    Jerry [is getting] more and more handsome.

    啤酒越来越贵 **píjiǔ yuè lái yuè guì**
    Beer [is getting] more and more expensive.

    草越来越少 **cǎo yuè lái yuè shǎo**
    Grass [is getting] less and less (There is less and less grass.)

Note that this is a **Subject Verb Object** structure, so whatever is becoming *more and more something* needs to come first in the sentence:

    我的问题越来越多 **wǒ de wèntí yuè lái yuè duō**
    I's problems more and more many (I have more and more problems.)

下   **xià** 326
to go down; to fall; to drop;

雨   **yǔ** 1008
rain

Looks like rain, doesn't it?

下雨   **xià yǔ**
to rain

"to fall" + "rain"

雪   **xuě** 1009
snow

"rain" 雨 **yǔ** radical, as seen in many weather-related words

下雪   **xià xuě**
to snow

"to fall" + "snow"

住   **zhù** 1010
to stay; to live

"person" 亻 **rén** radical and 主 **zhǔ** for pronunciation

可   **kě** 322
here: be worth of; be in need of

used to emphasize the verb after it

怜   **lián** 1011
to sympathize; to pity; feel tender regard for

忄(心) **xīn** "heart" radical for strong emotions

可怜   **kělián**
pitiful; pitiable; poor

"Worth of" + "to pity." 可 **kě** intensifies the following verb: "Oh how pityful" / "worthy of pity".

To be or to live somewhere

In chapter 7 we learned that in Chinese we always say where we do something before we say what we do, e.g.

齐老师和 Jerry 在床上 看星星
Qí lǎoshī hé Jerry zài chuáng shàng kàn xīng xing
Teacher Qi and Jerry are in bed watching the stars.

Then, you may be wondering why we said Jerry 住在公园 **Jerry zhù zài gōngyuán** *Jerry lives in a park*? Is *living somewhere* not an action? Should we not say Jerry 在公园住 **Jerry zài gōngyuán zhù** *Jerry in the park lives* instead? To make things easy, just think of 住 **zhù** as an exception. But also remember that 在 **zài** is a verb. Here, 住在 **zhùzài** is one action and means *to stay/live somewhere*. We can skip 在 **zài** and just say Jerry 住公园 **Jerry zhù gōngyuán** with the same meaning. In Chinese, when we say we are or live somewhere, we follow the verb *to be at* immediately with the place, according to the typical **Subject Verb Object** pattern:

↑ RULE
↳ EXCEPTION 住

Jerry 在家 **Jerry zài jiā** *Jerry is [at] home.*
我在中国 **wǒ zài Zhōngguó** *I am [in] China.*
她住(在)北京 **tā zhù (zài) Běijīng** *She lives [in] Beijing.*

Already 已经 yǐjīng

已经 **yǐjīng** *already* is an adverb and as such in Chinese must always precede a verb. Usually, sentences with 已经 **yǐjīng** are complete (something already took place) and therefore come with 了 **le** at the end:

Jerry 已经睡觉了 **Jerry yǐjīng shuì jiào le**
Jerry already sleep [complete] (Jerry is asleep already; Jerry already went to bed/to sleep; Jerry (has) already slept – depending on the context)

晚饭 **wǎn fàn**
晚饭 749, 203
dinner

"evening" + "meal"

我们已经吃了晚饭 **wǒmen yǐjīng chī le wǎnfàn**
We already eat [complete] dinner (We've already had dinner.)

他们已经认识了 **tāmen yǐjīng rènshi le**
They already know/meet [complete]
(They've already met/they already know each other.)

老师已经来了，没有？ **lǎoshī yǐjīng lái le, méi yǒu?**
Teacher already come [complete], no have?
(Has the teacher already come/arrived or not?/Has the teacher come yet?)

我已经跟你说了，Jerry不是一般的马
wǒ yǐjīng gēn nǐ shuō le, Jerry bú shì yì bān de mǎ
I already with you speak [complete], Jerry no is ordinary horse
(I told you already, Jerry is not an ordinary horse)

般　一般　**bān** 1028
kind; way; like

yìbān 516, 1028
ordinary; usual; common

Three kinds of "can"

We have now learned three different verbs that mean *can*:

1 可以 **kěyǐ** is the most general and universal one; it means we generally *can* or *are allowed to do something*, e.g.

明天我可以来你家吃饭 **míngtiān wǒ kěyǐ lái nǐ jiā chī fàn**
Tomorrow I can come and eat at your house. [because I have time]

人不可以吃人 **rén bù kěyǐ chī rén**
People can't eat people. [because it's wrong]

你可以给我一瓶啤酒吗？ **nǐ kěyǐ gěi wǒ yì píng píjiǔ ma?**
Can you give me a bottle of beer? [could you?]

在中国我们可以说中文
zài Zhōngguó wǒmen kěyǐ shuō zhōngwén
In China we can speak Chinese. [because in China we will be understood]

2 会 **huì** means *to know how, to have learned, to have acquired a skill* [and therefore to be able to do something], e.g.

我会说中文 **wǒ huì shuō Zhōngwén**
I can speak Chinese [because I learned and now I know how]

你会做饭吗？ **nǐ huì zuò fàn ma?**

Can you cook? [Do you know how?]

王小猫不会骑马 **Wáng xiǎomāo bú huì qí mǎ**

Wang Xiaomao can't ride horses.

[since she didn't learn it, not because the jealous teacher won't let her]

3 能 **néng** is similar to 可以 **kěyǐ** but with a bigger emphasis on the physical ability to do something; it can be translated as *to be able to*:

我很小，所以我不能打你 **wǒ hěn xiǎo, suǒyǐ wǒ bù néng dǎ nǐ**

I am small, so I can't beat you. [I am not able to]

他不能喝酒 **tā bù néng hē jiǔ**

he can't drink alcohol

[he is physically not able to, he will get sick if he does]

你能不能做这个？ **nǐ néng bù néng zuò zhè ge?**

Can you do this? [are you able to?]

我不能给你钱 **wǒ bù néng gěi nǐ qián**

I can't give you money. [I don't have it or something else is preventing me]

公园不能住了 **gōngyuán bù néng zhù le**

Park no can live [change] (*It's no longer possible to live in the park*.)

[because it's too cold and uncomfortable]

Fortune cookie:

包子 **bāozi**
steamed buns

包子 **bāozi** is a delicious and a popular snack. However, in slang 包子 **bāozi** refers to a stupid and not good looking person who posts fake profiles online to appear smart and good looking. Something like an internet "couch potato."

1027, 132

Part 2

老师的家很大，有两个大房间和一个厨房，
Lǎoshī de jiā hěn dà, yǒu liǎng gè dà fángjiān hé yí gè chúfáng,
Teacher's house very big, have two [item] big rooms and one [item] kitchen,
The teacher's house is big, there are two big rooms and a kitchen,

所以老师请 Jerry 跟他一起住。
suǒyǐ lǎoshī qǐng Jerry gēn tā yìqǐ zhù.
therefore teacher invite Jerry follow he together live.
so he invited Jerry to live together with him.

老师跟Jerry说：
Lǎoshī gēn Jerry shuō:
Teacher follow Jerry say:
The teacher told Jerry:

"亲爱的Jerry，我和你，就是我们，
"Qīn'ài de Jerry, wǒ hé nǐ, jiù shì wǒmen,
"Dear's Jerry, I and you, just is we,
"Dear Jerry, you and I, that is us,

应该住在一起。我们可以一起吃饭，
yīnggāi zhù zài yìqǐ. Wǒmen kěyǐ yìqǐ chī fàn,
should live together. We can together eat cooked rice,
we should live together. We can eat together,

一起听音乐，一起看星星。你不用付钱。
yìqǐ tīng yīnyuè, yìqǐ kàn xīngxing. Nǐ bú yòng fù qián.
together listen music, together watch stars. You no need pay money.
listen to music together, watch the stars together. You don't need to pay.

非常方便。我想住在这里你会觉得很开心。
Fēicháng fāngbiàn. Wǒ xiǎng zhù zài zhèlǐ nǐ huì jué de hěn kāixīn.
Extremely convenient. I think live here you can feel very cheerful.
Extremely convenient. I think you will feel happy living here.

房 **fáng** 1012
house; room

Refers to a physical apartment or building rather than the more abstract "home" 家 jiā; radical 戶 hù means "door" or "household;" 方 fāng, which we will learn in a moment, is for pronunciation.

房間 / 房间 **fángjiān** 1012, 728
room

House + space

廚 / 厨 **chú** 1013
kitchen

广 yǎn "house on a cliff" radical (in the traditional form 廚) is seen in characters that indicate halls where work is performed. In the simplified form, the dot has been abolished and 广 is replaced with 厂 hǎn, which means "cliff". This character in the simplified system on its own (not as a radical of another character) is the word for "factory" and is pronounced chǎng.

廚房 / 厨房 **chúfáng** 1013, 1012
kitchen

"kitchen" + "house/room"

跟 **gēn** 1014
to follow; with

𧾷 (足) zú radical means "foot;" 艮 gēn is for pronunciation. Originally a verb meaning "to follow", often used as a conjunction and translated as "with".

请你想一想。"
Qǐng nǐ xiǎng yì xiǎng."
Please you think one think."
Please, think about it."

一起 **yìqǐ** 516, 507 together

Always precedes a verb; see grammar explanations.

跟(誰)說 跟(谁)说 **gēn (shéi) shuō** 1014, (119), 321 to speak with (someone); to tell (someone)

"with" + (someone) + "speak"

親 亲 **qīn** 1015 a relative; intimate; personal; to kiss

親愛 亲爱 **qīn'ài** 1015, 313 dear

"intimate" + "to love"

應 应 **yīng** 1016 should; ought to

Originally means a response to some need, hence the 心 xīn "heart" radical in the traditional form; there, we can also see two short-tailed birds 隹 zhuī (repeated 亻 rén radical indicates double) responding to each other.

該 该 **gāi** 1017 should; deserve; fated to

This obligation is like a predetermination or a spell, hence the 讠 (言) yán "speech" radical; 亥 hài for pronunciation.

應該 应该 **yīnggāi** should; ought to

音 **yīn** 1018 sound; tone; musical note

樂 乐 **yuè** 1019 music

Ancient Chinese word indicating a whole ritual performance, including dancing, feasting, and all sorts of festivities.

音樂 音乐 **yīnyuè** music

"sounds" + "music"

星星 **xīngxing** 906 stars

用 **yòng** 1020 to use; to need

不用 **bú yòng** don't have to; don't need to

literally: "don't use"

付 **fù** 1021 to pay

付錢 付钱 **fù qián** 1021, 615 to pay

to pay ¨+ money

方 **fāng** 1022 square; direction

便 **biàn** 1023 fitting; at ease; relaxed

方便 **fāngbiàn** comfortable; convenient

開 开 **kāi** 1024 to open

In the traditional form, we see the "gate" 門 mén radical that suggests the meaning

開心 开心 **kāixīn** 1024, 311 to feel happy; to be glad; to be cheerful

"open" + "heart"

159

Jerry想了一想，就同意了。老师特别高兴。
Jerry xiǎng le yì xiǎng, jiù tóngyì le. Lǎoshī tèbié gāoxìng.
Jerry think [complete] one think, just agree [complete]. Teacher especially happy.
Jerry thought about it and agreed. The teacher was super happy.

同意 **tóngyì** 402, 157
to agree
"same" + "idea"

特 **tè** 1025
special; particular; unusual

牜 (牛) niú radical used in characters indicating animals; the character originally referred to a specially marked sort of cattle.

别 **bié** 1026
different; distinct; other

Note the slight difference between the traditional and the simplified forms.

特别 **tèbié**
special; especially; particularly

With

跟 **gēn** is usually translated as *with*, but it is actually a verb and means *to follow*. Chinese does not have prepositions (*in; at; for; from; to; with* etc.) and usually uses verbs where we use prepositions in English:

我在中国 **wǒ zài Zhōngguó** *I am in China*
[we use the verb 在 **zài** *to be present*; see chapter 4]

他给我做饭 **tā gěi wǒ zuò fàn** *he cooks for me*
[we use the verb 给 **gěi** *to give*; see chapter 7]

跟 **gēn** works in a similar way. It is important to remember that in any sentence with 跟 **gēn** the action comes at the end:

我跟你一起吃饭 **wǒ gēn nǐ yìqǐ chī fàn**
I follow you together eat → *I with you together eat* (*I eat together with you*)

他跟我们一起去中国 **tā gēn wǒmen yìqǐ qù Zhōngguó**
he follow us together go China → *he with us together goes to China*
(*he goes to China together with us*)

谁跟你一起看星星？ **shéi gēn nǐ yìqǐ kàn xīngxing**
Who follows you together watch the stars?
→ *Who with you together watches the stars?*
(*Who watches the stars together with you?*)

你想不想跟我一起听音乐？
nǐ xiǎng bù xiǎng gēn wǒ yìqǐ tīng yīn yuè?
You want or don't want to follow me together listen to music?
→ *Would you like with me together to listen to music?*
(*Would you like to listen to music together with me?*)

我跟你一起吃饭

你跟他一起睡觉吗？ **nǐ gēn tā yìqǐ shuì jiào ma?**

You follow him together sleep? → *You with him together sleep?*

(*Do you sleep together with him?*)

Note that in sentences with 跟 **gēn** it is idiomatic to use 一起 **yìqǐ**. It is not mandatory, but it just sounds right.

In negations, we put 不 **bù** or 没(有) **méi(yǒu)** (for past events) before 跟 **gēn**:

我不跟你一起去 **wǒ bù gēn nǐ yìqǐ qù**

I no follow you together go → *I don't with you together go*

(*I'm not going together with you*)

我没(有)跟他一起睡觉 **wǒ méi (yǒu) gēn tā yìqǐ shuì jiào**

I have not followed him together sleep → *I did not with him together sleep*

(*I did not sleep together with him*)

Finally, there is a fixed expression A 跟 B 说 **A gēn B shuō**, which always translates *A is telling/tells/told B*:

我跟你说 **wǒ gēn nǐ shuō** *I follow you say*

→ *I with you speak* → *I'm telling you / I tell you / I told you ...*

我想跟你说一件事儿 **wǒ xiǎng gēn nǐ shuō yí jiàn shì'er**

I wish follow you say one thing → *I would like to with you speak one thing*

→ *I'd like to tell you one thing* (件 **jiàn** is a measure word for 事 **shì**)

我跟你说，这个人真笨！ **wǒ gēn nǐ shuō, zhè gè rén zhēn bèn**

I'm telling you, this person is really stupid!

Alone or together?

一个人 **yí gè rén**, literally: *one person*, means *alone* regardless whether we are talking about a "person" or an animal; we must always use it before the verb:

Literally: *Jerry alone sleeps* (*Jerry sleeps alone*)

161

一起 **yìqǐ** *together* also needs to come before the verb:
> Jerry 和王小猫一起吃草 **Jerry hé Wáng Xiǎomāo yìqǐ chī cǎo**
> Literally: *Jerry and Wang Xiaomao together eat grass.*
> (*Jerry and Wang Xiaomao are eating grass together.*)

The verb 住 **zhù** *to live* is an exception. We can use it with 一起 **yìqǐ** in two ways:
> Jerry 和老师一起住 **Jerry hé lǎoshī yìqǐ zhù**
> *Jerry and teacher together live* (*Jerry and the teacher live together.*)

But when we use 住 **zhù** together with 在 **zài**, then we have to say:
> Jerry 和老师住在一起 **Jerry hé lǎoshī zhù zài yìqǐ**
> *Jerry and teacher live together.*

一起 **yìqǐ** can come after 在 **zài**:
> 我们都在一起 **wǒmen dōu zài yìqǐ** *We are [all] together.*

Orders and suggestions

In chapter 2, we learned about the particle 吧 **ba** that can be used to make a gentle request or to suggest an action to others or to oneself:
> 你吃吧 **nǐ chī ba** *You eat, ok? (Please, eat.)*
> 我也吃吧 **wǒ yě chī ba** *I also eat, ok. (Let me eat also.)*

There are other ways to make gentle requests in Chinese. The most common one is the repetition of the verb, with an optional 一 **yī** in between:
> 你吃(一)吃 **nǐ chī (yì) chī** *You eat (one) eat* (*Come eat, ok?*)
> 我看(一)看 **wǒ kàn (yí) kàn** *I look (one) look* (*Let me have a look, ok?*)

To make the request or suggestion even softer, we can still use 吧 **ba** at the end of the sentence:
> 你吃(一)吃吧 **nǐ chī (yì) chī ba** *Please, eat some, ok?*
> 我看(一)看吧 **wǒ kàn (yí) kàn ba** *Please, let me have a look, ok?*

If somebody completed the request or just did something *a little bit*, we can use 了 **le** between the repeated verbs:
> 我看了(一)看 **wǒ kàn le (yí) kàn** *I look [complete] (one) look*
> (*I had a look*)
> Jerry 想了(一)想 **Jerry xiǎng le (yì) xiǎng**
> *Jerry think [complete] (one) think* (*Jerry gave it a thought.*)

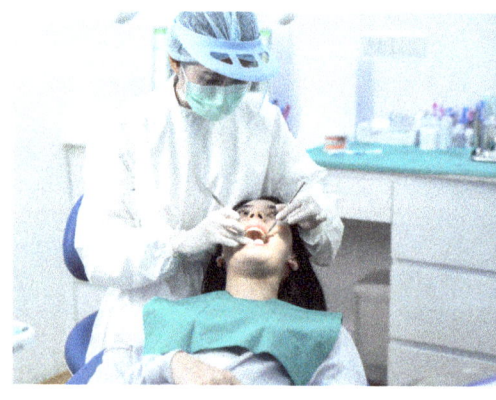

我看一看

1. Repeat numbers.

Example:

齐老师学几匹马的爱好？ （4）→ 齐老师学四匹马的爱好

The psychology of how many horses does teacher Qi study? – He studies the psychology of 4 horses.

a) 几个病人来看医生？(11)　　b) 王小猫有几个心理问题？(2)
c) 几个学生没有来上课？(14)　　d) 这个老人多大？(102)
e) 你的小孩子几岁了？(5)　　f) 马先生的家有几口人？(7)
g) 他吃了几个蛋糕？(6)　　h) 你认识几个外国人？(22)
i) 在美国新的手机多少钱？(812)　　j) Jerry有几个麻烦？(10)
k) 你有几个情人？(9)

2. Ask for YYY.

Example:

Jerry 爱YYY。→ Jerry爱谁？

Jerry loves YYY → Whom does Jerry love?

a) Jerry 的老朋友住在YYY。　　b) 我爱听YYY音乐。
c) 我想吃YYY。　　d) 你不应该喝YYY。
e) 学生YYY不用去学校。　　f) 我跟YYY一起去商店。
g) YYY认识他。　　h) 我在YYY做饭。
i) 我们YYY点下课。　　j) 我得去YYY。
k) 他病了YYY。

3. Make sentences using the vocabulary below.

a) 北京/想/我/住/在　　b) 没/吃饭/我/还/有
c) 了/她/已经/睡觉　　d) 已经/老师/了/下课
e) 去/我们/一起/吧
f) 公园/一个人/老师/今天/去/马/看
g) 她/我/想/跟/一起/去/也
h) 方便/做饭/在/很/不/公园里

4. Translation 翻译 fānyì

a) You should pay him.　　b) Can you feed the child?
c) Why don't you call her?　　d) I do not wish to sleep with the cat.
e) You should take some rest.　　f) Let me have a look.
g) Dad often cooks for mom.　　h) Come with me.
i) Children are trouble.　　j) It's raining now.

11 十一

床太小了
The bed is too small

Part 1

因为齐老师要和Jerry一起住，
Yīnwèi Qí lǎoshī yào hé Jerry yìqǐ zhù,
Because Qi Teacher want and Jerry together live,
Because teacher Qi and Jerry are going to live together,

所以要做好准备。老师的卧室不大，
suǒyǐ yào zuò hǎo zhǔnbèi. Lǎoshī de wòshì bú dà,
therefore want make good [finish] prepare. Teacher's bedroom no big,
therefore the teacher must get ready. The teacher's bedroom is small

可是很舒服，有一张小床，
kěshì hěn shūfu, yǒu yì zhāng xiǎo chuáng,
but very comfortable, have one [measure word for flat objects] small bed,
but comfortable, there is a small bed,

一张书桌和两把椅子。
yì zhāng shūzhuō hé liǎng bǎ yǐzi.
one [measure word for flat objects] desk and two [handle] chairs.
a desk and two chairs.

书桌上还有一台电脑。
Shūzhuō shàng hái yǒu yì tái diànnǎo.
Desk on still have one [measure word for machinery] computer.
On the desk, there also is a computer.

要 **yào** 204
want; to need; must; have to; going to; will

做好 **zuòhǎo**
to finish or complete doing something

An action "to do/to make" +"good" = "to make something with a good result" = "to finish [making] something". This function is called "resultative complement", we will learn more about it in chapter 13.

準
准 **zhǔn** 1101
level; standard; accurate

The simplified form 准 originally meant (and in traditional print still means) "to permit" because it was pronounced the same way as the more complex character 準, and because both characters kind of look alike, 准 was borrowed to replace the traditional form 準 and adopted its meaning; in the process the "water" radical 氵 lost one dot and became "ice" 冫.

備
备 **bèi** 1102
to be equipped with; to get ready

在床和书桌中间有一个衣柜，
Zài chuáng hé shūzhuō zhōngjiān yǒu yí gè yīguì,
Present bed and desk between have one [item] clothes closet,
Between the bed and the desk there is a closet,

準備
准备
zhǔnbèi
to prepare

"standard"+"get ready/equip with"

做好準備
做好准备
zuòhǎo zhǔnbèi
201, 103, 1101, 1102
to finish preparing; to get ready

臥
卧
wò 1103
to recline; to lie down; to rest

臥室
卧室
wòshì
1103, 702
bedroom

"to recline" + "room"

張
张
zhāng 1104
measure word for large flat objects, e.g. beds, tables, sheets of paper, tickets, etc., but also for the mouth

弓 gōng means "bow" (张 originally means "to stretch"), and 长(長) zhǎng "to grow" is for pronunciation

牀/床
床
chuáng 1105
bed

wooden 木 mù plank 爿 bǎn under a roofed structure 广; in traditional print, both 牀 and 床 can be used.

桌
zhuō 1106
table

also made of wood 木 mù

書桌
书桌
shūzhuō
209, 1106
desk

"documents" + "table"

把
bǎ 1107
measure word for things with a handle, e.g. chairs or umbrellas

Originally means "handle" or "handful;" also a verb "to hold; to grasp", hence the "hand" 扌(手) shǒu radical; 巴 bā is for pronunciation (we have seen it already in 吧 ba and 爸 bà).

椅
yǐ 1108
chair

also made of wood 木 mù

椅子
yǐzi 1108, 132
chair

"chair" + noun suffix

臺/台
台
tái 1109
platform; stand; *measure word for machinery*

腦
脑
nǎo 1110
brain

Radical 月 looks like "moon" (yuè), but is actually a short version of 肉 ròu "meat"; appears in characters for body organs.

電腦
电脑
diànnǎo
811, 1110
computer

"electronic" + "brain"

中間
中间
zhōngjiān
314, 728
between

"middle" + "space"

在A和B中間
在A和B中间
zài A hé B zhōngjiān
408, 302, 314, 728
between A and B

衣
yī 1111
clothes

櫃
柜
guì 1112
cupboard; cabinet

"Wood" radical 木 mù for furniture; in the traditional form, we can see the encasing 匚 and 貴 guì as a phonetic element.

165

里面有很多衣服。床下有一双高跟鞋。
lǐmiàn yǒu hěn duō yīfu. Chuáng xià yǒu yì shuāng gāogēnxié.
inside have very many clothes. Bed under have one [pair] high heels.
inside there are lots of clothes. Under the bed, there is a pair of high heels.

虽然老师的卧室很小，床也很小，
Suīrán lǎoshī de wòshì hěn xiǎo, chuáng yě hěn xiǎo,
Although Teacher's bedroom very small, bed also very small,
Even though the teacher's bedroom is small and the bed is also small,

不能跟Jerry一起睡，
bù néng gēn Jerry yìqǐ shuì,
no can follow Jerry together sleep,
and it is impossible to sleep in it together with Jerry,

但是家里还有别的房间，可以给Jerry住。
dànshì jiā li hái yǒu bié de fángjiān, kěyǐ gěi Jerry zhù.
but house inside still have other rooms, can give Jerry live.
but there are other rooms where Jerry can live.

衣櫃 / 衣柜 **yīguì**
wardrobe; closet for clothes
"clothes" + "cabinet"

面 **miàn** 1113
face; surface; side

裡面 / 里面 **lǐmiàn** 508, 1113
inside
"in" + "side"

服 **fú** 636
clothing; attire
We have seen this characer in 舒服 shūfu; here in a different meaning.

衣服 **yīfú** 1111, 636
clothes

雙 / 双 **shuāng** 1114
a pair
The traditional form has a couple of birds with short tails 隹 zhuī perched together. Cute. The simplified form is also creative.

跟 **gēn** 422
heel
This is yet another meaning in addition to "follow" (literally, "to be at one's heels").

鞋 **xié** 423
shoes
radical 革 gé means "leather"

高跟鞋 **gāogēnxié** 421, 422, 423
high heels
"high" + "heels" + "shoes"; but if you prefer, you are welcome to translate "tall with shoes", which is unintentionally meaningful :)

雖 / 虽 **suī** 1115
though; although
Why is it always the lovely 隹 zhuī "bird with a short tail" that gets amputated in order to "simplify" the characters?

雖然 / 虽然 **suīrán** 1115, 416
although; even though
"although" + "to be like this"

雖然...但是... / 虽然...但是... **suīrán ... dànshì ...** 1115,1116, 610, 107
although, ..., but ...

別的 / 别的 **biéde** 1026, 310
other
We can drop the 的 de when we say 别人 bié rén "other people".

Want

要 **yào** is a very strong verb. It means *to want* or *to need*. It is much stronger than 想 **xiǎng**, which merely expresses a wish. 要 **yào**, by comparison, expresses a very straightforward demand; therefore, we usually translate it as *going to* or *will*:

我想睡觉 **wǒ xiǎng shuì jiào** *I'd like to sleep*

我要睡觉 **wǒ yào shuì jiào** *I want/need to sleep → I am going to sleep*

Another difference between 要 **yào** and 想 **xiǎng** is that the latter always serves as a modal verb, i.e. we use it only with other verbs (e.g. *I'd like to sing*), whereas 要 **yào** can take direct objects, i.e. it can be directly followed by nouns:

我要你 **wǒ yào nǐ** *I want/need you*

她要钱 **tā yào qián** *she wants/needs money*

Jerry 要高跟鞋 **Jerry yào gāogēnxié** *Jerry wants/needs high heels*

By contrast, when 想 **xiǎng** is directly followed by a noun, it changes the meaning to *miss*, so it can take only things that can be missed as objects, e.g. people:

我想家 **wǒ xiǎng jiā** *I miss home*

老师想 Jerry **lǎoshī xiǎng Jerry** *Teacher misses Jerry*

要 **yào** often serves as a future marker: it indicates something is going to happen in the future; in this sense, it is similar to 会 **huì**, but again, it is much stronger:

明年我要去中国 **míngnián wǒ yào qù Zhōngguó**

I will go to China next year/I am going to go to China next year

要 **yào** expresses a certainty that something will happen, but 会 **huì** only a high likelihood; also, 要 **yào** may be used as *want to*, while 会 **huì** can mean *may*:

明年我要去中国 **míngnián wǒ yào qù Zhōngguó**

I want to go to China next year

明年我会去中国 **míngnián wǒ huì qù Zhōngguó**

I may go to China next year

There is a clear difference between these two when we use the negative:
不要 **bú yào** means *don't want/don't need*:

我不要你的钱 **wǒ bú yào nǐ de qián** *I don't want/need your money*

我不要去中国 **wǒ bú yào qù Zhōngguó** *I don't want to go to China*

It can also mean *don't, mustn't* or *shouldn't [do something]*:

你不要打他 **nǐ bú yào dǎ tā** *you should not beat him/do not beat him*

你不要去中国 **nǐ bú yào qù Zhōngguó** *don't go to China*

不会 **bú huì** means *will not; not likely to; would not; cannot.*
我不会去中国 **wǒ bú huì qù Zhōngguó**
I won't go to China / I'm not likely to go to China
我不会打他 **wǒ bú huì dǎ tā** *I would/will not not beat him*

You cannot say 我不会你的钱 **wǒ bú huì nǐ de qián**; but you can say 我不会要你的钱 **wǒ bú huì yào nǐ de qián** *I will not/would not want/need your money.*

Postpositions: table on

In English, words such as *on, under, in, out, next to, in front of, behind, left, right*, etc., always appear before the place they refer to, e.g. *on the table; behind the house*. In Chinese, it is the opposite. As we saw in chapter 7, *in* comes after, not before:

Jerry 在公园里吃草 **Jerry zài gōngyuán lǐ chī cǎo**
Jerry is eating grass in the park.

Similarly, we will not say *on the table*, but *table on*: 桌子上 **zhuōzi shàng**, or *bed under* instead of *under the bed*: 床下 **chuáng xià**.

里 **lǐ** *in*, 外 **wài** *out*, 上 **shàng** *on*, 下 **xià** *under*, 前 **qián** *in front*, and 后 **hòu** *in the back/behind*, are short versions of 里面 **lǐmian**, 外面 **wàimian**, 上面 **shàngmian**, 下面 **xiàmian**, 前面 **qiánmian**, and 后面 **hòumian**. Using the long version (meaning two syllables instead of one) is optional, e.g. (在) 桌子上面有高跟鞋 **(zài) zhuōzi shàngmian yǒu gāogēnxié** *there are high heels on the table* is the same as (在) 桌子上有高跟鞋 **(zài) zhuōzi shàng yǒu gāogēnxié**, except when they are separate words, i.e. when they are the subject of a sentence, e.g.:

里面有马 **lǐmian yǒu mǎ** *inside, there are horses*
[*inside* is a subject of the sentence; it is a place and it "has" horses]
前面有人 **qiánmian yǒu rén** *front has people (there are people in front)*
花园在后面 **huāyuán zài hòumian** *the garden is in the back*

面 **miàn** *face* is interchangeable with 边 **biān** *side* (上面 **shàngmian** = 上边 **shàngbiān**), with the exception of 旁 **páng** *next to*, 左 **zuǒ** *left*, and 右 **yòu** *right*, which are always 旁边 **pángbiān**, 左边 **zuǒbiān**, and 右边 **yòubiān**. 对 **duì** *opposite* is always 对面 **duìmian**.

Fortune cookie:

竹子 **zhúzi** *bamboo*

1137, 132

> Tones on these prefixes, especially -面 **miàn**, are optional. In the North, most speakers will pronounce the light tone, e.g. 后面 **hòumian**, but in Taiwan people like to pronounce both tones, i.e. 后面 **hòumiàn**.

Part 2

老师给Jerry的房间又大又亮，
Lǎoshī gěi Jerry de fángjiān yòu dà yòu liàng,
Teacher-give-Jerry's room both big and bright,
The room the teacher gave to Jerry is both big and bright,

可是家具不多，没有床，也没有桌子，
kěshì jiājù bù duō, méi yǒu chuáng, yě méi yǒu zhuōzi,
but furniture no much, no have bed, also no have table,
but it does not have a lot of furniture, there is no bed and no table,

只有一个沙发。Jerry说他不要家具，
zhǐ yǒu yí gè shāfā. Jerry shuō tā bú yào jiājù,
only have one [item] sofa. Jerry say he no want furniture,
just a sofa. Jerry says he does not want furniture,

有沙发就好了。房间很漂亮，
yǒu shāfā jiù hǎo le. Fángjiān hěn piàoliang,
have sofa just good [have become]. Room very pretty,
as long as there is a sofa it's ok. The room is nice,

有一个大窗户，后面有一个小花园；
yǒu yí gè dà chuānghù, hòumian yǒu yí gè xiǎo huāyuán;
have one [item] big window, behind have one [item] little flower garden;
there is a big window, and behind it there is a small flower garden.

又 **yòu** 1116
again
indicates a recurring action

又...又... **yòu (Adjective) yòu (Adjective)**
both ... and ...

具 **jù** 1117
appliance; utensil; tool

家具 **jiājù** 102, 1117
furniture
"home" + "appliances"

沙 **shā** 1118
sand
"water" 氵(水) shuǐ radical: sand was associated with rivers; 少 shǎo for pronunciation.

發 / 发 **fā** 1119
to send out; to issue; to emit

沙發 / 沙发 **shāfā**
sofa
One of the few words Chinese borrowed difectly from other languages; the characters composing it have completely unrelated meanings and are used just to imitate the sound: "shafa" sounds similar to "sofa"

不要 **bú yào** 121, 204
not want; not need

窗 **chuāng** 1120
window
穴 xué "cave" is a common radiclal in characters for holes and openings; supposedly looks like a window grill.

户 **hù** 1121
door

窗户 **chuānghù**
window
"Window" + "door"; the second character seems redundant here, but it is just meant to specify that we are talking about a big window, as opposed to a small one like at a ticket office (窗口 chuāngkǒu "window mouth/opening").

後面 / 后面 **hòumian** 927, 1113
behind; in the back
"behind" + "side"

花園 / 花园 **huāyuán** 729, 746
(flower) garden

Jerry春天和夏天可以去那儿吃花。
Jerry　chūntiān hé xiàtiān　kěyǐ　qù　nà'er　chī huā.
Jerry　spring and summer　can　go there　eat flowers.
In spring and in summer, Jerry can go there to eat flowers.

春　**chūn** 1122
　　spring
春天　**chūntiān** 709
　　spring
夏　**xià** 1123
　　summer
夏天　**xiàtiān** 709
　　summer

Don't forget that for seasons we add 天 tiān. We usually do not say 夏 alone.

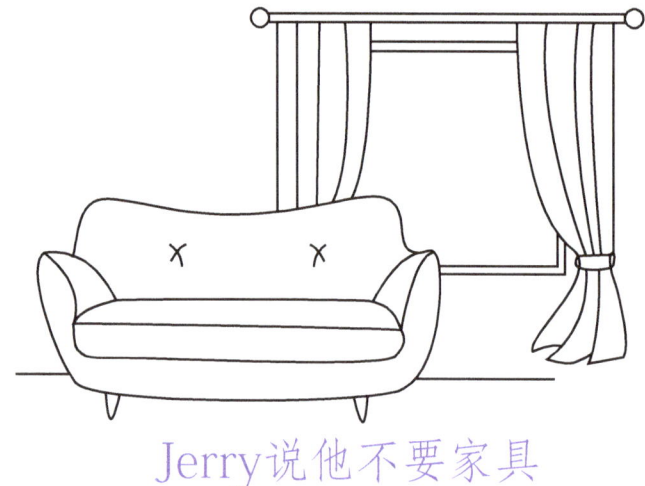

Jerry说他不要家具

Subordinate Clause?

No such thing in Chinese.
Let's look at the sentence:
　　老师给Jerry的房间 **lǎoshī gěi Jerry de fángjiān**
　　teacher-give-Jerry's room (the room that the teacher gave to Jerry)
　　　　description – object (vs. object – description)

In Chinese, we use 的 **de** to describe things; the description is always before 的 **de**, and what we describe is after. The description may be complex and even contain verbs, which in English need to be translated as a subordinate clause:
　　老师给Jerry的房间 **lǎoshī gěi Jerry de fángjiān**
　　room of [the kind] that teacher gave to Jerry

This whole phrase then can be a subject of a new sentence:
　　老师给Jerry的房间又大又亮
　　lǎoshī gěi Jerry de fángjiān yòu dà yòu liàng
　　teacher-give-Jerry's room both big and bright
　　= *The room that teacher gave to Jerry is both big and bright.*

Let's look at more sentences:

Jerry给大家做的饭很好吃 **Jerry gěi dàjiā zuò de fàn hěn hǎo chī**
Jerry-give-everybody-make's food very tasty
The food that Jerry cooked for everybody is tasty.

你给我听的音乐很难听 **nǐ gěi wǒ tīng de yīnyuè hěn nántīng**
You-give-me-listen's music very hard listening
The music that you gave me to listen to sounds terrible.

我学中文的姐姐住在北京
wǒ xué zhōngwén de jiějie zhù zài Běijīng
I-study-Chinese's elder sister live be in Beijing
My elder sister who studies Chinese lives in Beijing.

会说中文的马不多 **huì shuō zhōngwén de mǎ bù duō**
Can-speak-Chinese's horses no many
Horses that can speak Chinese are not many.

我在北京工作的朋友很帅
wǒ zài Běijīng gōngzuò de péngyou hěn shuài
I-be-at-Beijing-work's friend very hot
My friend who works in Beijing is hot.

In each case, it is 的 **de** that does the trick.

隻 只 **zhī** 1138
measure word for most animals and also for one out of a pair of things, e.g. eyes

The traditional form of 雙(双) shuāng "pair" is a double 隻. The idea is, we see "a pair" of 隹 zhuī "long-tailed birds" in 雙 and only one in 隻. Cute! The simplified form looks the same as 只 zhī "only" but is pronounced zhī

青蛙 **qīngwā** 1139, 1140
frog

嘴 **zuǐ** 1141
mouth

眼 **yǎn** 1142
eye

眼睛 **yǎnjing** 1142, 1143
eyes

條 条 **tiáo** 1144
twig; strip; measure word for long objects, dogs, and fishes

腿 **tuǐ** 1145
leg

Practice counting!

一只青蛙，一张嘴，两只眼睛，四条腿；
两只青蛙，两张嘴，四只眼睛，八条腿；
三只青蛙，...

Translation:
One frog, one mouth, two eyes, four legs;
Two frogs, two mouths, four eyes, eight legs;
Three frogs, ...

Part 3

要是Jerry想看电视，就可以去客厅，
Yàoshì　　Jerry xiǎng kàn diànshì,　　jiù　kěyǐ　qù　kètīng,
If　　　　　Jerry wish watch TV,　　just　can　go living room,
If Jerry wants to watch TV, then he can go to the living room,

那边有电视机，前面有几把椅子。
nàbiān yǒu　diànshìjī,　　qiánmian yǒu jǐ　bǎ　　yǐzi.
there have　　TV set,　　in front have several [handle] chairs.
there is a TV set there with some chairs in front.

Jerry不坐椅子，但是旁边还有很大的地方，
Jerry　bú zuò　　yǐzi,　　dànshì pángbiān hái yǒu hěn dà　de　dìfāng,
Jerry　no sit　　chair,　　but　next　still have very big['s] place,
Jerry does not sit on chairs, but there is lots of room next to the chairs,

他可以坐在地上。客厅右边是厨房，
tā　kěyǐ　zuò zài dì shàng.　Kètīng yòubiān shì chúfáng,
he　can　sit present ground on. Living room right side is kitchen,
so he can just sit on the floor. To the right of the living room is a kitchen,

左边是洗手间，到处都有很多啤酒
zuǒbiān shì　xǐshǒujiān,　　dàochu dōu yǒu hěn duō　píjiǔ
left side is　washroom,　　everywhere all have very much beer
and on the left there is a bathroom. Everywhere, there is lots of beer

（老师知道Jerry很喜欢喝）。
(lǎoshī　　zhīdào Jerry　hěn xǐhuan hē).
(teacher　　know Jerry very like　drink).
(the teacher knows that Jerry likes to drink very much).

因为现在跟Jerry一起住，
Yīnwèi　xiànzài gēn Jerry　　yìqǐ　zhù,
Because now　follow　Jerry　together live,
Now, when he is living with Jerry,

要是 **yàoshì** 204, 107
视 if

视 **shì** 1124
视 look at; regard; watch; vision

礻(示) shì radical for things that are transmitted spiritually, (originally means a spiritual kind of insight: being able to see into one's heart)

電視 **diànshì** 811
电视 television

"electronic" + "vision"

廳 **tīng** 1125
厅 hall

I know, the traditional form looks insane, but it's logical. We have the 广 yǎn radical for halls and 聽 tīng (traditional for "to listen") for pronunciation. The simplified form uses 丁 dīng for pronunciation and changed the radical to 厂 hǎn "cliff," which also indicates a roofed cover. We saw the same transition from 广 to 厂 in 廚 – 厨 chú "kitchen."

客廳 **kètīng**
客厅 815,1125
living room

"guest" + "hall"

邊 **biān** 1126
边 side; border; limit

"road" 辶 chuò radical

172

所以老师可能会买一张大床。 他想春天就买吧!
suǒyǐ lǎoshī kěnéng huì mǎi yì zhāng dà chuáng. Tā xiǎng chūntiān jiù mǎi ba!
therefore teacher maybe can buy one [item of flat objects] big bed. He think/wish spring just buy [suggestion]!
the teacher may perhaps buy a big bed. He's thinking why not buy one in spring?

那邊
那边
nàbiān
410, 1126
over there

"that" + "side"

電視機
电视机
diànshìjī
811, 1124, 620
TV set ("electronic watching machine")

This is the actual object (the TV set), not the TV you watch.

前
qián 1127
front

前面
qiánmian 1113
in front; the front

"front" + "side"

幾
几
jǐ 601
several; a few (see grammar explanations)

旁
páng 1128
side; next to

旁邊
旁边
pángbiān 1128, 1126
on the side

"next" + "side"

地
dì 1129
the earth; land; ground

modern Chinese word for earth; retains the ancient 土 tǔ radical

地方
dìfāng 1022
place; locality

"land" + "direction"

右
yòu 1130
right; to the right

右邊
右边
yòubiān
right side; on the right

左
zuǒ 1131
left; to the left

左邊
左边
zuǒbiān
left side; on the left

洗
xǐ 1132
to wash

"Water" 氵 shuǐ radical suggests the meaning, 先 xiān suggests the pronunciation.

洗手間
洗手间
xǐshǒujiān
1132, 904, 728
bathroom; washroom (wash + hands + space = "room for washing hands")

到
dào 1133
to arrive

至 zhì means "to reach the extreme; to attain" / "to; until". 刂 (刀) dāo "knife" is a popular radical related to weapons/cutting, but here it is for pronunciation.

處
处
chù 1134
a place; a spot; a location; a locality

到處
到处
dàochù
everywhere

"to arrive at a location" → "wherever one arrives"

喜
xǐ 1135
joy; joyful; to like; be fond of

歡
欢
huān 1136
pleased; glad; pleasures; joys

喜歡
喜欢
xǐhuan
to like; to be fond of

A "two syllable verb", consists of two synonyms: verbs with related meanings; see chapter 8.

可能
kěnéng
322, 916
perhaps; maybe; possible

"can" + "able to"

If

要是 **yàoshi** is another way to say *if* in Chinese (in chapter 9 we also learned 如果 **rúguǒ**). It literally means *[if] it needs to be so ...* The rest is straightforward:

> 要是你给我付钱，我会给你做饭
> **yàoshi nǐ gěi wǒ fù qián, wǒ huì gěi nǐ zuò fàn**
> *If you give me pay money, I can give you make food.*
> (If you pay me, I will cook for you.)

> 要是你爱我，就不要吃我的饭
> **yàoshi nǐ ài wǒ, jiù bú yào chī wǒ de fàn**
> *If you love me, just no want eat my rice*
> (If you love me, then don't eat my rice.)

> 要是你有时间，请来我家看星星
> **yàoshi nǐ yǒu shíjian, qǐng lái wǒ jiā kàn xīngxing**
> *If you have time, please come to my house to watch the stars.*

> **Attention**
>
> 要是 **yàoshi** (same as 如果 **rúguǒ**) is <u>not</u> a question word! It can only be used in conditional sentences, e.g. *if A, then B*. We may never use it like in English *I don't know if she will come tonight* or *I'm not sure if he knows her*.

The curious matter of the word 几 jǐ

In chapter 6 we learned that 几 **jǐ** is a question word meaning *how many* for numbers below 10. But in a different context the same 几 **jǐ** is not a question word at all and means *a few* (less than 10). A sentence 你有几个好朋友 **nǐ yǒu jǐ gè hǎo péngyou** can be a question and mean *How many good friends do you have?* or a statement *You have a few good friends*. Only context will determine which is which.

> 她想问你几个问题 **tā xiǎng wèn nǐ jǐ gè wèntí**
> *She would like to ask you a few questions.*

or: *How many questions would she like to ask you?*

(We can see from the context that the question option is less likely, because to ask this question we would probably not use the verb 想 **xiǎng** *to wish*.)

> 这几个人很笨 **zhè jǐ gè rén hěn bèn**
> *These few people are stupid. (This bunch of people are stupid.)*

The context here determines it cannot be a question at all, because we have the demonstrative pronoun *this* 这 **zhè**.

我几天没睡觉了 **wǒ jǐ tiān méi yǒu shuì jiào le**
I a few days no have sleep. [continuation]
(I haven't slept for a few days now/It's been a few days since I slept.)

This could also be a question *How many days have I not slept?/How many days since I last slept?*

这几天我很忙 **zhè jǐ tiān wǒ hěn máng**
These few days I very busy. (I'm busy these days.)

这几天 **zhè jǐ tiān** is a fixed way of saying *these days; lately*.

Like versus would like

In chapter 8 we learned a lot about the verb 想 **xiǎng**, which can mean *to wish* or *would like to*. English speakers often confuse it with the verb 喜欢 **xǐhuan** *to like*. These two are, of course, quite different:

我想吃饭
wǒ xiǎng chī fàn *I'd like to eat*

→ 我喜欢吃饭
wǒ xǐhuan chī fàn *I like to eat*

我想睡觉 **wǒ xiǎng shuìjiào**
I'd like to sleep

→ 我喜欢睡觉 **wǒ xǐhuan shuì jiào**
I like to sleep

我想打你 **wǒ xiǎng dǎ nǐ**
I want to beat you up

→ 我喜欢打你 **wǒ xǐhuan dǎ nǐ**
I like beating you up

我想你 **wǒ xiǎng nǐ** *I miss you*

→ 我喜欢你 **wǒ xǐhuan nǐ** *I like you*

1. Transcribe from pinyin to characters.
a) Shūzhuō, yīguì, yǐzi, shāfā dōu shì jiājù.
b) Wòshì, kètīng, xǐshǒujiān, chúfáng dōu shì fángjiān.
c) Lǐmiàn, wàimiàn, shàngmiàn, xiàmiàn, zuǒbiān, yòubiān, hái yǒu pángbiān, dàochù dōu yǒu māo; zhè gè dìfāng zhēn qíguài.

2. Transcribe to pinyin.
a) 我们还没有做好准备
b) 不可能
c) 电脑在桌上
d) 衣柜里有高跟鞋
e) 我去找别人

3. Choose 要 or 想.
a) 你__干什么？
b) 我不__你的钱，我__你的爱。
c) 我__家。
d) 我__这个人很笨。
e) 你__吗？
f) 明年我一定__去中国。
g) 我很__跟你一起去。
h) 你不__这样__！
i) 你__工作吗？
j) 我__听音乐。
k) 我不__跟你过夜。
l) 她__吃中国饭。
m) 我__去中国学中文。
n) 我__去公园看小羊驼。

羊 **yáng** 1146
lamb; sheep

驼 **tuó** 1147
camel

羊驼 **yángtuó**
1146, 1147
alpaca

4. Where are these things/people? Make sentences in Chinese.
E.g. The cat is in the closet ...

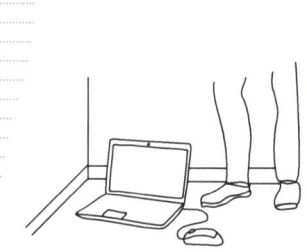  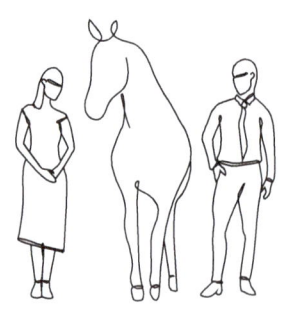  

5. Translate these sentences using 的.
a) Steamed buns that my mom makes are delicious.
b) The horse the teacher is riding is pretty.
c) My boyfriend who studies Chinese in China is rich.
d) The clothes dad bought for mom were expensive.
e) I don't like people who don't eat tofu.
f) The thing you did was not right.
g) The person you love is weird.
h) People who often go to China do not necessarily know how to speak Chinese.
i) Where is the TV set I bought?
j) Who is the person that calls you every day at 6AM?
k) My 5 year old younger brother already has a cell phone.
l) People who have not paid cannot enter.

6. Connect the sentences with 要是.
Example:
你吃我的猫。我吃你的小羊驼。 → 要是你吃我的猫，我（就会）吃你的小羊驼。

a) 你不给我钱。我不给你看我男朋友的照片。　f) 床太小。我们不能一起睡。
b) 你不付钱。我告诉妈妈。　　　　　　　　　g) 你觉得这里太贵。我们去找别的地方。
c) 你不洗手。你不能吃饭。　　　　　　　　　h) 天气太冷。我们在家里休息。
d) 你不喜欢他。不要请他喝茶。　　　　　　　i) 办公室没有窗户。我不想在这里工作。
e) 他来。我们可以一起看电视。　　　　　　　j) 沙发上有青蛙。我坐地（坐在地上）。

7. 想 vs. 喜欢 – which sentences match?
a) 我喜欢你的男朋友。　　　我想在你的沙发上休息休息，可以吗？

b) 我想去中国。　　　　　　我想跟你一起喝，怎么样？

c) 我喜欢做饭。　　　　　　我想请他喝个酒。

d) 我喜欢看电视。　　　　　因为我喜欢吃中国饭。

e) 你喜欢喝啤酒吗？　　　　今天我想做包子。

f) 我喜欢你的家。　　　　　我得买新的电视机。

g) 老师喜欢骑马。　　　　　我想找一个中国男朋友。

h) 我喜欢说中文。　　　　　我想在那儿上大学。

i) 我喜欢北京。　　　　　　她想买一匹。

14 Jerry 在哪儿上厕所?
Where does Jerry go to the toilet?

Part 1

齐老师和Jerry在一起过得非常开心。
Qí lǎoshī hé Jerry zài yìqǐ guò de fēicháng kāixīn.
Qi Teacher and Jerry present together pass [to the degree of] extremely cheerful.
Teacher Qi and Jerry are extremely happy when they spend time together.

老师每天都起得很早。
Lǎoshī měi tiān dōu qǐ de hěn zǎo.
Teacher every day all rise [to the degree of] very early.
Every day, the teacher gets up early.

他先洗澡再吃早饭。
Tā xiān xǐ zǎo zài chī zǎofàn.
He first shower then eat morning cooked rice.
He first showers and then eats breakfast.

老师吃饭吃得少,而且吃得快。
Lǎoshī chī fàn chī de shǎo, érqiě chī de kuài.
Teacher eat cooked rice eat [to degree of] few, and also eat [to degree of] fast.
The teacher eats little and he eats fast.

他早上喜欢喝咖啡,吃火腿炒鸡蛋和面包;
Tā zǎoshang xǐhuan hē kāfēi, chī huǒtuǐ chǎo jīdàn hé miànbāo;
He morning like drink coffee, eat ham stir-fry chicken egg and bread;
In the morning he likes to drink coffee, eat scrambled eggs with ham and bread;

得 **de** 521
complement of degree

originally a verb pronounced dé meaning "to reach; to obtain; to achieve;" see grammar explanations

起(牀) **qǐ (chuáng)** 507, (1105)
起(床) to get up (from bed)

"To rise" + "bed"; 起 qǐ "to rise" takes an object 床 chuáng "bed," but we can skip it if the context is clear.

澡 **zǎo** 1201
to wash; to bathe

"Water" 氵 shuǐ radical

洗澡 **xǐ zǎo** 1132
to take a shower

"to wash" + "to bathe"

再 **zài** 1202
again

先 ... 再 ... **xiān ... zài ...** 405, 1202
first ... and then ...

早飯 / 早饭 **zǎofàn** 301, 203
breakfast

"morning" + "rice"

吃早飯 / 吃早饭 **chī zǎofàn** 202, 301, 203
to have breakfast

In Chinese we say "to eat" and not "to have".

咖啡 **kāfēi** 1203, 1204
coffee

These two characters are exceptional in that they do not have any independent meaning on their own, i.e. both can only exist together in this combination; they were made up to represent the sound "coffee" (kafei) by adding mouth 口 kǒu radicals to characters 加 jiā "to add" and 非 fēi "not so," which we have seen in 非常 fēicháng "extraordinary".

火 **huǒ** 1205
fire

An intensely beautiful character that actually looks like flames, one of the elements and a common radical.

腿 **tuǐ** 1145
leg

月(肉) ròu "flesh" radical for meaning (body part), 退 tuì "retreat/return" for pronunciation

火腿 **huǒtuǐ**
ham

"fire" + "leg"= "leg on fire"?

炒 **chǎo** 1206
to stir-fry

火 huǒ "fire" radical and 少 shǎo for pronunciation

雞 / 鸡 **jī** 1207
chicken

The traditional form has 隹 zhuī "a bird with a short tail" for a radical, but, as we have observed before, Chinese script reformers particularly disliked it, so they removed it whenever possible; here, they've replaced it with a more general radical 鸟 niǎo "bird" to create a simplified "chicken". 奚 xī in the traditional form is for pronunciation.

雞蛋 / 鸡蛋 **jīdàn** 1207, 909
egg

"Chicken" + "egg"; the syllable "dàn" can have many meanings (e.g. in 但是 dànshì), so we need to specify that we mean a "chicken" dàn → a chicken egg.

火腿炒雞蛋 / 火腿炒鸡蛋 **huǒtuǐ chǎo jīdàn** 1205, 1145, 1206, 1207, 909
eggs fried with ham

麵 / 面 **miàn** 1208
wheat flour; meal; noodles; things made of wheat flour

The traditional form has 麥 mài "wheat" radical to suggest the meaning and 面 miàn for pronunciation; the simplified was reduced to 面 miàn alone, which originally means "face; surface" (see vocabulary chapter 11); the simplified character now means both "flour" and "face."

包 **bāo** 1027
to wrap/pack/roll; a bundle/package/bag/roll

an extremely useful character that looks kind of like what it means

麵包 / 面包 **miànbāo** 1208, 1027
bread; bread roll ("meal" + "roll")

179

老师不喜欢喝牛奶。
lǎoshī bù xǐhuan hē niúnǎi.
teacher no like drink milk.
the teacher does not like to drink milk.

Jerry 早上不吃饭，只喝几瓶啤酒；
Jerry zǎoshang bù chī fàn, zhǐ hē jǐ píng píjiǔ;
Jerry morning no eat cooked rice, only drink several bottle beer;
Jerry does not eat in the morning, he just drinks a few bottles of beer;

虽然他喝得很多，但是他不会醉。
suīrán tā hē de hěn duō, dànshì tā bú huì zuì.
although he drink [to the degree of] very much, but he no can drunk.
even though he drinks a lot, he does not get drunk.

喝咖啡的时候，Jerry 喜欢加牛奶。
Hē kāfēi de shíhou, Jerry xǐhuan jiā niúnǎi.
Drink-coffee's time, Jerry like add milk.
When he drinks coffee, Jerry likes to add milk.

他说牛和马是朋友。
Tā shuō niú hé mǎ shì péngyou.
He say cow and horse are friend.
He says cows and horses are friends.

牛 **niú** 1209
cow

This character is a common radical, usually in animal-related characters; we've seen it in 物 wù "objects; outside things; matter; animals".

奶 **nǎi** 341
breasts; milk

女 nǚ "female" is for the meaning, 乃 nǎi for pronunciation.

牛奶 **niúnǎi**
cow's milk

瓶 **píng** 1210
bottle

并 bìng suggests the pronunciation and 瓦 wǎ "earthenware" indicates the meaning.

醉 **zuì** 1211
drunk; to get drunk

We've seen the element 酉 yǒu "wine vessel" in 酒 jiǔ "alcohol". Here, it carries the same meaning. 卒 zú is for pronunciation.

加 **jiā** 1212
to add

We've seen this character in 咖 kā 咖啡 kāfēi, where it was modified by adding 口 kǒu "mouth" to create a character for the sound "kā"

Fortune cookie:

方便面 **fāngbiàn miàn**
instant noodles

1022, 1023, 1208

Verb complements

Every time we want to describe how an action is performed, we need to use a special grammatical function called a **complement**, because it "completes" and further explains the meaning of the verb. There are different kinds of complements in Chinese and we will learn all of them in the following chapters. In this chapter we will focus on the **complement of degree**, which describes the degree or extent to which an action is performed.

In English, when we want to say how we do something, we simply use a description word, such as an adverb, e.g. *I walk <u>fast</u>, she speaks Chinese <u>well</u>, you live <u>far</u>*, or otherwise describe it, e.g. *we eat <u>a lot</u>, I sing <u>with joy</u>* etc. That does not work in Chinese. Instead, we need to use a special function word 得 **de** after the verb, which literally means *to obtain; to get; to reach [the point/extent/degree of]*:

 pǎo 1226
to run

> Jerry 跑得快 **Jerry pǎo de kuài**
> *Jerry runs reaching the point/degree of fast* → *Jerry runs fast*

> 王小猫拉得少 **Wáng Xiǎomāo lā de shǎo**
> *Wang Xiaomao poop reaching the degree of little*
> → *Wang Xiaomao doesn't poop much*

Remember that verbs in Chinese often come with a default object, e.g. we translate 吃饭 **chī fàn** as *to eat*, but it literally means *to eat cooked rice*: 吃 **chī** is the verb *to eat* and 饭 **fàn** is the object (a noun). 得 **de** needs to always come after the verb it complements; therefore, when the verb is followed by an object, as is often the case in Chinese, e.g. Jerry 吃饭 **Jerry chī fàn** *Jerry eats [cooked rice]*, if we want to use 得 **de**, we need to repeat the verb after the object:

> Jerry 吃饭吃得慢 **Jerry chī fàn chī de màn**
> *Jerry eat cooked rice eat reaching the degree of slow* → *Jerry eats slowly.*

We may never say ~~Jerry 吃饭得慢 Jerry chī fàn de màn~~, with 得 **de** following directly after the noun. Since this sounds a little clumsy, we can move the object to the front of the verb whenever we use 得 **de**; this is convenient, especially with longer objects: Instead of Jerry 说中文说得好 **Jerry shuō zhōngwén shuō de hǎo** *Jerry speak Chinese speak reaching the degree of good*, we can say Jerry 中文说得好 **Jerry zhōngwén shuō de hǎo** (*Jerry Chinese speak reaching the point/degree of good* → *Jerry speaks Chinese well*). If it is easier for you though, feel free to say the verb twice instead of moving the object.

> Do not confuse the possessive particle 的 **de** that we've learned before with the complement of degree 得 **de** that we have learned just now. They sound exactly the same, but they have nothing in common with each other and they are used completely differently.

Finally, the degree to which an action is performed may be more abstract or descriptive, not just *fast*, *slow*, *good*, etc., but also *happy* or *drunk*. This can mean that a sentence can have a very different structure from what a sentence expressing the same idea would have in English. Look at a few examples:

老师骑Jerry骑得很高兴 **lǎoshī qí Jerry qí de hěn gāoxìng**
Teacher ride Jerry ride reaching the point of very happy
→ *The teacher rides Jerry happily. / Riding Jerry makes the teacher happy.*

王小猫喝酒喝得很醉 **Wáng Xiǎomāo hē jiǔ hē de hěn zuì**
Wang Xiaomao drink alcohol drink to the point of very drunk
→ *Wang Xiaomao is getting really drunk.*

In questions, we ask about the complement and not the verb, i.e. we ask about how the action is performed and not what action it is; we can form the question by using 吗 **ma** or by alternating the description word:

你睡得好吗？ **nǐ shuì de hǎo ma?**
You sleep to the degree of good [question particle]?
→ *Do/did you sleep well?*

or:

你睡得好不好 **nǐ shuì de hǎo bù hǎo?**
You sleep to the degree of good not good? → *Do/did you sleep well?*

We may also use the question word 怎么样 **zěnmeyàng** *how*:

你睡得怎么样？ **nǐ shuì de zěnmeyàng?**
You sleep to the degree of how? → *How did you sleep?*

老师做饭做得怎么样？ **lǎoshī zuò fàn zuò de zěnmeyàng?**
Teacher make food make to the degree of how?
→ *How does the teacher cook?*

In negations, 不 **bù** is part of the complement "*not tasty*; *not well*" etc. and not the verb (*to sleep*; *to cook*):

我睡得不好 **wǒ shuì de bù hǎo** *I sleep to the degree of no good.*

老师唱歌唱得不好听 **lǎoshī chàng gē chàng de bù hǎo tīng**
Teacher sing songs sing to the degree of no good [to] listen.

Again, idiomatic English translation would be *the teacher doesn't sing nicely*, rather than *the teacher sings not nicely*.

> Attention! In English we would say *I don't sleep well*, which is negating the verb and not the description; in Chinese, we say something closer to *I sleep unwell*; however, there is no way of saying 我不睡得好 **wǒ bù shuì de hǎo** *I not sleep to the degree of good (I don't sleep well)*.

First and again

先 **xiān** and 再 **zài** are both adverbs; therefore, they must always come before a verb:

你先吃吧 **nǐ xiān chī ba** You first eat [suggestion] → Let you eat first!

我们先休息休息 **wǒmen xiān xiūxi xiūxi** We first rest rest
→ Let us first take some rest

请你再来 **qǐng nǐ zài lái** Please you again come → Please, come again!

明年我要再去中国 **míngnián wǒ yào zài qù Zhōngguó**
Next year I will again go to China. → Next year, I'm going to China again.

要是你再吃我的饭，我会请你男朋友喝啤酒
yàoshì nǐ zài chī wǒ de fàn, wǒ huì qǐng nǐ nán péngyou hē píjiǔ
If you again eat my food, I may invite your boyfriend to drink beer.
→ If you eat my food again, I will take your boyfriend out for beer.

> 再 **zài** can only refer to actions that can be repeated in the future; it cannot be used for things that happened again in the past, e.g. *I came again*.

先 **xiān** + action 再 **zài** + action connects two actions happening one after another, like in "first ... then ..."

我先洗澡再大便 **wǒ xiān xǐzǎo zài dàbiàn**
I first shower [and] then I poop

她先吃蛋糕再喝啤酒 **tā xiān chī dàngāo zài hē píjiǔ**
She first eat cake then drink beer. (She eats cake first and then drinks beer.)

大便 **dà biàn**
101, 1023
poo; to poo

"Big convenience;" can you guess what 小便 **xiǎo biàn** "little convenience" would mean? Yes, it means "pee/to pee".

Part 2

Jerry 虽然不洗澡，但是他很干净；
Jerry   suīrán bù xǐ zǎo,   dànshì tā hěn gānjìng;
Jerry   although no shower,   but   he very clean;
Although Jerry does not shower, he is clean;

他也不刮脸，可是他的脸很可爱。
tā yě bù guā liǎn,   kěshì   tā dē liǎn hěn kě'ài.
he also no shave face,   but   he's face very lovely (cute).
he does not shave, either, but his face is lovely (cute).

有的时候老师帮Jerry刷牙。
Yǒu de shíhou   lǎoshī bāng Jerry   shuā yá.
Sometimes   teacher help Jerry brush teeth.
Sometimes, the teacher helps Jerry to brush his teeth.

因为老师的厕所没有门，
Yīnwèi   lǎoshī de cèsuǒ méi yǒu mén,
Because   teacher's   toilet   no have door,
Because the teacher's toilet has no door,

所以Jerry不喜欢在家里上厕所。
suǒyǐ   Jerry bù xǐhuan zài jiā li shàng cèsuǒ.
therefore Jerry no like present house inside mount toilet.
therefore Jerry does not like to go to the toilet at home.

老师问Jerry："你要方便一下吗？
Lǎoshī   wèn Jerry: "Nǐ yào fāngbiàn yí xià ma?
Teacher ask Jerry: "You want relieve [one down] [question]?
Teacher asks Jerry: "Do you need to relieve yourself?

没事儿，你可以去外面的花园里。"
Méi shì'er,   nǐ   kěyǐ   qù wàimian de huāyuán li."
No [have] matter, you can go outside's flower garden."
No problem, you can go into the flower garden outside."

乾 / 干   **gān** 1213
          dry

We've seen 干 before in chapter 8 as a simplification of 幹 gàn "to do". Here, it is used again to simplify another character with a similar pronuncntaition (gàn~gān); thus, in simplified spelling 干 can have two pronunciations and different meanings; originally, 干 gān means "shield". It also refers to the "Celestial Stems" 天干 tiān gān--the 12 Chinese zodiac signs.

淨 / 净   **jìng** 1214
          clean

For reasons unknown the original "water" 氵 shuǐ radical, which also makes sense semantically (water~clean), has been "simplified" to 冫 bīng "ice". Apparently, the concerned language reformers thought the character will be easier to write with one less dot.

乾淨 / 干净   **gānjìng**
              clean

刮   **guā** 1215
      to scrape; to shave

刂 dāo "knife" for scraping

有的时候老师帮Jerry刷牙。

刮臉 / 刮脸
guā liǎn 1215, 523
to shave (face)

可愛 / 可爱
kě'ài 322, 313
lovely; cute; lovable

"worth to" + "to love"; compare to 可怜 kělián "poor"

有的
yǒu de 214, 310
some

"there are those who/that ..."

有(的)時候 / 有(的)时候
yǒu (de) shíhou 214, 310, 727, 902
sometimes ("some" + "time"; "there are times (when)")

幫 / 帮
bāng 1216
to help

刷
shuā 1217
to brush

牙
yá 1218
tooth; teeth

We saw this character as a phonetic element in 呀; here in its original meaning.

刷牙
shuā yá
to brush teeth

廁 / 厕
cè 1219
lavatory; toilet

Note that the simplified not only reduces 貝 to 贝, but also changes 广 to 厂 (same as in 廚 → 厨 chú "kitchen" and 廳 → 厅 tīng "hall")

所
suǒ 809
place; office

We've seen this character as a function word in 所以; here in its original meaning.

廁所 / 厕所
cèsuǒ
toilet; WC; restroom

Chinese people are not shy to use the word "toilet", rather than the more euphemistic "restroom" or "bathroom."

上廁所 / 上厕所
shàng cèsuǒ 217, 1219, 809
to go to the toilet; to use the toilet

方便
fāngbiàn 1022, 1023
to relieve oneself

We've seen this word before in chapter 10, where it meant "convenient". So does it here, except in a verbal form "to convenience oneself" or "to make oneself feel comfortable".

外面
wàimian 325, 1113
outside

As a suffix -面 -mian usually loses the tone; but it is also correct to read "wàimiàn".

185

老师说Jerry的大便是有机肥料，
Lǎoshī shuō Jerry de dàbiàn shì yǒujī féiliào,
Teacher say　Jerry's　　poop　is organic fertilizer,
The teacher says Jerry's poop is an organic fertilizer,

对花特别好。
duì huā tèbié hǎo.
towards flowers especially good.
extremely good for the flowers.

Jerry拉得很多，每天至少十五公斤，
Jerry lā de hěn duō, měi tiān zhìshǎo shí wǔ gōngjīn,
Jerry poops [to the degree of] very much, every day at least 15 kg,
Jerry poops a lot, at least 15kg every day,

老师还可以卖给别人.
lǎoshī hái kěyǐ mài gěi bié rén.
teacher still　can　sell give other people.
the teacher can even sell it to other people.

大便	**dà biàn** 101, 1023 poo; to poo	
有機 有机	**yǒujī** 214, 620 organic	

机 jī here means "organism" or "the natural mechanism/engine"; "to have" + "organisms" = "organic; natural".

肥　　**féi** 1220
　　　fat; fertilizer

another character with 月(肉) ròu "flesh" radical

料　　**liào** 1221
　　　stuff; material; (grain) feed

Refers to raw food materials of all kinds; note the 米 mǐ "uncooked rice grain" radical.

肥料　**féiliào**
　　　fertilizer; manure

"fat" + "material"

對 对　**duì** 436
　　　for; to

literally "to face something/somebody", here used as a preposition "for (the flowers)"

拉　　**lā** 1222
　　　to discharge (stool; urine); to empty the bowels; to pull; to draw; to haul

The basic meaning is "to pull," hence the 扌(手) shǒu "hand" radical.

至　　**zhì** 1223
　　　to arrive at; to reach (a point); superlative degree--the most

至少　**zhìshǎo** 820
　　　at least

"the most" + "few" = "the most least"

斤　　**jīn** 1224
　　　a unit of weight, Chinese pound (0.5 kg)

This character is a common radical and originally means "an ax".

公斤　**gōngjīn** 342
　　　kilogram

賣 卖　**mài** 1225
　　　to sell

Notice the similarity with 买(買) mǎi "to buy".

Some

有(的) **yǒu (de)** followed by a noun means *some*.

There are some fixed phrases, such as 有(的)时候 **yǒu (de) shíhou**, literally *there are times [when ...]* → *sometimes*, or 有人 **yǒu rén**, literally *there is a person* → *somebody*; in such phrases, 的 **de** is optional:

有(的)时候我想吃你 **yǒu (de) shíhou wǒ xiǎng chī nǐ**
There is time I wish eat you (Sometimes, I want to eat you)

有人告诉我你喜欢吃草 **yǒu rén gàosu wǒ nǐ xǐhuan chī cǎo**
There is a person tell me you like [to] eat grass.
(Somebody told me you like to eat grass.)

有人给我打了一个电话 **yǒu rén gěi wǒ dǎ le yí gè diànhuà**
There is person give me hit [complete] a telephone.
(Somebody gave me a phone call.)

有人敲门 **yǒu rén qiāo mén**
There is [a] person knock [on the] door. (Somebody's knocking on the door.)

If we keep 的 **de**, 有的人 **yǒu de rén** usually refers to *some people* (more than one), but that's not a strict rule:

有的人不喜欢喝酒 **yǒu de rén bù xǐhuan hē jiǔ**
Some people don't like to drink alcohol.

有的人觉得我很可爱 **yǒu de rén juéde wǒ hěn kě'ài**
Some people think I'm cute.

有的人11点才起床 **yǒu de rén 11 diǎn cái qǐ chuáng**
Some people 11 o'clock only rise from bed. (Some people don't get up till 11.)

With other nouns we keep 的 **de**:

有的马不漂亮 **yǒu de mǎ bú piàoliang** *Some horses are not pretty.*

有的学生不喜欢齐老师 **yǒu de xuésheng bù xǐhuan Qí lǎoshī**
Some students don't like teacher Qi.

有的女人不喜欢男人 **yǒu de nǚrén bù xǐhuan nánrén**
Some women don't like men.

有人告诉我你喜欢吃草

How to use the toilet

We learned how to ask for things politely, how to invite people and how to make suggestions. We saw that we can either repeat the verb:

你看一看 **nǐ kàn yí kàn** You look one look (Have a look)

or use 吧 **ba**:

吃吧 **chī ba** eat [suggestion] (Please, eat; Let you eat!)

In addition to those two ways, we can also add 一下 **yí xià** (literally: *one [time] down*) after the verb; this has no meaning that we can translate easily, it simply softens the intensity of the action and can be understood as *just one bit*:

你吃一下 **nǐ chī yí xià** You eat [one down], ok? (Please, eat/Have a bite)

我看一下 **wǒ kàn yí xià** I look [one down] (Let me have a look.)

休息一下 **xiūxi yí xià** Rest [one down] (Take some rest.)

我去方便一下 **wǒ qù fāngbiàn yí xià** *I go convenience [one down]*
(Let me go and relieve myself)
→ polite and euphemistic way of asking permission to use the toilet

Attention: 一下 **yí xià** must follow a verb. If the verb takes an object, we put 一下 **yí xià** in between:

你吃一下饭 **nǐ chī yí xià fàn** You eat [one down] rice, ok?
(Please, eat some food./Have some food.)

我去方便一下

对 duì "right"

对 **duì** is a meaningful little word. Most often, it means *right* or *correct* and is most commonly used as the Chinese equivalent of *yes*, like in this little dialogue:

— 你爱我吗？ **nǐ ài wǒ ma?** *Do you love me?*
— 对 **duì** Literally: *Correct.* (*That's right; Yes.*)

We can also use it literally to say something is *right* or *correct*:

这个字写得不对
zhè ge zì xiě de bú duì
Literally: *This character write to degree of not correct.*
(*This character is written incorrectly.*)

你的想法不对 **nǐ de xiǎngfǎ bú duì**
Your way of thinking/idea/opinion is not right (is wrong)

你说得对 **nǐ shuō de duì**
You speak to the degree of correct.
(*You're right.*)

However, 对 **duì** actually is a verb and means *to be directed at; to face; to address*. It often translates as the English preposition *to; towards*:

她对我不客气 **tā duì wǒ bú kèqi**
She towards me [is] not kind
→ *She is unkind/mean to me*

你对我不好 **nǐ duì wǒ bù hǎo**
You towards me are bad
(*You treat me badly; You are bad to me.*)

我对你说，这个问题很大！
wǒ duì nǐ shuō, zhè ge wèn tí hěn dà
I towards you speak, this problem very big.
(*I'm telling you, this is a huge problem!*)

1. Tongue Twister:

山南有个崔粗腿，　　Shān nán yǒu gè Cuī Cūtuǐ,
山北有个崔腿粗。　　shān běi yǒu gè Cuī Tuǐcū.
两人上山来比腿。　　Liǎng rén shàng shān lái bǐ tuǐ,
也不知是崔粗腿的腿粗，Yě bù zhī shì Cuī Cūtuǐ de tuǐ cū,
还是崔腿粗的腿粗。　háishì Cuī Tuǐcū de tuǐ cū.

South of the mountain there is one Cui the Coarse Leg,
north of the mountain there is one Cui whose leg is coarse.
The two of them climb on top of the mountain to compare their legs.
We still cannot tell whether it is Cui the Coarse Leg's leg that's coarse,
or is it Cui whose leg is coarse's leg that's coarse.

2. Transliterate from pinyin to characters:
a) nǐ shuō de duì
b) tā shuì de hěn wǎn
c) qǐng nǐ zuò yí xià
d) yǒu de rén hē jiǔ hē de tài duō
e) wǒ zhǐ chī yǒujī de jīdàn
f) lǎoshī gōngzuò de hěn máng
g) wǒ gēge duì wǒ bú kèqi
h) yǒu de shíhou wǒ gěi bàba māma dǎ diànhuà

3. Transliterate from characters to pinyin and translate to English:
a) 老虎不吃面
b) 你可以帮我一个忙吗？
c) 他为什么来得那么早？
d) 你怎么跑得这么快？
e) 有的女的不喜欢男的
f) 我们要想别的办法
g) 大便对花有用
h) 虽然我哥哥很可爱，但是他没有用
i) 你为什么对我那么不客气？

有用　**yǒu yòng**
214, 1020
useful

"to have" + "to use"

4. Use the words from the list to form questions and answers with the complement of degree according to the pattern:

Pattern: Jerry　吃草　快
→Q: Jerry 吃草吃得怎么样？ ("How does Jerry eat grass?")
A: Jerry 吃草吃得快 ("Jerry eats grass fast")

a) Jerry　喝　啤酒　很多 (Jerry drinks beer a lot)
b) 老师　喝　啤酒　很醉 (Teacher drinks beer until drunk)
c) Jerry　做　日本饭　好吃 (Jerry cooks Japanese food well)
d) Jerry 看电视　很高兴 (Jerry watches TV happily)
e) 马先生　洗手　不干净 (Mr. Ma does not wash his hands clean)
f) Jerry 上课　早 (Jerry goes to class early)
g)） 王小猫　听　音乐　不太多 (Wang Xiaomao doesn't listen to music much)
h) 齐老师　说　法文　还行 (Teacher Qi speaks French OK)

i) 学生 准备 中文课 还可以 (The students prepare for Chinese class alright)
j) 妈妈 做饭 还好 (Mom cooks fine)
k) 齐老师 骂学生 不好听 (Teacher Qi curses students and it sounds bad)
l) 这个人 骑自行车 很慢 (This man bikes slowly)
m) Jerry 学 英文 真不错 (Jerry learns English really well)
n) 我男朋友 炒鸡蛋 很香 (My boyfriend fries eggs so they are delicious)
o) 学生 在大学 过 开心 (Students are cheerful at the College)

5. Make sentences using 先 xiān and 再 zài.
a) 老师/刮脸/洗澡
b) 小猫/洗脸/喝牛奶
c) 马先生/喝醉/打人
d) 我哥哥/看电视/睡觉
e) 有的老师/骂学生/问问题

6. Fill in the blank; Use 的 or 得
a) 他吃饭吃＿＿很快。
b) 我＿＿老师不帅。
c) 我＿＿朋友炒鸡蛋炒＿＿很香。
d) 我＿＿书在哪里？
e) 老师＿＿房间很干净。
f) 他说话说＿＿很慢！
g) 他喝我＿＿啤酒喝＿＿很醉！
h) 你女朋友不美，而且她做饭做＿＿不好吃。
i) 我每天都起床起＿＿很早！
j) 老师＿＿厕所没有门！

說話
说话

shuō huà
321, 812
to speak; to talk

"to speak" + "words"

7. Reply/make invitations using 一下 yí xià according to the pattern.
Example:
可以休息休息吗？[May I take some rest?] → 请你休息一下 [Please, take some rest]
a) 你可以给我看一看这张照片吗？
b) 我要听音乐。
c) 我有一个问题想跟你说，可以吗？
d) 我想问你一个问题，可以吗？
e) 这里可以坐吗？
f) 我想吃这个包子，可以吗？
g) 怎么吃鸡蛋？--（answer: 炒）
h) 我喝这瓶牛奶，怎么样？
i) 你要做什么？--（answer: 方便）

13 十三

Part 1

东方红，Jerry 棒
East is red, Jerry is awesome

Jerry 的身体特别棒。
Jerry de shēntǐ tèbié bàng.
Jerry's body especially awesome.
Jerry's body is extremely awesome (fit).

每天早上吃饭了以后，
Měi tiān zǎoshang chī fàn le yǐhòu,
Every day morning eat cooked rice [complete] after,
Every morning after having eaten,

齐老师骑Jerry去学校。
Qí lǎoshī qí Jerry qù xuéxiào.
Qi teacher ride Jerry go school.
Teacher Qi rides Jerry to school.

这样，Jerry有机会锻炼身体。
Zhè yàng, Jerry yǒu jīhuì duànliàn shēntǐ.
This way, Jerry have opportunity exercise body.
This way, Jerry has an opportunity to exercise.

虽然老师住得很远，
Suīrán lǎoshī zhù de hěn yuǎn,
Although teacher live [to the degree of] very far,
The teacher lives far,

身 **shēn** 1301
body; self

Refers to the phyisical body as well as the personality / identity

體
体 **tǐ** 1302
body; shape; form; substance; essence

Refers to physical aspects of the body. There is a lot going on in the traditional form; radical 骨 gǔ means "bones", 豊 lǐ is a "vessel" or "container". Thus, the physical body as "container of bones". The simplified form is very reduced, yet meaningful; "a person" 亻rén and a "root" 本 běn.

身體
身体 **shēntǐ**
body; health

Not only means "body," but also physical condition of a person; to ask "how is your health?", we say 你身体好吗? nǐ shēntǐ hǎo ma?

棒 **bàng** 1303
strong/fit; awesome

Originally means "stick", hence "wood" 木 mù; also means "beat with a stick", which makes you as resistant as wood. 棒 describes a tough, worked out body, but is also a slang word for "awesome".

但是Jerry 跑得很快，马上就到。
dànshì   Jerry   pǎo de hěn kuài, mǎshàng jiù dào.
but Jerry run [to the degree of] very fast, immediately just arrive.
but Jerry runs fast and arrives right away.

老师觉得又方便又舒服。
Lǎoshī jué de yòu fāngbiàn yòu shūfu.
Teacher think both convenient and comfortable.
The teacher thinks it's both convenient and comfortable.

虽然骑马以后屁股很痛，但是老师说他不管。
Suīrán qí mǎ yǐhòu   pìgu hěn tòng, dànshì   lǎoshī shuō tā bù guǎn.
Although ride horse after   butt very hurt,   but   teacher say he no care.
Although his butt hurts after riding a horse, he says he doesn't care.

以後 / 以后 **yǐhòu** 719, 927
after; later (see grammar notes)

機 / 机 **jī** 620
here: crucial point; chance; opportunity

机 jī has many meanings; we have seen: 司机 sījī "driver," where it means "machine" and 有机 yǒujī "organic," where it means "organism."

會 / 会 **huì** 320
here: moment

機會 / 机会 **jīhuì**
opportunity; chance

"chance" + "moment"

鍛 / 锻 **duàn** 1304
to forge

Radical 钅(金) jīn "metal" for meaning; 段 duàn "section" for pronunciation. Both are common (we have seen 钅 in 钱 qián "money," which originally means "silver").

鍊 / 炼 **liàn** 1305
to smelt; to refine

Another metal-related verb, hence the 金 jīn radical (traditional) – interchangable with 火 huǒ "fire" in simplified form (we need fire to smelt metal).

鍛鍊 / 锻炼 **duànliàn**
to toughen; to work out

Also "to temper steel," hence the metal-forging related characters.

遠 / 远 **yuǎn** 1306
far

辶 chuò "road" radical for meaning; same phonetic element 袁 (元) as in 園/园 yuán "garden".

跑 **pǎo** 1226
to run

⻊(足) zú "foot" radical for "to run"; 包 bāo "to wrap; bag": phonetic element in characters pronounced "bao/pao"

馬上 / 马上 **mǎshàng**
at once; right away; very fast; very soon;

"As if on a horseback". An adverb – needs to be followed by a verb.

屁 **pì** 1307
fart

尸 shī "corpse" radical for meaning; 比 bǐ "to compare" for pronunciation; it sounds nefarious, but corpse is a common radical in body-related characters.

股 **gǔ** 1308
thigh; hip; lower back

月 (肉) ròu "meat" radical common in characters for body parts.

屁股 **pìgu**
butt

"fart hip" :)

痛 **tòng** 1309
to ache; to hurt; pain

疒 chuáng "illness" for the meaning; we've seen it in 病 bìng "illness." 甬 yǒng for pronunciation

Part 2

Jerry 学得很努力。
Jerry xué de hěn nǔlì.
Jerry study [to the degree of] very diligent.
Jerry studies diligently.

虽然Jerry是一匹马，但是他中文说得很好
Suīrán Jerry shì yì pǐ mǎ, dànshì tā zhōngwén shuō de hěn hǎo
Although Jerry is one [measure word for horses] horse, but he Chinese language speak [to the degree of] very good
Even though Jerry is a horse, he speaks Chinese well

　　（他还会说日文，德文和别的语言）；
　　(tā hái huì shuō rìwén, déwén hé bié de yǔyán);
　　(he still can speak Japanese language, German language and other language);
　　(he can also speak Japanese, German, and other languages);

　　虽然他没有手，但是汉字也写得很好看。
　　suīrán tā méi yǒu shǒu, dànshì hànzì yě xiě de hěn hǎo kàn.
　　although he no have hand, but Chinese characters also write [to the degree of] very good [to] look at (good looking).
　　even though he has no hands, he writes Chinese characters really beautifully.

　　上课的时候Jerry常常唱中国歌；
　　Shàng kè de shíhou Jerry cháng cháng chàng Zhōngguó gē;
　　Attend-class's time Jerry often sing China song;
　　During class, he often sings Chinese songs;

　　他唱得很好听。
　　tā chàng de hěn hǎo tīng.
　　he sing [to the degree of] very good [to] listen (sounds good).
　　he sings really beautifully.

　　他最喜欢的一首歌是"东方红"。
　　Tā zuì xǐhuan de yì shǒu gē shì "Dōngfāng hóng."
　　He most-like's one [measure word for songs] song is "East Red."
　　His favorite song is "East Is Red".

努　**nǔ** 1310
to exert oneself; to make an effort

力 lì "power; force" radical; 奴 nú is for pronunciation, but it also means "slave", which adds to the meaning of the character.

力　**lì** 1311
power; force; strength

common radical that we have seen in other characters, such as 男 nán "male" ("field force"); here used in its original meaning

努力　**nǔlì**
diligent; to make great effort; to exert oneself

日文　**rìwén** 346, 315
Japanese language

日 rì comes from 日本 Rìběn "Japan" ("the Sun" + "root/origin" = "The Land of the Rising Sun")

德　**dé** 345
virtue

Ancient concept of "virtue" + "power" by means of which everything that happens, happens; here phonetic part in 德国 Déguó "Germany", which may appear to mean "country of virtue", but is in fact an abbreviation of 德意志 déyìzhì, the phonetic transcription of "Deutsch (German)." See chapter 3.

德文　**déwén**
German language

那首歌很有名。
Nà shǒu gē hěn yǒu míng.
That [measure word for songs] very have name (famous).
That song is very famous.

語
语
yǔ 1312
language; speech, spoken language

言 (讠) yán "speech" radical, 吾 wú for pronunciation

言
yán 1313
speech; words; language

We've seen 言 many times before as a radical; here in its original meaning. No simplified form (as a radical simplified to 讠).

語言
语言
yǔyán
language

Modern Chinese likes two-syllable words, hence combination of "spoken language" + "speech".

漢
汉
hàn 1314
Han (*ethnic Chinese*); Chinese

Han is originally the name of a river, hence "water" 氵 shuǐ radical; it was the name of the first major Chinese dynasty that ruled all of China - Han Dynasty (206 BCE-220 CE), and later adopted as a name of the Chinese people: the Han nationality, which today designates ethnic Chinese (as opposed to Uyghurs, Tibetans, Manchus, and other nationalities living in China).

漢字
汉字
hànzì
1314, 130
Chinese characters

"Han (Chinese)" + "characters"

寫
写
xiě 1315
to write

Note that the simplified character, apart from being much reduced, also uses a different "roof" radical with one less stroke: 冖 instead of 宀.

verb +
(的) 時候
(的) 时候
verb + (**de**) **shíhou**
(310), 727, 902
at the time when (something happens)

的 de is optional; see grammar explanations

唱
chàng 1316
to sing

口 kǒu "mouth" is needed for singing and 昌 chāng is for pronunciation.

歌
gē 1317
song

唱歌
chàng gē
to sing

"to sing" + "songs"

好聽
好听
hǎo tīng
103, 510
to sound good; to be nice to hear/listen to

"good" + "listen"

最 + *adj.*
zuì 1318
most

首
shǒu 1319
measure word for songs and poems

Originally means "head".

東
东
dōng 1320
east

The sun 日 born in a (mulberry) tree 木, which grows in the East.

方
fāng 1022
here: (*geographical*) direction; region

東方
东方
dōngfāng
1320, 1022
the East

Literally "Eastern direction". Refers to a geographical region, i.e. East Asia or Orient.

紅
红
hóng 1321
red

"Silk" 糹: a piece of silk cloth colored in vermilion red; 工 gōng is for pronunciation (gōng~hóng).

Language

文 **wén** means *language* and we saw it in chapter 3. It originally means *written language*, so we could say 学中文 **xué Zhōngwén** *study Chinese*, but not 说中文 **shuō Zhōngwén** *speak [written] Chinese*. Nowadays, speakers use 文 **wén** for both written and spoken language.

However, the correct word for spoken language is 语 **yǔ** and people still use it a lot, especially in mainland China. We build the vocabulary with 语 **yǔ** the same way we do with 文 **wén**, except for the word *Chinese language*, where we use 汉 **hàn** instead of 中 **zhōng**:

汉语 **hànyǔ** 1314, 1312 Literally: *Han Language*
(= 中文 **zhōngwén** *Chinese language*; **Han** are the ethnic Chinese)
英语 **yīngyǔ** 323 *English*   (= 英文 **yīngwén**)
日语 **rìyǔ** 346 *Japanese*   (= 日文 **rìwén**)
法语 **fǎyǔ** 344 *French*   (= 法文 **fǎwén**)
德语 **déyǔ** 345 *German*   (= 德文 **déwén**)
西班牙语 **xībānyáyǔ** 524, 1349, 1218 *Spanish* (= 西班牙文 **xībānyáwén**)

When things happen

In chapter 9 we discussed the difference between 时间 **shíjiān** *time* (concept) and 时候 **shíhou** *time*, which we use to indicate when things happen, or to answer the question 什么时候 **shénme shíhou** *when*. The construction **Action** + 的时候 **de shíhou** means *when (something is happening)*, *at the time of ...* or *during*. In fact, this is a typical construction with 的 **de** that we saw in chapter 4: **A**的**B**, where **A** describes **B**, e.g.

漂亮的男孩子 **piàoliang de nánháizi** *pretty boy*
睡觉的朋友 **shuìjiào de péngyou**
sleeping friend (a friend who is sleeping)

To put it simply, whatever comes before 的 **de** is a description of whatever comes after it. Similarly, in **Action** + 的时候 **shíhou** *Action's time*. The action describes 时候 **shíhou** *time*:

上课的时候 **shàngkè de shíhou** *in class' time*
("when in class," "at the time of class" or "during class")

Let's look at a longer sentence:

上课的时候，Jerry唱中国歌
Shàng kè de shíhou, Jerry chàng Zhōngguó gē
　　　1　　　　　　2
(1) To be in class's time, (2) Jerry sings Chinese songs.

As we can see, it consists of two parts: (1) and (2). This is a temporal clause, where two events are happening at the same time. We can translate the whole sentence as *(1) When in class, (2) Jerry sings Chinese songs.*

Here are some more examples:

洗澡的时候，老师想Jerry
xǐzǎo de shíhou, lǎoshī xiǎng Jerry
　　　1　　　　　2
(1) Showering's time, (2) the teacher thinks [about] Jerry.
(When the teacher showers, he thinks about Jerry.)

跳舞的时候，Jerry很开心
tiàowǔ de shíhou, Jerry hěn kāixīn
　　　1　　　　　2
(1) Dancing's time, (2) Jerry is happy.
(When Jerry is dancing, he is happy.)

一个人的时候，王小猫吃蛋糕
yí gè rén de shíhou, Wáng Xiǎomāo chī dàngāo
　　　　1　　　　　　2
(1) Alone's time, (2) Wang Xiaomao eats cake.
(When Wang Xiaomao is alone, she eats cake.)

难过的时候，Jerry 喝啤酒
nánguò de shíhou, Jerry hē píjiǔ
　　　1　　　　　2
(1) Sad's time, (2) Jerry drinks beer.
(When he is sad, Jerry drinks beer.)

Part 3

Jerry唱歌的时候，老师和学生都听得很高兴。
Jerry chàng gē de shíhou, lǎoshī hé xuésheng dōu tīng de hěn gāoxìng.
Jerry sing-song's time, teacher and student all listen [to the degree of] very happy.
When Jerry sings, the teacher and the students listen happily.

老师也喜欢给学生唱歌，可是他一开始唱，
Lǎoshī yě xǐhuan gěi xuésheng chàng gē, kěshì tā yì kāishǐ chàng,
Teacher also like give student sing song, but he one (as soon as) start sing,
The teacher also likes to sing to the students, but as soon as he starts singing,

大家就从教室里跑出去。
dàjiā jiù cóng jiàoshì li pǎo chū qù.
everybody just from classroom inside run out go.
everybody runs out of the classroom.

虽然老师住得很远，
但是Jerry 跑得很快，
马上就到。

始 **shī** 1322
beginning; start; to begin; to originate

開始
开始 **kāishǐ** 1024
to begin; to start

"to open" + "beginning"

從
从 **cóng** 1323
(to go; to start; to pass) from

The first meaning of this character is "to follow," hence the two 人 rén following each other; the traditional form has also the path they are walking 辵.

教 **jiào** 1324
to instruct; teaching; doctrine

教室 **jiàoshì** 702
classroom

"teaching" + "room"

出 **chū** 1325
to exit

Two mountains 山 shān on top of each other; like in a mountain range: one mountain appears ("exits") behind another.

出去 **chū qù** 330
to exit; to go out

"exit" + "go"

跑出去 **pǎo chū qù**
1226, 1325, 330
to run out; to go out running

"to run" + "exit" + "go"

Running away

In the phrase 跑出去 **pǎo chū qù** *to run out* we can observe the so-called "complex directional complement". In general, a directional complement tells us in what direction the action is performed. But let's have a closer look! In 跑出去 **pǎo chū qù** we see three verbs:

    1) 跑 **pǎo** *to run*   2) 出 **chū** *to exit*   3) 去 **qù** *to go*

The last of those verbs, 去 **qù** *to go*, is the directional complement, because it indicates the direction of running → away from the speaker:

    从教室里跑出去 **cóng jiàoshì li pǎo chū qù**
    from classroom in run exit go → *to run out of the classroom*
    (the speaker is inside)

Another such verb is 来 **lái** *to come*; it also indicates the direction → towards the speaker:

    从教室里跑出来 **cóng jiàoshì li pǎo chū lái**
    from classroom in run exit come → *to run out of the classroom*
    (the speaker is outside) → *to come running out of the classroom*

As you can see, in English we can translate both *to run out of the classroom* without the information about the speaker.

The second element is the verb 出 **chū** *to exit*. Likewise, it indicates a movement out. It can be replaced with the verb 进 **jìn** *to enter* for the opposite effect:

    跑进去 **pǎo jìn qù** *run enter go* → *to run in* (the speaker is outside)
    跑进来 **pǎo jìn lái** *run enter come* → *to run in* (the speaker is inside)

The combinations 进来 **jìn lái** *to come in*, 进去 **jìn qù** *to go in*, 出来 **chū lái** *to come out*, 出去 **chū qù** *to go out*, are complex directional complements (they consist of two verbs, both indicating the direction of an action).

Lastly, 跑 **pǎo** *to run* is the main verb (action) that is performed in, out, toward, or away from the speaker; we can use other verbs of motion here:

    带进来 **dài jìn lái** *carry enter come* → *to carry in* (the speaker is inside)
    骑出去 **qí chū qù** *ride exit go* → *to ride out* (the speaker is inside)

他从教室里跑出去

他从教室里跑出来

Part 4

除了唱歌以外，Jerry还有别的爱好。
Chú le chàng gē yǐwài   Jerry hái yǒu bié de àihào.
Exclude [complete] sing song [apart from], Jerry still have other hobby.
Apart from singing, Jerry also has other hobbies.

他特别爱运动：打球，游泳，跑步；
Tā tèbié ài yùndòng: dǎ qiú, yóu yǒng, pǎo bù;
He especially love sport: hit ball, swim swim, run step;
He especially loves sports: playing ball, swimming, running;

他也喜欢看电影。
tā yě xǐhuan kàn diànyǐng.
he also like watch movie.
he also likes to watch movies.

他常常跟老师一起去电影院。
Tā cháng cháng gēn lǎoshī yìqǐ qù diànyǐngyuàn.
He often follow teacher together go movie theater.
He often goes to the movie theater together with the teacher.

老师买票。
Lǎoshī mǎi piào.
Teacher buy ticket.
The teacher buys the tickets.

看完电影以后，老师还带Jerry去餐厅吃饭。
Kàn wán diànyǐng yǐhòu,   lǎoshī hái dài Jerry qù cāntīng chī fàn.
Watch finish movie after, teacher still take Jerry go restaurant eat cooked rice.
After the movie, the teacher also takes Jerry to eat at a restaurant.

除 **chú** 1326
to get rid of; to remove; to exclude; to except

除了 X 以外 **chúle X yǐwài**
1326, 329, 719, 325
except for X; apart from X; besides X

"having excluded X away"

運 运 **yùn** 1327
to carry; to transport; move things around

"Road" 辶 radical for the meaning; the traditional form also has a car 車 chē under the roof ⼍; the simplified character uses 云 yún "cloud" for pronunciation.

動 动 **dòng** 1328
to move

運動 运动 **yùndòng**
sports; physical exercises; motion

球 **qiú** 1329
ball or anything shaped like a ball; sphere; globe

Radical 王 (玉) yù "jade" suggests that the globe is made of precious stone.

打球 **dǎ qiú** 810
to play ball

"to hit" + "ball"

游泳 **yóu** 1330 to swim; to float; to drift

泳 **yǒng** 1331 a swim; a style of swimming

游泳 **yóuyǒng** to swim

"to swim" + "a swim"; both characters have "water" 氵(水) shuǐ radicals.

步 **bù** 1332 a pace; a step; to walk; to pace

跑步 **pǎobù** 1226 to jog; to run

"to run" + "a pace"

影 **yǐng** 1333 shadow; shade

電影 / 电影 **diànyǐng** 811, 1333 movie; film

"electricity" + "shadow"

電影院 / 电影院 **diànyǐngyuàn** 811, 1333, 915 movie theater; cinema ("movie" + "court")

票 **piào** 1334 ticket

完 **wán** 1335 to finish; to end

看完 **kàn wán** 208 to finish watching

verb "to watch" + result "to finish"

帶 / 带 **dài** 908 *here*: to take (someone somewhere)

餐 **cān** 1336 a meal; food

Are you wondering why this character was not simplified? Me too ... 食 shí underneath means "food" and is the radical.

餐廳 / 餐厅 **cāntīng** 1336, 1125 restaurant

"meal" + "hall"

一樣 / 一样 **yí yàng** 516, 730 same

"one" + "model/pattern"

Making exceptions

除了 ... 以外 **chú le ... yǐ wài**, literally: *Having excluded ... out*, is a clause that means *apart from ... / except for ... / besides ...*

We put the thing we want to exclude in the blank between the two parts of the clause:

除了Jerry以外，老师没有别的朋友
chú le Jerry yǐ wài, lǎoshī méi yǒu biéde péngyou
Having excluded Jerry out, teacher no have other friends
(Except for Jerry, the teacher has no other friends.)

除了汉语以外，Jerry还会说日语和德语
chú le hànyǔ yǐ wài, Jerry hái huì shuō rìyǔ hé déyǔ
Having excluded Chinese out, Jerry still can speak Japanese and German
(Apart from Chinese, Jerry can also speak Japanese and German.)

除了天天喝酒以外，王小猫还吃快餐
chú le tiān tiān hē jiǔ yǐ wài, Wáng Xiǎomāo hái chī kuài cān
Having excluded day [by] day drinking alcohol out, Wang Xiaomao still eats fast food
(Apart from drinking alcohol every day, Wang Xiaomao also eats fast food.)

Quickly about finishing things

One of the most common and useful complements in Chinese is the so-called **resultative complement** – it indicates the result of an action. Most often it is another verb completing the main one, e.g. the verb 完 **wán** *to end; to finish*:

吃完 **chī wán** *eat finish* → *to finish eating*
看完 **kàn wán** *watch/read finish* → *to finish watching/reading*
写完 **xiě wán** *write finish* → *to finish writing*
做完 **zuò wán** *do/make finish* → *to finish doing/making*

好 **hǎo** can also be a resultative complement and mean *to do something to completion; to finish*, very similar to 完 **wán**:

吃好 **chī hǎo** *eat good* → *to complete eating; have eaten; finish eating*

写好 **xiě hǎo** *write good*
→ *to complete writing; have written; finish writing*

做好 **zuò hǎo** *do/make good*
→ *to complete doing/making; to have done/made; to finish doing/making*

做好准备 **zuò hǎo zhǔnbèi** *make finish prepare*
→ *to complete getting ready; to have made preparations*

准备好 **zhǔnbèi hǎo** *prepare good*
→ *to complete preparing; to have prepared; to finish preparing*

好 **hǎo** and 完 **wán** are very similar; the former conveys a sense of completion (*I have eaten well* so now I am done eating), whereas the latter just means that the action has stopped because it was finished.

Fortune cookie:

乒乓球 Ping Pong
pīng pāng qiú

1347, 1348, 1329

Part 5

Jerry跟别的学生不一样。
Jerry gēn bié de xuésheng bù yí yàng.
Jerry follow other student no one model.
Jerry is different from other students.

比如，王小猫和马先生上课的时候不理老师；
Bǐ rú, Wáng Xiǎomāo hé Mǎ xiānsheng shàng kè de shíhou bù lǐ lǎoshī;
E. g., Wang Little Cat and Ma Mister attend-class's time no acknowledge teacher;
For example, Wang Xiaomao and Mr. Ma in class don't pay attention to the teacher;

他们一直上网，发短信，自拍。
tāmen yìzhí shàng wǎng, fā duǎn xìn, zì pāi.
they continuously go on web, send short letter, self photograph.
they go online, send text messages and take selfies all the time.

下课以后他们都吃快餐。
Xià kè yǐhòu tāmen dōu chī kuài cān.
Go off class after they all eat fast food.
After class they eat fast food.

A 跟 B (不) 一樣
A 跟 B (不) 一样

A gēn B (bù) yí yàng
422, (121), 516, 730

A is (not) the same as B; A is (not) like B

"A with B (not) one pattern/same"

比 **bǐ** 1337
to compare

We've just seen it as a phonetic element in 屁 pì.

如 **rú** 917
to be like; to be similar to; to be as good as

比如 **bǐ rú**
for example

"compared to" + "to be just as"

理 **lǐ** 312
to pay attention to; to acknowledge

used a lot in negative sentences; we've seen it in 心理 xīnlǐ "psychology;" here another meaning.

不理 **bù lǐ**
to not pay attention to; disregard; ignore

直 **zhí** 1338
straight

一直 **yìzhí**
continuously; all the time; non stop; *also*: go straight

網
网 **wǎng** 1339
net

The traditional character has "silk" 糸 to suggest a fabric and 冈 gāng for pronunciation; the simplified does look like a net …

上網
上网 **shàng wǎng**
to go online (on the internet)

"to ascend" + "the net"

發
发 **fā** 1119
to send out; to issue; to emit

We saw this character in 沙发 shāfā "sofa", where it was used for pronunciation; here, it functions in its original meaning.

短 **duǎn** 1340
short (lengthwise)

信 **xìn** 739
letter; message

We saw this character in 相信 xiāngxìn "to believe", where it had a different meaning "to trust".

短信 **duǎnxìn**
text message; SMS

Comparisons

一样/不一样 **yí yàng/bù yí yàng** means *same/not same (different)*

我们买一样的衣服
wǒmen mǎi yí yàng de yīfu *We buy the same clothes*

人人都不一样 **rén rén dōu bù yí yàng**
Person person all not same (All people are different)

We use 跟 **gēn** *with* to make a comparison:

A 跟 B 一样/不一样 **A gēn B yí yàng/bù yí yàng**
A with B same/not same → A is (not) the same as B

我的高跟鞋跟你的（高跟鞋）一样
wǒ de gāogēnxié gēn nǐ de (gāogēnxié) yí yàng
I's high heels with you's (high heels) same
(My high heels are the same as your (high heels))

男人跟女人不一样 **nánrén gēn nǚrén bù yí yàng**
Men with women not same (Men and women are not the same.)

最 **zuì** means *most* and is used to create the superlative; it can be used both with adjectives and verbs:

Jerry 最棒 **Jerry zuì bàng** *Jerry [is] most awesome.*

我最喜欢睡觉 **wǒ zuì xǐhuan shuìjiào**
I most like sleep (Most of all I like sleeping/I like sleeping best).

發短信
发短信 **fā duǎnxìn** 1119, 1340, 739
to text; to send a text message

自 **zì** 424
oneself; one's own; self

拍 **pāi** 1341
to take a picture

This character originally means "to pat; to clap", hence the hand 扌(手) shǒu radical; 白 bái "white" is for pronunciation.

自拍 **zì pāi**
to take a selfie
"to self-photograph"

快餐 **kuài cān** 823, 1336
fastfood
"quick" + "meal"

1. Make sentences including the date/time.

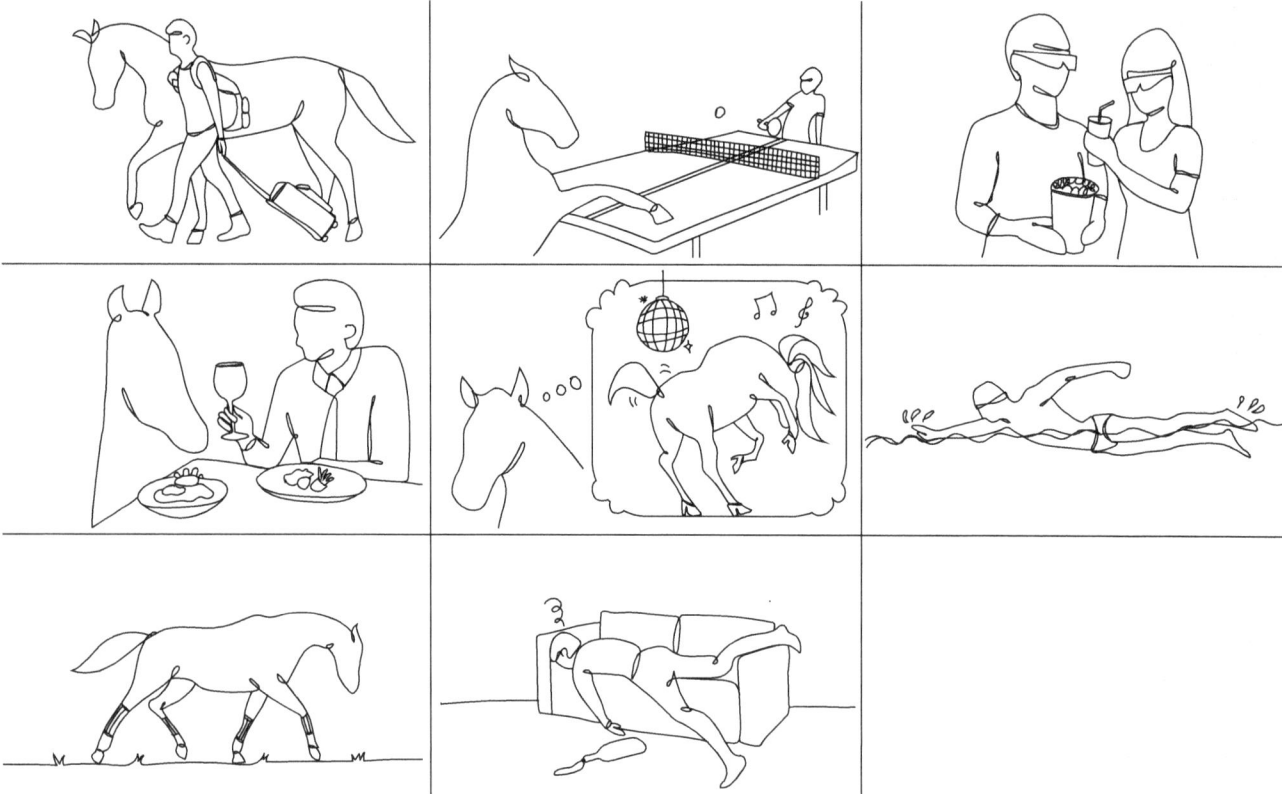

Next year in the summer on July 4th the teacher and Jerry are going to Korea.
This Monday afternoon Jerry plays ping pong.
Friday night at 8:30 Wang Xiaomao and Mr. Ma are going to the movies.
Next week the teacher will take Jerry to a Spanish restaurant
Last Saturday night Jerry went dancing in a bar .
Next month the teacher will go swimming every day.
Every morning from 10 to 11 Jerry goes jogging in the park.
Every Thursday Mr. Ma is drunk.

2. Translate 翻译 fānyì from English using complement of degree.
a) Although every day her work keeps her busy [she works busily], she's not tired.
b) Jerry is awesome at ping pong [he plays ping pong awesomely].
c) My younger sister is a fast swimmer.
d) Even though Wang Xiaomao studies diligently, she doesn't speak Chinese well.
e) Mr. Ma does not live far.
f) I need to get up early tomorrow.

3. Transliterate to characters.
a) wǒ bù lǐ nǐ
b) tā shuō de duì
c) zhè jiā cāntīng hěn guì
d) nǐ chī wán le ma?
e) wǒmen de zhōngwén lǎoshī hěn bàng
f) tā lái de zǎo

4. Transliteration characters to pinyin
a) 我睡得很晚
b) 她吃得早
c) 猫跑出去了
d) 你要洗衣服吗？
e) 我刷牙刷得累。
f) 洗衣机洗衣服洗得干净。

5. Fill in blanks using vocabulary from the list:
以后　才　别的　先　没有　应该　就　完　跑出去
上　马上

a) 来了北京 ____ ，我才开始学中文。
b) 看 ____ 电视以后，Jerry和别的马去公园喝啤酒。
c) 吃饭了以后，大家都 ____ 刷牙。
d) 吃了爸爸做的饭以后，妈妈 ____ 就生病了。
e) 除了Jerry以外，我不认识 ____ 会说话的马。
f) 马先生 ____ 了厕所以后没洗手。
g) 王小猫没有付钱，就从商店里 ____ 了。
h) 好学生看完书以后 ____ 去睡觉。
i) 不好的学生起了床以后马上 ____ 上网。
j) 有文化的人 ____ 敲门再进去。

6. Connect sentences with 的时候.

a) 有的人上网　　　　　　　　不理别人
b) 生病　　　　　　　　　　　得休息，喝水，不要喝酒
c) Jerry看他老朋友的照片　　　老师很吃醋
d) 有的人上厕所　　　　　　　爱听音乐
e) 齐老师洗澡　　　　　　　　唱歌
f) 上课　　　　　　　　　　　不应该用手机
g) 在电影院看电影　　　　　　不要说话
h) 老师生气　　　　　　　　　骂学生
i) 王小猫难过　　　　　　　　买花
j) 忙的人饿　　　　　　　　　吃快餐

7. Running away: Match the images with correct descriptions.

跑进来
跑出来
跑进去
跑出去

a)

b)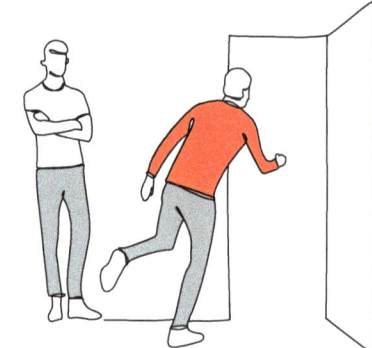

c)

d)

有一天Jerry出去跑步的时候，
Yǒu yì tiān Jerry chū qù pǎo bù de shíhou,
Have one day Jerry exit go run step's time,
One day Jerry went out for a run

老师一个人在家里打扫房间。
lǎoshī yí gè rén zài jiā li dǎ sǎo fángjiān.
teacher one [item] person exist home inside sweep room.
and the teacher was home alone cleaning the rooms.

他先吸地再去洗厕所。
Tā xiān xī dì zài qù xǐ cèsuǒ.
He first suck ground again go wash toilet.
He first vacuumed the floor and then went to clean the toilet.

冲了马桶以后转身要擦浴缸，发现浴缸
Chōng le mǎtǒng yǐhòu zhuǎn shēn yào cā yùgāng, fāxiàn yùgāng
Flush [complete] toilet seat turn body want wipe bathtub, notice bathtub
After rinsing/flushing the toilet seat he turned to wipe the bathtub

里有Jerry的手机。
li yǒu Jerry de shǒujī
inside have Jerry's cell phone.
and saw that Jerry's cell phone was in it.

那很奇怪。
Nà hěn qíguài.
That very strange.
That was strange.

那么棒的新买的苹果机，又贵又漂亮
Nàme bàng de xīn mǎi de píngguǒ jī, yòu guì yòu piàoliang
So awesome's new buy's apple machine, again expensive again pretty,
Such an awesome new iPhone, expensive and beautiful,

怎么放在浴缸里呢？
zěnme fàng zài yùgāng li ne?
how come put exist bathtub inside and [what about]?
why put it in the bathtub?

掃
扫
sǎo 1350
to sweep; to clear away

hand 扌(手) radical for meaning

打掃
打扫
dǎ sǎo 810, 1350
to sweep; to clean

"to hit" + "to sweep"

吸
xī 1351
to suck; inhale

口 kǒu "mouth" for the meaning

吸地
xī dì 1351, 1129
to vacuum

"to suck" + "the floor"

沖
冲
chōng 1352
to rinse; to flush

氵 "water" shuǐ radical in the traditional character, for meaning; using one less stroke and making it 冫 bīng "ice" in the simplified makes no logical or practical sense, unless you want to clean your toilet with ice cubes or ice cold water; it is what it is; 中 zhōng is for pronunciation.

桶
tǒng 1353
bucket; barrel

木 mù "wood" for the meaning; 甬 yǒng for pronunciation is an element often used in characters pronounced "tong", like e.g. 痛.

馬桶
马桶
mǎtǒng
3, 1353
toilet seat

"horse" + "bucket"; don't ask...

老师拿来看的时候突然有信息进来，说：
Lǎoshī ná lái kàn de shíhou tūrán yǒu xìnxī jìn lái, shuō:
Teacher take come look's time suddenly have message enter come, say:
When the teacher picked it up and looked at it, a new message came in

"亲爱的，你在哪儿呢？
"Qīn'ài de, nǐ zài nǎ'er ne?
"Dear's you where now [and what about]?
"Darling, where are you?

你说我们10点要出发。
Nǐ shuō wǒmen shí diǎn yào chūfā
You say we 10 o'clock want depart.
You said we were leaving at 10.

轉
转
zhuǎn 1354
to turn; to change; to switch

车 (車) chē "car; vehicle" radical: usually means "turn while driving; switch vehicles" (e.g. planes), so it is used for navigation; 专 (專) zhuān "special" is phonetic

擦
cā 1355
to wipe; to rub

hand 扌(手) radical for meaning; 察 chá "to check" is phonetic

轉身
转身
zhuǎn shēn 1354, 1301
to turn around

"turn" + "body"

浴
yù 1356
to bathe

氵"water" shuǐ radical for meaning; 谷 gǔ "valley" is phonetic

缸
gāng 1357
vat; jar

缶 fǒu is an ancient earthen jar and is often used in characters that indicate pottery vessels; 工 gōng "work" is for pronunciation.

浴缸
yùgāng
bathtub

"bath" + "vat"

發現
发现
fāxiàn 1119, 733
to notice; to realize; to discover; to find out

"to come out to existence" + "the present reality"

蘋
苹
píng 1342
apple

"Grass" 艹 cǎo radical: apples are plants; the traditional form has 頻 pín for pronunciation; the simplified uses 平 píng that we know from 平常 píngcháng "usually" but still retains "grass".

蘋果
苹果
píngguǒ 918
apple

"apple" + "fruit" - two syllables to avoid ambiguity

蘋果機
苹果机
píngguǒjī 1342, 918, 620
iPhone ("apple" + "machine")

放
fàng 1343
to put; to place

We see the familiar 方 fāng for pronunciation.

拿
ná 1344
to take

手 shǒu "hand" radical.

拿來
拿来
ná lái 1344, 216
to pick up

"to take" + "to come"

信息
xìnxī 739, 807
message

"letter" + "news"

進來
进来
jìn lái 705, 216
to come in

"to enter" + "to come"

出發
出发
chū fā 1325, 1119
to depart; leave; set out; start off

"to exit" + "to come out"

我在这儿等你，我的箱子都准备好了"。
Wǒ zài zhè'er děng nǐ,　 wǒ de xiāngzi dōu zhǔnbèi hǎo le".
I exist here　wait you,　　I's suitcase all prepare good [complete]."
I am waiting for you here, my suitcases are ready."

老师头昏眼花，他不能呼吸。
Lǎoshī tóu hūn yǎn huā,　　tā bù néng hūxī.
Teacher head dark eyes flowers, he no able to breathe
The teacher felt dizzy and he couldn't breathe.

手机从手里掉在地上了。
Shǒujī cóng shǒu li diào zài dì shàng le.
The cell phone from hand inside drop exist ground on top [complete]
The cell phone fell from his hand to the floor.

老师在马桶上坐下，忘了时间。
Lǎoshī zà mǎtǒng shàng zuò xià,　　wàng le shíjiān.
Teacher exist toilet seat on top sit down, forget [complete] time.
The teacher sat down on the toilet seat and forgot about the time (passing).

等　**děng** 1358
to wait

箱　**xiāng** 1359
box; case; trunk

⺮(竹) zhú "bamboo" radical to suggest the meaning--boxes and cases in China were made of bamboo; 相 xiāng is a fairly common phonetic element, we have seen it before in 想 xiǎng "to think"

箱子　**xiāngzi** 132
suitcase; trunk

"box" + a suffix indicating a noun

頭 头　**tóu** 1345
head; beginning

In the traditional form, we see 頁 yè, which originally means "head," and 豆 dòu "beans" for pronunciation; the simplified form is just an invention.

昏　**hūn** 1360
dusk; dark; dim; muddled

花　**huā** 729
here: cloudy; blurred

As we have seen, 花 has many meanings; the first one is "flower," but it can also mean "to spend (money)" see chapters 7 and 8; here, you can think of it as "becoming flowery"--scrambled and unclear.

頭昏眼花
头昏眼花　**tóu hūn yǎn huā**
1345, 1360, 1142, 729
dizzy; giddy; confused; fainting

"head muddled eyes flowered/blurred"

呼　**hū** 1361
to breathe out; to exhale

呼吸　**hūxī** 1361, 1351
to breathe

"to exhale" + "to inhale"

掉　**diào** 1362
to drop; to fall; to come off

hand 扌(手) shǒu radical to suggest the meaning

忘　**wàng** 1346
to forget

心 xīn "heart/mind" for forgetfulness; 亡 wáng for pronunciation; we saw the exact same combination of radicals in 忙 máng "busy".

So ...

What is going to happen to Jerry?

Why is Jerry leaving?
Will he come back?
What is teacher Qi going to do?

If you want to find out – keep on learning Chinese!

Oh, Jerry! – Part 2 – will be available from 2024.

The ISBN will be 978-3-945174-26-5.

Stay tuned:
www.skapago.eu/jerry/bonus

Would you like to learn more languages?

Skapago can help you even with other languages. What about learning **Swedish** with Alfred the ghost, **Norwegian** with Nils the doll or **German** with Jens and Jakob, the sparrows from Berlin?
More information:
www.skapago.eu

Alphabetic Word List

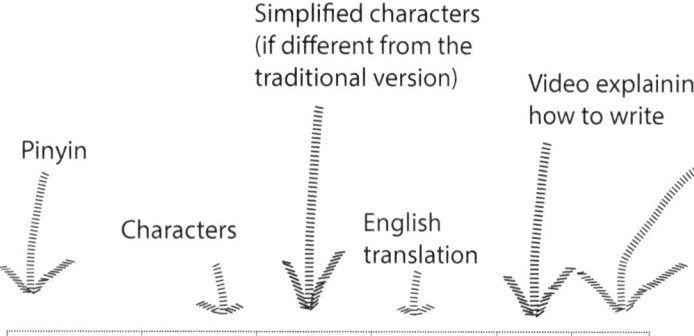

Pinyin	Characters	Simplified	English translation	Video	Chapter
a	啊		an exclamatory particle	407	4
A gēn B (bù) yí yàng	A 跟 B(不)一樣	A 跟 B(不)一样	A is (not) the same as B; A is (not) like B	A, 422, B, (121), 516, 730	13
ài	愛	爱	to love	313	3
āi	哎		an interjection of surprise mixed with regret	919	9
āi yā	哎呀		exclamation of surprise, grief, exasperation; "oh well!"	919, 509	9
àihào	愛好	爱好	hobby; interest; love	313, 103	3
àirén	愛人	爱人	spouse	313, 122	6
ān	安		peace; safe; safety	525	5

Pinyin	Characters	Simplified	English translation	Video	Chapter
ba	吧		Particle expressing a wish, a suggestion, or a guess	219	2
bà	爸		father	317	3
bǎ	把		measure word for things with a handle, e.g. chairs or umbrellas	1107	11
bā	八		eight	541	5G
bàba	爸爸		dad	317	3
bàba māma	爸爸媽媽	爸爸妈妈	parents	317, 1	3
bái	白		white	901	9
bài	敗	败	to defeat; to be defeated	527	5LT
bǎi	百		hundred	544	5G
bàn	辦	办	to manage; to handle; to deal with; to solve	701	7

Pinyin	Traditional	Simplified	Meaning	Ref	Lesson
bàn	半		half	735	7
bǎn	板		board; plank	430	4G
bān	般		kind; way; like	1028	10G
bān	班		class	1349	13G
bànfǎ	辦法	办法	solution; way of dealing with something	701, 344	7
bàng	棒		strong; fit; awesome	1303	13
bāng	幫	帮	to help	1216	12
bàngōngshì	辦公室	办公室	office	701, 342, 702	7
bāo	包		to wrap; to pack; to roll; a bundle; a package; a bag; a roll	1027	10LT, 12
bāozi	包子		steamed bun	1027, 132	10LT
bèi	備	备	to be equipped with; to get ready	1102	11
běi	北		North	413	4
Běidà	北大		Beijing University	413, 101	6E
Běijīng	北京		Beijing	413, 414	4
Běijīng dàxué	北京大學	北京大学	Beijing University		4
bèn	笨		stupid; dumb	926	9
běn	本		root; origin	347	3G
bì	幣	币	currency	830	8G
bǐ	比		to compare	1337	13
bǐ rú	比如		for example	1337, 917	13
biàn	便		fitting; at ease; relaxed	1023	10
biān	邊	边	side; border; limit	1126	11
bié	別	别	different; distinct; other	1026	10
biéde	別的	别的	other	1026, 310	11
bìng	病		sick; ill; illness; disease	802	8
bù	不		no, not	121	1
bù	步		a pace; a step; to walk; to pace	1332	13
bù hǎo yìsi	不好意思		sorry; my bad; excuse me	121, 103, 157, 502	7
bù kě	不可		not able to; cannot; unable	121, 322	5
bù kě sī yì	不可思議	不可思议	incomprehensible; unfathomable; beyond comprehension	121, 322, 502, 503	5
bù lǐ	不理		to not pay attention to; to disregard; to ignore	121, 312	13

Pinyin	Traditional	Simplified	Meaning	Ref	Ch
bú shì A, ér shì B	不是A,而是B		not A, but rather B	121, 107, A, 616, 107, B	8
bù shūfu	不舒服		uncomfortable; feeling unwell; sick; under the weather	121, 814, 636	8
bú yào	不要		not want; not need	121, 204	11
bú yòng	不用		don't have to; don't need to	121, 1020	10
bú dàn ... érqiě	不但。。。而且		not only ..., but also ...	121, 610, 616, 617	6
cā	擦	擦	to wipe; to rub	1355	13
cái	纔/才	才	not until; only when; *see grammar explanations*	504	5
cài	菜		vegetable	826	8LT
cān	餐		a meal; food	1336	13
cāntīng	餐廳	餐厅	restaurant	1336, 1125	13
cǎo	草		grass	207	2
cè	廁	厕	lavatory; toilet	1219	12
cèsuǒ	廁所	厕所	toilet; WC; restroom	1219, 809	12
chá	茶		tea	531	5LT
cháng	常		common, ordinary	625	6
cháng	長	长	long	744	7LT
chàng	唱		to sing	1316	13
cháng cháng	常常		often	625	9
cháng chéng	長城	长城	The Great Wall	744, 745	7LT
chàng gē	唱歌		to sing	1316, 1317	13
chǎo	炒		to stir-fry	1206	12
chē	車	车	car; vehicle	426	4G
chéng	成		to become; to form; to fix; to establish; ready-made	333	3G
chéng	城		wall	745	7LT
chénggōng	成功		success	333, 528	5LT
chéngyǔ	成語	成语	idiom; set phrase	333, 334	3G
chī	吃		to eat	202	2
chī cù	吃醋		to be jealous	202, 929	9LT
chī fàn	吃飯	吃饭	to eat	202, 203	2
chī zǎofàn	吃早飯	吃早饭	to have breakfast	202, 301, 203	12
chōng	沖	冲	to rinse; to flush	1352	13
chú	廚	厨	kitchen	1013	10
chú	除		to get rid of; to remove; to exclude; to except	1326	13

pinyin	traditional	simplified	meaning	ref	ch
chù	處	处	a place; a spot; a location; a locality	1134	11
chū	出		to exit	1325	13
chū fā	出發	出发	to depart; to leave; to set out; to start off	1325, 1119	13
chū qù	出去		to exit; to go out	1325, 330	13
chú X yǐwài	除了 X 以外		except for X; apart from X; besides X	1326, 329 X 719, 325	13
chuáng	牀 / 床	床	bed	1105	11
chuāng	窗		window	1120	11
chuānghù	窗戶		window	1120, 1121	11
chúfáng	廚房	厨房	kitchen	1013, 1012	10
chūn	春		spring	1122	11
chūntiān	春天		spring	1122, 709	11
cí	瓷		porcelain; china	419	4LT
cíqì	瓷器		chinaware; porcelain	419, 420	4LT
cóng	從	从	(to go; to start; to pass) from	1323	13
cù	醋		vinegar	929	9LT
cuò	錯	错	wrong; mistake	514	5
dà	大		big	101	1
dǎ	打		to hit	810	8
dà biàn	大便		poo; to poo	101, 1023	12
dǎ diànhuà	打電話	打电话	to make a phone call	810, 811, 812	8
dà jiā hǎo	大家好		hello everybody	101, 102, 103	1
dǎ qiú	打球		to play ball	810, 1329	13
dǎ sǎo	打掃	打扫	to sweep; to clean	810, 1350	13
dài	帶	带	to carry; to bring	908	9
dài	帶	带	*here*: to take (someone somewhere)	908	13
dàjiā	大家		everybody	101, 102	1
dàn	但		but; yet	610	6
dàn	蛋		egg	909	9
dāng	當	当	to work as; to serve as; to have to; must; just at	515	5
dàngāo	蛋糕		*Western style* cake	909, 910	9
dāngrán	當然	当然	of course	515, 416	5
dànshi	但是		but	610, 107	
dào	道		The Way; road; way; method; doctrine	623	6
dào	到		to arrive	1133	11
dàochu	到處	到处	everywhere	1133, 1134	11
dàxué	大學	大学	University; College	101, 123	2G

Pinyin	Traditional	Simplified	Meaning	Ref	Ch
dàxué	大學	大学	university	101, 123	4
de	的		possessive particle; of/'s	310	3
de	得		complement of degree	521	12
dé	德		virtue	345	3G
dé	得		to get; to achieve; to be able to; to the degree of	521	5
dé	德		virtue	345	13
déguó	德國	德国	Germany	345, 316	3G
děi	得		must; to have to	521	9
děng	等		to wait	1358	13
déwén	德文		German language	345, 315	13
déyǔ	德語	德语	German language	345, 1312	13G
dì	弟		younger brother	336	3G
dì	第		prefix for ordinal numbers; number in a sequence	924	9
dì	地		the earth; land; ground	1129	11
dì èr	第二		second (in a row)	924, 535	9
dì èr tiān	第二天		the next day	924, 535, 709	9
diàn	電	电	electricity; electronic	811	8
diàn	店		shop; store	819	8
diǎn	點	点	a dot; a point; unit of time (hours)	734	7
diànhuà	電話	电话	telephone	811, 812	8
diànnǎo	電腦	电脑	computer	811, 1110	11
diànshì	電視	电视	television	811, 1124	11
diànshìjī	電視機	电视机	TV Set	811, 1124, 620	11
diànyǐng	電影	电影	movie; film	811, 1333	13
diàn yǐng yuàn	電影院	电影院	movie theater; cinema	811, 1333, 915	13
diào	掉		to drop; to fall; to come off	1362	13
dìdi	弟弟		younger brother	336	3G
dìfāng	地方		place; locality	1129, 1022	11
dìng	定		to decide; to fix; to settle	614	6
diū	丟		to lose; to miss; to go missing; to be missing	522	5
diū liǎn	丟臉	丢脸	to lose face; to be disgraced; to be ashamed	522, 523	5
dòng	動	动	to move	1328	13
dōng	東	东	east	1320	13
dōngfāng	東方	东方	the East	1320, 1022	13
dòu	豆		beans	331	3LT

Pinyin	Traditional	Simplified	Meaning	Page	Lesson
dōu	都		all	303	3
dòufu	豆腐		bean curd; tofu	331, 332	3LT
duàn	鍛	锻	to forge	1304	13
duǎn	短		short (lengthwise)	1340	13
duànliàn	鍛鍊	锻炼	to take physical exercise; to toughen; to work out	1304, 1305	13
duǎnxìn	短信		text message; SMS	1340, 739	13
duì	對	对	to face; to address; to treat; correct; *often used as "yes" or "that's right"*	506	5
duì	對	对	correct; that's right!; yes	436	6
duì	對	对	for; to	436	12
duì bù qǐ	對不起	对不起	to be sorry	436, 121, 507	5
duó	多		How? How much?	512	7
duō	多		many; much	512	5
duó dà	多大		How old?	512, 101	7
duō jiǔ	多久		how long?	512, 808	8
duōme	多麼	多么	so; thus	512, 128	8G
duōshao	多少		how much? how many? (for numbers over 10)	512, 820	8
è	餓	饿	hungry	205	2
ér	兒	儿	son; child	609	6
ér	兒	儿	the sound "r" added after a noun; diminutive	609	6
ér	而		and; also; nevertheless; and yet	616	6
èr	二		two	535	5G
ér shì	而是		but rather	616, 107	8
érqiě	而且		and; besides; and also	616, 617	6
érzi	兒子	儿子	son	609, 132	6
fǎ	法		French; law rule; method; way of doing something	344	3G, 5, 7
fā	發	发	to send out; to issue; to emit	1119	11
fā duǎnxìn	發短信	发短信	to text; to send a text message	1119, 1340, 739	13
fǎguó	法國	法国	France	344, 316	3G, 5
fán	煩	烦	irritated; anoyed; tired of; bothered; inconvenienced	1002	10
fàn	飯	饭	cooked rice; food	203	2
fáng	房		house; room	1012	10
fàng	放		to put; to place	1343	13

221

Pinyin	Traditional	Simplified	Meaning	Ref	Lesson
fāng	方		square; direction	1022	10
fāng	方		here: (geographical) direction; region	1022	13
fāngbiàn	方便		comfortable; convenient; to relieve oneself	1022, 1023	10, 12
fāngbiàn miàn	方便麵	方便面	instant noodles	1022, 1023, 1208	12LT
fángjiān	房間	房间	room	1012, 728	10
fāxiàn	發現	发现	to notice; to realize; to discover; to find out	1119, 733	13
fǎyǔ	法語	法语	French language	344, 1312	13G
féi	肥		fat; fertilizer	1220	12
fēi	非		negation particle; "is not"	624	6
fēicháng	非常		extremely; extraordinarily	624, 625	6
féiliào	肥料		fertilizer; manure	1220, 1221	12
fēn	分		minute, Chinese penny (0.01 yuan)	747	7G, 8G
fú	服		to serve; to obey; to accept; to acclimatize; clothing; attire	636	6G, 8, 11
fù	付		to pay	1021	10
fǔ	腐		rotten; corrupt; spoiled	332	3LT
fù qián	付錢	付钱	to pay	1021, 615	10
fúwù	服務	服务	to serve	636, 637	6G
fúwùyuán	服務員	服务员	servant; waiter	636, 637, 635	6G
gāi	該	该	should; deserve; fated to	1017	10
gàn	幹	干	to do	817	8
gǎn	敢		to dare	736	7
gān	乾	干	dry	1213	12
gàn ma	幹嗎		why? what for?	817, 125	8
gàn shénme	幹什麼	干什么	what are you doing? what for?	817, 127, 128	8
gāng	缸		vat; jar	1357	13
gānjìng	乾淨	干净	clean	1213, 1214	12
gào	告		to report; to tell; to inform	712	7
gāo	高		tall; high	421	4G, 9
gāo	糕		cake	910	9
gāogēnxié	高跟鞋		high heels	421, 422, 423	4G, 11
gàosu	告訴	告诉	to tell (a person); to let know	712, 713	7
gāoxìng	高興	高兴	happy; glad; high-spirited	421, 911	9

Pinyin	Trad	Simp	Meaning	Page	Lesson
gè	個	个	measure word for general objects and people	517	5
gē	歌		song	1317	13
gē	哥		elder brother	335	3G
gēge	哥哥		elder brother	335	3G
gěi	給	给	to give	725	7
gěi A dǎ diànhuà	給A打電話	给A打电话	to give A a phone call	725, A, 810, 811, 812	8
gěi Jerry guò shēngrì	給Jerry過生日	给Jerry过生日	to organize a party for Jerry	725, 818, 124, 710	9
gēn	跟		heel	422	4G, 11
gēn	跟		to follow; with	1014	10
gēn (shéi) shuō	跟(誰)說	跟(谁)说	to speak with (someone); to tell (someone)	1014, (119), 321	10
gōng	公		lord	342	3G
gōng	功		a merit; an achievement; a practice; a skill	528	5LT
gōng	工		work; craft	604	6

Pinyin	Trad	Simp	Meaning	Page	Lesson
gōng	公		public; communal; official duties	342	7, 10
gōngjīn	公斤		kilogram	342, 1224	12
gōngyuán	公園	公园	park	342, 746	7G, 10
gōngzuò	工作		job; work; to work	604, 605	6
gǒu	狗		dog	638	6G
gǒu'er	狗兒	狗儿	doggy	638, 609	6G
gǔ	股		thigh; hip; lower back	1308	13
guā	刮		to scrape; to shave	1215	12
guā liǎn	刮臉		to shave (face)	1215, 523	12
guài	怪		strange; odd; uncanny; monstrous; freak; monster	627	6
guǎn	管		to heed; to pay attention to; to care	724	7
guān	關	关	related; relationship; to involve; to negotiate; to go between	611	6
guān	官		government office	634	6G
guānxi	關係	关系	connection(s); bonds; relationship	611, 612	6
guānyuán	官員	官员	officer; clerk	634, 635	6G
guì	貴	贵	expensive; noble; honorable	115	1

223

Pinyin	Traditional	Simplified	Meaning	Ref	Ch
guì	櫃	柜	cupboard; cabinet	1112	11
guó	國	国	country; state	316	3
guò	過	过	to cross; to pass; to spend (time)	818	8
guǒ	果		fruit; result; outcome	918	9
guò shēngrì	過生日	过生日	to celebrate birthday	818, 124, 710	8
guò yè	過夜	过夜	spend the night; sleep over; stay overnight	818, 923	9
guójiā	國家	国家	country	316, 102	5G
hái	孩		child	608	6
hái	還	还	still; also; in addition to; on top of	718	7
háizi	孩子		child	608, 132	6
hán	韓	韩	South Korea	529	5E
hàn	漢	汉	Han (*ethnic Chinese*); Chinese	1314	13
hánguó	韓國	韩国	South Korea	529, 316	5E
hánguórén	韓國人	韩国人	South Korean person	529, 316, 122	5E
hànyǔ	漢語	汉语	Chinese language	1314, 1312	13G
hànzì	漢字	汉字	Chinese characters	1314, 130	13
hào	號	号	number	715	7
hào	好		to like; to be fond of	103	3
hǎo	好		good, well	103	1
hǎo chī	好吃	好吃	tasty; delicious	103, 128	2
hǎo tīng	好聽	好听	to sound good; to be nice to hear/listen to	103, 510	13
hàomǎ	號碼	号码	number	715, 905	9
hé	和		and; with	302	3
hē	喝		to drink	210	2
hěn	很		very	304	3
hěn duō	很多		a lot; many	304, 512	5
hóng	紅	红	red	1321	13
hòu	候		to wait; time; season	902	9
hòu	後	后	behind; after	927	9
hòu huǐ	後悔	后悔	to reget	927, 928	9
hòumian	後面	后面	behind; in the back	927, 1113	11
hù	戶		door	1121	11
hǔ	虎		tiger	306	3
hū	呼		to breathe out; to exhale	1361	13
huá	滑		to skate	429	4G
huà	畫	画	to paint; painting	613	6
huà	化		to transform; to change; to influence; to civilize	737	7

Pinyin	Traditional	Simplified	Meaning	Ref	Ch
huà	話	话	words; spoken language	812	8
huā	花		flower; to spend; cloudy; blurred	729	7, 8, 13
huà huà'er	畫畫兒	画画儿	to paint	613, 609	6
huà'er	畫兒	画儿	painting	613, 609	6
huábǎn	滑板		skating board	429, 430	4G
huábǎnchē	滑板車		scooter	429, 430, 426	4G
huàjiā	畫家	画家	painter	613, 102	6
huān	歡	欢	pleased; glad; pleasures; joys	1136	11
huāyuán	花園	花园	(flower) garden	729, 746	11
huí	回		to return; to go back; to turn back	925	9
huì	會	会	to know how; can; to be likely to; will; moment	320	3, 8, 13
huǐ	悔		to regret; to repent; to remorse	928	9
huí qù	回去		to go back	925, 330	9
hūn	昏		dusk; dark; dim; muddled	1360	13
huǒ	火		fire	1205	12
huǒtuǐ	火腿		ham	1205, 1145	12
huǒtuǐ chǎo jīdàn	火腿炒雞蛋	火腿炒鸡蛋	eggs fried with ham	1205, 1145, 1206, 1207, 909	12
hūxī	呼吸		to breathe	1361, 1351	
jǐ	幾	几	how many? (for numbers less than 10); several; a few	601	6
jī	機	机	machine; crucial point; chance; key moment; opportunity	620	6, 13
jī	雞	鸡	chicken	1207	12
jǐ diǎn	幾點	几点	What time is it?	601, 734	7
jiā	家		home, family; measure word for businesses, e.g. restaurants, shops, etc.	102	1, 13E
jiā	加		to add	1212	
jiājù	家具		furniture	102, 1117	11
jiān	間	间	space; room	728	7
jiàng	醬	酱	thick sauce (traditionally made of soya beans)	220	2LT
jiàngyóu	醬油	酱油	soy sauce	220, 221	2LT
jiào	叫		to call	126	1
jiào	覺	觉	a sleep; a nap	921	9

jiào	教		to instruct; teaching; doctrine	1324	13
jiǎo	餃	饺	dumpling	628	6LT
jiàoshì	教室		classroom	1324, 702	13
jiǎozi	餃子	饺子	dumpling	628, 132	6LT
jiārén	家人		family members	102, 122	3G
jīdàn	雞蛋	鸡蛋	egg	1207, 909	12
jiě	姐		elder sister	337	3G, 5
jiějie	姐姐		elder sister	337	3G, 5
jīhuì	機會	机会	opportunity; chance	620, 320	13
jìn	進	进	to enter	705	7
jīn	今		present; now	708	7
jīn	斤		*a unit of weight, Chinese pound (0.5 kg)*	1224	12
jìn lái	進來	进来	to come in	705, 216	13
jìng	淨	净	clean	1214	12
jīng	京		capital	414	4
jīng	經	经	to pass through; to undergo	1005	10
jīnnián	今年		this year	708, 716	7
jīntiān	今天		today	708, 709	7
jiù	就		just; see grammar explanations	501	5
jiù	就		just; only	501	9
jiǔ	酒		wine, alcoholic beverage	212	2
jiǔ	九		nine	542	5G
jiǔ	久		long time	808	8
jiǔ	韭		green garlic	825	8LT
jiǔbā	酒吧		bar	212, 219	6G
jiǔcài	韭菜		green garlic chives	825, 826	8LT
jù	具		appliance; utensil; tool	1117	11
jué	覺	觉	to perceive; to feel	520	5
juéde	覺得	觉得	to feel; to think; to be of an opinion	520, 521	5
kāfēi	咖啡		coffee	1203, 1204	12
kāi	開	开	to open	1024	10
kāishǐ	開始	开始	to begin; to start	1024, 1322	13
kāixīn	開心	开心	to feel happy; to be glad; to be cheerful	1024, 311	10
kàn	看		to watch, to look at, to read silently, to visit (= to see somebody)	208	2
kàn bìng	看病		to see a doctor; to get checked up (*for an illness*)	208, 802	8
kàn shū	看書	看书	to read, to study	208, 209	2
kàn wán	看完		to finish watching	208, 1335	13

pinyin	trad	simp	meaning	page	lesson
kè	課	课	lesson, class	218	2
kè	刻		a quarter of an hour	748	7G
kè	客		guest	815	8
kě	可		but; however; may; can; be able to; be worth of; be in need of	322	3, 5, 10
kě'ài	可愛	可爱	lovely; cute; lovable	322, 313	12
kělián	可憐	可怜	pitiful; pitiable; poor	322, 1011	10
kěnéng	可能		perhaps; maybe; possible	322, 916	11
kèqi	客氣	客气	kind; polite	815, 816	8
kěshì	可是		but; however	322, 107	3
kètīng	客廳	客厅	living room	815, 1125	11
kěyǐ	可以		can; be able to	322, 719	7
kǒu	口		mouth; *measure word for family members*	602	6
kù	酷		cool	324	3
kuài	筷		chopsticks	131	1LT
kuài	塊	块	a piece; measure word for money	821	8
kuài	快		fast; quick; soon	823	8
kuài cān	快餐		fastfood	823, 1336	13
kuàizi	筷子		chopsticks	131, 132	1LT

pinyin	trad	simp	meaning	page	lesson
lā	拉		to discharge (*stool; urine*); to empty the bowels; to pull; to draw; to haul	1222	12
lái	來	来	to come, to arrive; often used to invite somebody to do something "let('s)"	216	2
lǎo	老		old	108	1
lǎoshī	老師		teacher	108, 109	1
lǎoshī hǎo	老師好	老师	Hello Teacher	108, 109, 103	
lǎowài	老外		foreigner; outsider	108, 325	3
le	了		*aspect particle indicating the action has been completed*	329	3
lèi	累		tired	732	7
lěng	冷		cold	1007	10
lì	力		power; force; strength	1311	13

227

lǐ	理		reason; logic; cause; truth; right; law; principles; texture; [*usually used in negative sentences*] to pay attention to; to acknowledge	312	3
lǐ	裡	里	in; inside	508	5
lǐ	禮	礼	rites; ceremony; etiquette	722	7
lián	憐	怜	to sympathize; to pity; to feel tender regard for	1011	10
liàn	鍊	炼	to smelt; to refine	1305	13
liǎn	臉	脸	face	523	5
liàng	亮		bright, light, shiny	913	9
liǎng	兩	两	two of	607	6
liào	料		stuff; material; (grain) feed	1221	12
lǐmiàn	裡面	里面	inside	508, 1113	11
líng	零/〇		zero	533, 534	5G
liù	六		six	539	5G
lǐwù	禮物	礼物	gift; present	722, 723	7
lǜ	律		law; rule	629	6G
lǜshī	律師	律师	lawyer	629, 109	6G

ma	嗎	吗	*question particle*	125	1
má	麻		hemp; numb; to numb; to tingle	1001	10
mà	罵	骂	to curse; to yell at; to dress down	5	PT
mǎ	馬	马	horse	3	1
mǎ	碼	码	digit; number	630	6G
mǎ	碼	码	a code; a sign or symbol indicating number	905	9
mā	媽	妈	mother	1	3
mǎ mǎ hū hū	馬馬虎虎	马马虎虎	so-so; fifty-fifty; mediocre; average	3, 3, 306, 306	3
mǎ yī	馬醫	马医	horse doctor	3, 606	6
máfan	麻煩	麻烦	troublesome; inconvenient; trouble; inconvenience; to bother	1001, 1002	10
mài	賣	卖	to sell	1225	12
mǎi	買	买	to buy	726	7
māma	媽媽	妈妈	mom	1	3
màn	慢	慢	slow	4	PT
máng	忙		busy	307	3
mǎnóng	碼農	码农	computer programmer	630, 631	6G
māo	貓	猫	cat	113	1

Pinyin	Traditional	Simplified	Meaning	Page	Lesson
mǎshàng	馬上	马上	at once; right away; very fast; very soon;	3, 217	13
mǎtǒng	馬桶	马桶	toilet seat	3, 1353	13
me	麼	么	what?	128	1
méi	沒	没	there is not	213	2
mèi	妹		younger sister	338	3G
měi	美		beautiful	319	3
měi	每		every; each	804	8
méi (yǒu) bànfǎ	沒(有)辦法	没(有)办法	there is nothing I can do about it; what to do?; there is no way	213, (214), 701, 344	7
méi (yǒu) guānxi	沒(有)關係	没(有)关系	it does not matter; nevermind	213, 214, 611, 612	6
méi cuò	沒錯	没错	true; correct; "no mistake"	213, 514	5
měi nǚ	美女		beautiful woman; a beauty	319, 513	5E
méi shì	沒事		everything is alright	213, 707	8
méi wèntí	沒(有)問題		no problem	213, (214), 111, 215	2
méi yǒu wén huà	沒有文化	没有文化	rude; uncivilized	213, 214, 315, 737	7
měiguó	美國	美国	America	319, 316	3
měiguórén	美國人	美国人	American person (people)		3
mèimei	妹妹		younger sister	338	3G
měiyuán	美元		American dollar	319, 828	8G
men	們	们	suffix used after a personal pronoun to indicate plural	133	1G, 2
mén	門	门	door; gate	704	7
miàn	面		face; surface; side	1113	11
miàn	麵	面	wheat flour; meal; noodles; things made of wheat flour	1208	12
miànbāo	麵包	面包	bread; bread roll	1208, 1027	12
mín	民		the people; nation	829	8G
míng	名		name	129	1
míng	明		bright; future	827	8G, 9
míng nián	明年		next year	827, 716	8G
míng tiān	明天		tomorrow	827, 709	8G
míngbai	明白		to understand; to comprehend; to get (the meaning)	710, 714, 901	9
míngzi	名字		name	129, 130	1

229

Pinyin	Traditional	Simplified	Meaning	Ref	Ref2
mó	摩		to rub; to scrape	427	4G
mótuō	摩托		motor	427, 428	4G
mótuōchē	摩托車	摩托车	motorcycle	427, 428, 426	4G
mǔ	母		mother	530	5LT
ná	拿		to take	1344	13
nà	那		that	410	4
nà	那		then; in that case	410	6
nǎ	哪		which?	318	3
ná lái	拿來	拿来	to pick up	1344, 216	13
nǎ wèi	哪位		Politely "who are you?"	318, 505	5
nà'er	那兒	那儿	there	410, 609	6G, 9
nǎ'er	哪兒	哪儿	where	318, 609	6G
nàbiān	那邊	那边	over there	410, 1126	11
nǎi	奶		paternal grandmother; breasts; milk	341	3G, 12
nǎinai	奶奶		paternal grandmother	341	3G
nǎlǐ	哪裡	哪里	where?; where on earth, not at all	318, 508	5
nàme	那麼	那么	so; thus	410, 128	8
nán	男		male	511	5
nán	難	难	difficult	618	6
nán kàn	難看	难看	ugly	618, 208	6
nánguò	難過	难过	sad	618, 818	8
nánpéngyou	男朋友		boyfriend	511, 411, 412	5
nánrén	男人		man	511, 122	5
nǎo	腦	脑	brain	1110	11
ne	呢		and what about?	120	1
ne	呢		right now; at this moment	120	2
néng	能		can; to be able to	916	9
nǐ	你		you	114	1
nǐ nà'er	你那兒	你那儿	your place; at your place; at your house	114, 410, 609	
nián	年		year	716	7
nián nián	年年		every year; annually	716	8G
niánqīng	年輕	年轻	young	716, 740	7
nǐmen	你們	你们	you (plural)	114, 128	1G
niú	牛		cow	1209	12
niúnǎi	牛奶		cow's milk	1209, 341	12
nóng	農	农	farming; farmer	631	6G
nǔ	努		to exert oneself; to make an effort	1310	13
nǚ	女		woman; female	513	5

pinyin	traditional	simplified	meaning	ref	ch
nǚ de	女的		woman	513, 310	5
nǚér	女兒	女儿	daughter	513, 609	6
nǔlì	努力		diligent; to make great effort; to exert oneself	1310, 1311	13
nǚpéngyou	女朋友		girlfriend	513, 411, 412	5
o	哦		oh	409	4
pāi	拍		to take a picture	1341	13
páng	旁		side; next to	1128	11
pángbiān	旁邊	旁边	on the side	1128, 1126	11
pǎo	跑		to run	1226	12G, 13
pǎo chū qù	跑出去		to run out; to go out running	1226, 1325, 330	13
pǎobù	跑步		to jog; to run	1226, 1332	13
péng	朋		friend	411	4
péngyou	朋友		friend	411, 412	4
pí	啤		beer	211	2
pì	屁		fart	1307	13
pǐ	匹		*measure word for horses*	547	5G, 6E, 10
piàn	片		a piece; a slice; a chip	519	5
piào	漂		pretty	912	9
piào	票		ticket	1334	13
piàoliang	漂亮		pretty	912, 913	9
pìgu	屁股		butt	1307, 1308	13
píjiǔ	啤酒		beer	211, 212	2
píng	平		flat; level; even; equal	803	8
píng	瓶		bottle	1210	12
píng	蘋	苹	apple	1342	13
pīng	乒		the crack of a rifle or pistol	1347	13LT
píng cháng	平常		usually	803, 625	8
pīng pāng	乒乓		rattle	1348	13LT
pīng pāng qiú	乒乓球		table tennis; ping pong	1348, 1329	13LT
píngguǒ	蘋果	苹果	apple	1342, 918	13
píngguǒjī	蘋果機	苹果机	iPhone	1342, 918, 620	13
pó	婆		old woman; husband's mother	343	3G
qí	騎	骑	to ride	2	PT
qí	齊	齐	orderly, correct, tidy; Chinese family name	106	1
qí	騎	骑	to ride (a horse; a bike)	2	4
qí	奇		strange; wondrous; bizarre	626	6
qì	器		utensil; ware	420	4TL

231

pinyin	trad	simp	meaning	ref	lesson
qì	氣	气	air; ether; gas; vapor; the atmosphere	816	8
qǐ	起		to rise; to get up; to stand up	507	5
qī	七		seven	540	5G
qī	期		period of time; designated time; time limit	907	9
qǐ (chuáng)	起(牀)	起(床)	to get up (from bed)	507, 1105	12
qián	錢	钱	money	615	6
qián	前		front	1127	11
qiān	千		thousand	545	5G
qiánmian	前面		in front; the front	1127, 1113	11
qiāo	敲		to knock	703	7
qiāo mén	敲門	敲门	to knock on the door	703, 704	7
qiě	且		moreover; besides	617	6
qíguài	奇怪		strange; weird	626, 627	6
qīn	親	亲	a relative; intimate; personal; to kiss	1015	10
qīn'ài	親愛	亲爱	dear	1015, 313	10
qíng	情		feelings; emotions	621	6
qǐng	請	请	to ask for; to invite; to request; please	110	1
qīng	輕	轻	light	740	7
qīng	青		azure; green-blue; turqoise	1139	11LT
qíng rén	情人		lover	621, 122	6
qīngwā	青蛙		frog	1139, 1140	11LT
qǐngwèn	請問	请问	excuse me, may I ask	110, 111	1
qiú	球		ball or anything shaped like a ball; sphere; globe	1329	13
qiū	秋		autumn	1003	10
qiūtiān	秋天		autumn	1003, 709	10
qù	去		to go	330	3
qù nián	去年		last year	330, 716	8G
rán	然		so; thus; such; in such a way	416	4
rén	人		person, human being	122	1
rèn	認	认	to recognize; to admit; to accept	403	4
rén rén	人人		people; everybody	122, 122	13G
rénmín	人民		the people; the nation; the masses	128, 829	8G
rénmínbì	人民幣	人民币	People's Currency; RMB	128, 829, 830	8G
rènshi	認識	认识	to be acquainted with; to know someone	403, 404	4

Pinyin	Traditional	Simplified	Meaning	Pages	Lesson
rì	日		sun	346	3G
rì	日		day; sun	710	7
rìběn	日本		Japan	346, 347	3G
rìwén	日文		Japanese language	346, 315	3G
rìwén	日文		Japanese language	346, 315	13
rìyǔ	日語	日语	Japanese language	346, 1312	13G
rú	如		to be like; to be similar to; to be as good as	917	
rú	如		to be like; to be similar to; to be as good as	917	13
rúguǒ	如果		if	917, 918	9
sān	三		three	536	5G
sǎo	掃	扫	to sweep; to clear away	1350	13
shā	沙		sand	1118	11
shāfā	沙發	沙发	sofa	1118, 1119	11
shàng	上		on; to be on top; to get onto; to come on top; to mount; to climb; to ascend	217	2
shāng	商		business; trade; commerce	633	6G, 8
shàng cèsuǒ	上廁所	上厕所	to go to the toilet; to use the toilet	217, 1219, 809	12
shàng dàxué	上大學	上大学	go to University/College; attend University	217, 101, 123	6E
shàng gè xīngqī	上個星期		last week	217, 517, 906, 907	9
shàng kè	上課	上课	to go to class, to be in class, to start class, to have class	217, 218	2
shàng wǎng	上網	上网	to go/be online	217, 1339	13
shāngdiàn	商店		shop; store	633, 819	8
shāngrén	商人		businessman; merchant	633, 122	6G
shàngwǔ	上午		before noon; AM	217, 401	4
shǎo	少		few	820	8
shéi/shuí	誰	谁	who?	119	1
shén	甚/什		what?	127	1
shēn	身		body; self	1301	13
shēng	生		to give birth to; an adept	124	1
shēng bìng	生病		to get sick	124, 802	8
shēng qì	生氣	生气	to get upset	124, 816	9
shēngrì	生日		birthday	124, 710	7
shénme	什麼	什么	what?	127, 128	1

233

Pinyin	Traditional	Simplified	Meaning	Page	Lesson
shénme shíhou	什麼時候	什么时候	when?	127, 128, 727, 902	9
shēntǐ	身體	身体	body; health	1301, 1302	13
shí	識	识	to know	404	4
shí	十		ten	543	5G
shí	時	时	time; season	727	7
shì	是		to be sth./sb.	107	1
shì	室		room	702	7
shì	事		matter; thing; business; agenda	707	7
shì	視	视	look at; regard; watch; vision	1124	11
shǐ	始		beginning; start; to begin; to originate	1322	13
shī	師	师	master	109	1
shī	失		to lose	526	5LT
shībài	失敗	失败	a defeat; a failure; to fail	526, 527	5LT
shíhou	時候	时候	(a point in) time; time (when); at the time (when)	727, 902	9
shíjian	時間	时间	time (the concept); time (the duration)	727, 728	7
shǒu	手		hand	904	9
shǒu	首		measure word for songs and poems	1319	13
shǒujī	手機	手机	cellphone	904, 620	9
shū	書	书	book	209	2
shū	舒		to relax; to make oneself comfortable	814	8
shuā	刷		to brush	1217	12
shuā yá	刷牙		to brush teeth	1217, 1218	12
shuài	帥	帅	handsome; cute	418	4
shuài gē	帥哥	帅哥	handsome bro; handsome dude; hot guy	418, 335	5E
shuāng	雙	双	a pair	1114	11
shūfu	舒服		comfortable; feeling good; relaxed	814, 636	8
shuì	睡		to sleep	920	9
shuǐ	水		water	1363	13E
shuì jiào	睡覺	睡觉	to sleep	920, 921	9
shuō	說	说	to speak	321	3
shuō huà	說話	说话	to speak; to talk	321, 812	12E
shūzhuō	書桌	书桌	desk	209, 1106	11
sì	四		four	537	5G
sǐ	死		to die	824	8

Pinyin	Traditional	Simplified	Meaning	Page	Chapter
sī	思		thoughts; to think; to ponder, to cosider	502	5
sī	司		to be in charge of; to preside over	619	6
sī yì	思議	思议	to consider; to comprehend; to imagine	502, 503	5
sījī	司機	司机	driver	619, 620	6
sòng	送		to present (a gift)	721	7
sù	訴	诉	to tell; to accuse; to file a suit	713	7
suàn	算		to count; to calculate	328	3
suàn le	算了		nevermind; forget it!	328, 329	3
suì	歲	岁	measure word for years of age	717	7
suī	雖	虽	though; although	1115	11
suīrán	雖然	虽然	although; even though	1115, 416	11
suīrán ... dànshì ...	雖然 ... 但是 ...	虽然 ... 但是 ...	although, ..., but ...	1115, 1116, 610, 107	11
suǒ	所		a place; that which	809	8
suǒ	所		place; office	809	12
suǒyǐ	所以		therefore	809, 719	8
tā	他		he	117	1
tā	她		she	118	1, 5
tā	牠/它	它	it	822	8
tái	臺/台	台	platform; stand; measure word for machinery	1109	11
tài	太		too (much)	720	7
tài ... le	太 ... 了		extremely ...	720, 329	7
tāmen	他們	他们	they (male or mixed)	117, 133	2G
tāmen	她們	她们	they (female olny)	118, 133	2G
tāmen	牠/它們	它们	they (objects or animals)	822, 133	
tè	特		special; particular; unusual	1025	10
tèbié	特別	特别	special; especially; particularly	1025, 1026	10
tí	題	题	subject, topic	215	2
tǐ	體	体	body; shape; form; substance; essence	1302	13
tiān	天		day; heaven; sky	709	7
tiān	天		heaven; God	709	8
tiān tiān	天天		every day; day by day; daily	709	10
tiānqì	天氣	天气	weather	709, 816	10

Pinyin	Traditional	Simplified	Meaning	Pages	Lesson
tiáo	調	调	to mix; to adjust; to tune	632	6G
tiáo	條	条	twig; strip; measure word for long objects, dogs, and fishes	1144	11LT
tiáo jiǔ	調酒	调酒	to mix alcohol; to make cocktails	632, 212	6G
tiáojiǔshī	調酒師	调酒师	bartender; mixologist	632, 212, 109	6G
tīng	聽	听	to hear; to listen	510	5
tīng	廳	厅	hall	1125	11
tīng (shéi de) huà	聽(誰的)話	听(谁的)话	to listen (to somebody); to consider someone's opinion; to obey; to be obedient	510, (119, 310), 812	9
tīng shuō	聽說	听说	to have heard	510, 321	5
tóng	同		same; alike; similar; to be or become the same; together with	402	4
tòng	痛		to ache; to hurt; pain	1309	13
tǒng	桶		bucket; barrel	1353	13
tóngxué	同學	同学	classmate	402, 123	4
tóngyì	同意		to agree	402, 157	10
tóu	頭	头	head; beginning	1345	13
tóu hūn yǎn huā	頭昏眼花	头昏眼花	dizzy; giddy; confused; fainting	1345, 1360, 1142, 729	13
tū	突		sudden; to break through	415	4
tuǐ	腿		leg	1145	11LT, 12
tuó	駝	驼	camel	1147	11E
tuō	托		to support with a hand	428	4G
tūrán	突然		suddenly	415, 416	4
verb + (de) shíhou	verb + (的)時候	verb + (的)时候	at the time when (something happens)	(310), 727, 902	13
wā	蛙		frog	1140	11LT
wài	外		outside; foreign	325	3
wàigōng	外公		maternal grandfather	325, 342	3G
wàiguó	外國	外国	foreign country	325, 316	3
wàiguórén	外國人	外国人	foreigner	325, 316, 122	3
wàimian	外面		outside	325, 1113	12
wàipó	外婆		maternal grandmother	325, 343	3G
wàixīngrén	外星人		alien; extra-terrestial	325, 906, 128	9Ex
wán	完		to finish; to end	1335	13
wǎn	晚		late; evening	749	7G

wǎn	晚	晚	late; evening	922	9
wǎn fàn	晚飯	晚饭	dinner	749, 203	10G
wáng	王		king	116	1
wàng	望		to gaze into the distance	742	7
wàng	忘		to forget	1346	13
wǎng	網	网	net	1339	13
wǎnshang	晚上		evening; in the evening	749, 217	7G, 10
wèi	為	为	for the sake of; to do; to act; to be	308	3
wèi	位		position; rank; polite *measure word for people*	505	5
wèi	喂		hello	813	8
wèi shénme	為什麼	为什么	why?	308, 127, 128	3
wén	文		language; letters; script	315	3
wèn	問	问	to ask a question	111	1
wén huà	文化		culture	315, 737	7
wèntí	問題	问题	question, problem	111, 215	2
wò	臥	卧	to recline; to lie down; to rest	1103	11
wǒ	我		I	104	1
wǒ de tiān	我的天		oh my God	104, 310, 709	8
wǒ kàn	我看		in my opinion; I think...; the way I see it	104, 208	9
wǒmen	我們	我们	we, us	104, 133	2
wòshì	臥室	卧室	bedroom	1103, 702	11
wù	務	务	affair; task; duty	637	6G
wù	物		object; material thing	723	7
wǔ	午		noon	401	4
wǔ	五		five	538	5G
xí	習	习	to learn; to practice	805	8
xì	係	系	to bind; to attach; to connect with	612	6
xǐ	洗		to wash	1132	11
xǐ	喜		joy; joyful; to like; to be fond of	1135	11
xī	西		west	524	5
xī	希		to hope; to expect; to wish	741	7
xī	息		breath; to breathe; to rest; to pause	807	8
xī	吸		to suck; to inhale	1351	13
xī dì	吸地		to vacuum	1351, 1129	13
xǐ zǎo	洗澡		to take a shower	1132, 1201	12
Xī'ān	西安		Xi'an City	524, 525	5

pinyin	traditional	simplified	meaning	page	lesson
xià	下		down; under; to go down; to descend; to get off	326	3
xià	下		to go down; to fall; to drop;	326	10
xià	夏		summer	1123	11
xià kè	下課	下课	to get off class; to finish class	326, 218	3
xià xuě	下雪		to snow	326, 1009	10
xià yǔ	下雨		to rain	326, 1008	10
xiàn	現	现	to appear; present	733	7
xiān	先		first	405	4
xiān ... zài ...	先 ... 再 ...		first ... and then ...	405, 1202	12
xiǎng	想		to think; to wish; to want to; would like to	743	7
xiāng	相		mutual; reciprical; each other; towards another person	738	7
xiāng	香		fragrant; delicious; yummy	914	9
xiāng	箱		box; case; trunk	1359	13
xiāngxìn	相信		to believe	738, 739	7
xiāngzi	箱子		suitcase; trunk	1359, 132	13
xiānsheng	先生		mister; sir; master	405, 124	4
xiànzài	現在	现在	now	733, 408	7
xiào	校		schoolhouse	903	9
xiǎo	小		small	112	1
xiǎo māo	小貓	小猫	little cat; kitten; here: given name		1
xiǎojiě	小姐		miss; young lady	112, 337	5G
xiàtiān	夏天		summer	1123, 709	11
xiàwǔ	下午		afternoon; PM	326, 401	4
xībānyá	西班牙		Spain	524, 1349, 1218	13G
xībānyáyǔ	西班牙語	西班牙语	Spanish language	524, 1349, 1218, 1312	13G
xié	鞋		shoe(s)	423	4G, 11
xiè	謝	谢	to thank	305	3
xiě	寫	写	to write	1315	13
xièxie	謝謝	谢谢	thanks	305, 305	3
xǐhuan	喜歡	喜欢	to like; to be fond of	1135, 1136	11
xìn	信		honesty; trust; to believe; to trust; to rely upon; letter; message	739	7, 13
xīn	心		heart; mind	311	3
xīn	新		new	431	4
xíng	行		to move; to go; alright; to be OK	425	4G, 7

Pinyin	Traditional	Simplified	Meaning	Pages	Lesson
xìng	姓		surname	105	1
xìng	興	兴	enthused; excited; stimulated; elated	911	9
xīng	星		star; heavenly body; planet	906	9
xīngqī	星期		week	906, 907	9
xīngqīèr	星期二		Tuesday	906, 907, 535	9G
xīngqīliù	星期六		Saturday	906, 907, 539	9G
xīngqīrì	星期日		Sunday	906, 907, 710	9G
xīngqīsān	星期三		Wednesday	906, 907, 536	9G
xīngqīsì	星期四		Thursday	906, 907, 537	9G
xīngqītiān	星期天		Sunday	906, 907, 709	9G
xīngqīwǔ	星期五		Friday	906, 907, 538	9G
xīngqīyī	星期一		Monday	906, 907, 516	9G
xīngxing	星星		stars	906	10
xīnlǐ	心理		psychology	311, 312	3
xīnlǐ yīshēng	心理醫生	心理医生	psychologist	311, 312, 606, 124	9
xìnxī	信息		message	739, 807	13
xiōng	兄		elder brother	339	3G
xiōngdì jiěmèi	兄弟姊妹		brothers and sisters; siblings	339, 336, 348, 338	3G
xǐshǒujiān	洗手間	洗手间	bathroom; washroom	1132, 904, 728	11
xiū	休		to rest; to take a break; to cease	806	8
xiūxi	休息		to rest; to take a break	806, 807	8
xīwàng	希望		to hope	741, 742	7
xǐyījī	洗衣機	洗衣机	washing machine	1132, 1111, 620	13E
xué	學	学	to study	123	1
xuě	雪		snow	1009	10
xuésheng	學生	学生	student	123, 124	1
xuéxí	學習	学习	to study; to learn	123, 805	8
xuéxiào	學校	学校	school	123, 903	9
ya	呀		Particle expressing surprise, often used as an exclamation mark	509	5
yá	牙		tooth; teeth	1218	12

Pinyin	Traditional	Simplified	Meaning	Ref 1	Ref 2
yán	言		speech; words; language	1313	13
yǎn	眼		eye	1142	11LT
yáng	羊		lamb; sheep	1146	11E
yàng	樣	样	style, mode, form, appearance	730	7
yángtuó	羊駝	羊驼	llama; alpaca	1146, 1147	11E
yǎnjing	眼睛		eyes	1142, 1143	11LT
yào	要		to want	204	2
yào	要		to want; to need; must; have to; going to; will	204	11
yàoshì	要是		if	204, 107	11
yé	爺		paternal grandfather	340	3G
yè	夜		night	923	9
yě	也		also, too, either	206	2
yéye	爺爺		paternal grandfather	340	3G
yì	議	议	to comment; to discuss; to suggest	503	5
yì	意		idea; intention	157	5
yǐ	以		by means of; because of; to take	719	7
yǐ	已		stop; cease; end; already (finished)	1004	10
yǐ	椅		chair	1108	11
yī	一		one; (one) whole	516	5G, 9
yī	醫	医	medical science; medicine; here: (medical) doctor	606	6
yī	衣		clothes	1111	11
yí gè rén	一個人	一个人	alone; by oneself	516, 517, 122	8
yí yàng	一樣	一样	same	516, 730	13
yí yè	一夜		the whole night	516, 923	9
yìbān	一般		ordinary; usual; common	516, 1028	10G
yídìng	一定		certainly; surely	516, 614	6
yīfú	衣服		clothes	1111, 636	11
yīguì	衣櫃	衣柜	wardrobe; closet for clothes	1111, 1112	11
yǐhòu	以後	以后	after; later	719, 927	13
yǐjing	已經	已经	already	1004, 1005	10
yīn	因		cause; reason	309	3
yīn	音		sound; tone; musical note	1018	10
yǐng	影		shadow; shade	1333	13
yīng	英		hero; English; flower	323	3
yīng	應	应	should; ought to	1016	10
yīnggāi	應該	应该	should; ought to	1016, 1017	10
yīngguó	英國	英国	England	323, 316	3G

Pinyin	Traditional	Simplified	Meaning	Pages	Lesson
yīngwén	英文		English language	323, 315	3
yīngyǔ	英語	英语	English language	323, 1312	13G
yīnwèi	因為	因为	because	309, 308	3
yīnwèi ... suǒ yǐ ...	因為 ... 所以 ...	因为 ... 所以 ...	because ..., therefore ...	308, 309, 808, 719	8
yīnyuè	音樂	音乐	music	1018, 1019	10
yìqǐ	一起		together	516, 507	10
yīshēng	醫生	医生	medical doctor	606, 124	9
yìsi	意思		meaning; sense; interest	157, 502	5
yǐwéi	以為	以为	to have assumed mistakenly	719, 308	8
yīxué	醫學	医学	medical studies	606, 123	6G
yīyuàn	醫院	医院	hospital	606, 915	9
yìzhí	一直		continuously; all the time; non stop; also: go straight	516, 1338	13
yǐzi	椅子		chair	1108, 132	11
yòng	用		to use; to need	1020	10
yǒng	泳		a swim; a style of swimming	1331	13
yóu	油	油	oil	221	2LT
yóu	游		to swim; to float; to drift	1330	13
yòu	又		again	1116	11
yòu	右		right; to the right	1130	11
yǒu	有		to have; there is	214	2
yǒu	友		friend; companion	412	4
yǒu (de) shíhou	有 (的) 時候	有 (的) 时候	sometimes	214, (310), 727, 902	12
yòu Adj. yòu Adj.	又 Adjective 又 Adjective		both ... and ...	1116	11
yǒu bìng	有病		double meaning of "sick"	214, 802	9
yǒu de	有的		some	214, 310	12
yǒu míng	有名		famous	214, 129	6
yǒu qián	有錢	有钱	rich	214, 615	6
yǒu yìsi	有意思		interesting	214, 157, 502	5
yǒu yòng	有用		useful	214, 1020	12E
yòubiān	右邊	右边	right side; on the right	1130, 1126	11
yǒujī	有機	有机	organic	214, 620	12
yóuyǒng	游泳		to swim	1330, 1331	13
yù	浴		to bathe	1356	13
yǔ	語	语	language; speech	334	3G

pinyin	traditional	simplified	meaning	ref	ch
yǔ	雨		rain	1008	10
yǔ	語	语	language; speech	1312	13
yuán	員	员	a person engaged in some field of activity; member	635	
yuán	園	园	garden	746	7G
yuán	元		Chinese yuan (currency)	828	8G
yuán	園	园	garden	746	10
yuàn	院		a yard; a courtyard; a designation for government offices or public places	915	9
yuǎn	遠	远	far	1306	13
yuè	月		month; moon	714	7
yuè	越		get over; exceed	1006	10
yuè	樂	乐	music	1019	10
yuè lái yuè	越來越 + Adjective	越来越 + Adjective	more and more + adjective; exceedingly + adjective	1006, 216	10
yuè lái yuè lěng	越來越冷	越来越冷	colder and colder; more and more cold	1006, 216, 1007	10
yùgāng	浴缸		bathtub	1356, 1357	13
yùn	運	运	to carry; to transport; to move things around	1327	13
yùndòng	運動	运动	sports; physical exercises; motion	1327, 1328	13
yǔyán	語言	语言	language	1312, 1313	13
zài	在		to be present; to be somewhere; to exist; at the present moment	408	4, 7
zài	再		again	1202	12
zài A hé B zhōngjiān	在A和B中間	在A和B中间	between A and B	408, 302, 314, 728	11
zǎo	早		early; morning	301	3
zǎo	澡		to wash; to bathe	1201	12
zǎofàn	早飯	早饭	breakfast	301, 203	12
zǎoshàng	早上		morning; in the morning	301, 217	3
zěn	怎		how; what; why	711	7
zěnme	怎麼	怎么	how; why; how come	711, 128	7
zěnme bàn	怎麼辦	怎么办	what to do? how to deal? (with something)	711, 128, 701	7
zěnme le	怎麼了	怎么了	how now? what's up? what's going on?	711, 128, 329	8
zěnmeyàng	怎麼樣	怎么样	how? how about? in what way?	711, 128, 730	7

Pinyin	Traditional	Simplified	Meaning	Ref	Lesson
zhāng	張	张	measure word for large flat objects, e.g. beds, tables, sheets of paper, tickets, etc., but also for the mouth	1104	11
zhào	照		to shine upon; to flash; to photograph; to reflect	518	5
zhǎo	找		to look for	406	4
zhàopiàn	照片		photograph	518, 519	5
zhè	這	这	this	417	4
zhè yàng	這樣	这样	this way; in this fashion; so	417, 730	7
zhè'er	這兒	这儿	here	417, 609	6G
zhème	這麼	这么	so; thus	417, 128	8G
zhēn	真		real; true	327	3
zhēnde	真的		really	327, 310	3
zhí	直		straight	1338	13
zhì	至		to arrive at; to reach (a point); superlative degree--the most	1223	12
zhǐ	只		only	603	6
zhī	之		*possessive particle; "of"*	546	5LT
zhī	知		to know	622	6
zhī	隻	只	*Measure Word for most pets and animals, such as cats; and one out of a pair of things, eg. eyes, etc*	639	6E
zhīdào	知道		to know (how; something)	622, 623	6
zhìshǎo	至少		at least	1223, 820	12
zhōng	中		middle; center; Chinese	314	3
zhōngguó	中國	中国	China	314, 316	3
zhōngguó rén	中國人	中国人	Chinese person; Chinese people	314, 316, 122	3
zhōngjiān	中間	中间	between	314, 728	11
zhōngwén	中文		Chinese language	314, 315	3
zhōngwén kè	中文課	中文课	Chinese language class	314, 315, 218	6E
zhú	竹		bamboo	1137	11LT
zhù	住		to stay; to live	1010	10
zhǔ	主		main; principal; master; leader; chief	731	7
zhuǎn	轉	转	to turn; to change; to switch	1354	13
zhuǎn shēn	轉身	转身	to turn around	1354, 1301	13
zhǔn	準	准	level; standard; accurate	1101	11

pinyin	trad	simp	meaning	char refs	lesson
zhǔnbèi	準備	准备	to prepare	1101, 1102	11
zhuō	桌		table	1106	11
zhǔyì	主意		idea	731, 157	7
zhúzi	竹子		bamboo	1137, 132	11LT
zì	字		word, character	130	1
zì	自		self; personal; oneself; one's own	424	4G, 13
zǐ	子		noun suffix; (male) child; son *x*	132	1LT, 6
zì pāi	自拍		to take a selfie	424, 1341	13
zìxíngchē	自行車	自行车	bicycle	424, 425, 426	4G
zuì	醉		drunk; to get drunk	1211	12
zuì	最 + adj.		most	1318	13
zuǐ	嘴		mouth	1141	11LT
zuó	昨		yesterday; past	801	8
zuò	做		to do, to make	201	2
zuò	作		to do; to compose	605	6
zuò	坐		to sit	706	7
zuǒ	左		left; to the left	1131	11
zuó wǎn	昨晚	昨晚	yesterday night; last night	801, 922	9
zuǒbiān	左邊	左边	left side; on the left	1131, 1126	11
zuòhǎo	做好		to finish or complete doing something	201, 103	11
zuòhǎo zhǔnbèi	做好準備	做好准备	to finish preparing; to get ready	201, 103, 1101, 1102	11
zuótiān	昨天		yesterday	801, 709	8

Key to the exercises

1

2
a) 大家好 [Hello everybody]
b) 我是老师 [I am a teacher]
c) 他不是人 [He's not a human]
d) 他是学生吗? [Is he a student?]
e) 他是谁? [Who is he?]
f) wǒ xìng wáng [My last name is Wang]?
g) tā jiào shénme míngzi [What's his name?]
h) wǒ shì lǎoshī [I am a teacher]
i) qǐngwèn, nǐ guì xìng [Excuse me, what is your last name?]
j) nǐ shì xuésheng ma? [Are you a student]

3
a) 他叫 Jerry。
b) 我是人。
c) 我不是老师。
d) 他是谁?

4
a) 你叫什么名字? nǐ jiào shénme míngzi
b) 她是谁? tā shì shéi
c) 我是学生。wǒ shì xuésheng
d) 我不是老师。wǒ bú shì lǎoshī
e) 请问 qǐngwèn

5
a) 他不是人吗? [Is he not a human?]
b) 他叫什么名字呢? [And what is your name?]
c) 你是谁呢? [And who is he?]
d) 他是学生，你呢? [He is a student, what about you?]
e) 你姓王吗? [Is your last name Wang?]
f) 谁叫 Jerry 呢? [Is your name Jerry?]
g) 谁是老师呢? [And who is the teacher?]
h) 谁姓齐呢? [And whose last name is Qi?]
i) 你贵姓呢? [And what is your last name?]
j) 你是王小猫吗? [Are you Wang Xiaomao?]

6
a) Jerry 不是学生。
b) Jerry 不是人。
c) 齐老师是人。

7
a) Qí lǎoshī bú shì hǎo rén [Teacher Qi is not a good person]
b) Jerry shì hǎo xuésheng [Jerry is a good student]
c) Wáng Xiǎomāo bú shì xiǎo māo, tā jiào Xiǎomāo [Wang Xiaomao is not a little cat, her name is Little Cat]
d) tā bú jiào Xiǎomǎ, tā jiào Xiǎomāo [Her name is not Little Horse, her name is Little Cat]
e) xuésheng bú shì lǎo rén [Students are not old people]
f) xiǎo mǎ wèn xiǎo māo: Jerry shì shéi? [little horse asks little cat: Who is Jerry?]
g) qǐng wèn, nǐ xué shénme? [Excuse me, what do you study?]

2

2
a) 我吃饭呢。[I am eating right now]
b) 没问题。[No problem]
c) 你不吃吗? [You don't eat?]
d) 他（她）不看书。[He (she) does not read]
e) 我们上课。[We go to class]
f) 我要问问题。[I want to ask questions]

3
a) wǒ bù chī, wǒ bú è
b) wǒ wèn nǐ
c) rén bú shì mǎ, mǎ yě bú shì rén
d) tā bú kàn shū
e) Jerry hē píjiǔ
f) wǒ yào chī māo

4
a) 他看书呢
b) 她喝啤酒!
c) 我们吃饭!
d) 你有问题吗?
e) 你们要看她吗?

5
老师看书呢。
Jerry 喝啤酒呢。
王小猫吃饭呢.

6
a) 我也吃饭
b) 王老师喝啤酒呢
c) 我不是学生
d) 他是谁? (吗 is redundant)
e) 我姓齐 (贵 is redundant)
f) 他是谁?
g) 他们要不要来? (吗 is redundant)

7
a) 是，Jerry 喝啤酒。
b) 齐老师不饿。
c) 王小猫不吃草，她吃饭。
d) Jerry 是马。
e) 王小猫吃饭呢。
f) Jerry 喝啤酒呢。
g) Jerry 不要吃饭。
h) 老师没有问题。

8
a) 王老师吃不吃饭呢? [Is Teacher Wang eating right now?]
b) 你做什么呢? [What are you doing right now?]
c) 齐小猫也吃草。[Qi Xiaomao also eats grass.]
d) 我也不是人。[I am not a human, either.]
e) 你吃什么饭? [What food do you eat?]
f) 我们也喝啤酒呢。[We are also drinking beer right now.]
g) 你们要不要喝啤酒? [Do you want to drink beer?]

3

2
他是法国人。 He is from France.
他是日本人。 He is from Japan.
他是中国人。 He is from China.

3
a) 算了，我哥哥要吃草！
b) 我爸爸，我妈妈和我都学中文。
c) 我会说中文，也会说日文。
d) 你为什么不喝啤酒？
e) 做饭是我的爱好 / 我的爱好是做饭。

4
a) 我不吃草。
b) 我爸爸妈妈是中国人。
c) 我不说中文，我说英文。
d) 你学什么？
e) 你妈妈忙吗？
f) 我爱做饭。

5
a) nǐ máng bù máng?
b) wǒ hěn máng, tā yě hěn máng.
c) tā yě shì lǎowài.
d) nǐ shì yīngwén lǎoshī.
e) nǐ hǎo ma?
f) wǒ qǐng Jerry chī Zhōngguó zǎofàn, kěshì tā bú yào chī fàn, tā yào chī cǎo.

6
a) So so.
b) I am a foreigner/outsider.
c) You are a Chinese language teacher.
d) I study the psychology of cats.
e) Tigers don't eat cats, tigers eat people.
f) Chinese characters are hard to learn.

7
a) 我们都很忙。
b) 他们都是老外。
c) 妈妈和爸爸都吃豆腐。
Important note: 吃豆腐 means "to eat tofu", but it also means "to get laid" or "to get some," so be careful when using it …
d) 英文和中文Jerry都会说。
e) 王小猫和齐老师都不喝啤酒。

8
a) 我是XXX人。
b) 我是/不是学生。
c) 我会/不会说中文。
d) 我喝/不喝啤酒。
e) 我爸爸妈妈是XXX人。
f) 我学XXX。
g) 我的爱好是XXX。

9
a) 齐老师很忙因为他学马的心理和爱好。
b) 王小猫学中文。
c) 王小猫是美国人。她不是中国人。
d) Jerry学人的爱好。
e) 齐老师不是中国人。

10
a) 我的猫很酷，可是它有心理问题。
b) 我哥哥很好看，可是爸爸妈妈都不爱他。
c) 我的马不是人，可是它爱喝啤酒。
d) 中文很不好学，可是我爱学中文。
e) 她是老外，可是她不老。
f) 老虎吃马，可是马不吃老虎。

11
a) 老虎很饿
b) 老外很酷
c) 老师是外国人
d) 啤酒很贵
e) 王小猫是学生
f) 我是中国人
g) 我妈妈很美
h) 我的学生是老外
i) 美国很大
j) 中国饭很好吃
k) 你很忙
l) 草很好看
m) 他的中文很好
n) 我是爸爸

4

1
a) 你是不是老师？
b) 他/她很老。
c) 她/他是北京大学的老师。
d) 你找谁？
e) 那是什么人？
f) 他/她学什么？
g) 他很帅。
h) 他/她是我妈妈的朋友。

2
a) Nǐ zhǎo shéi? [Who are you looking for?]
b) Qí lǎoshī bú zài. [Teacher Qi is not here.]
c) Nǐ wèishénme xué zhōngwén? [Why do you study Chinese?]
d) Tā qí mǎ lái shàng kè. [He comes to class on a horseback.]
e) Zhè shì wǒmen dàxué de mǎ. [This is a horse from our University.]
f) Tā hěn shuài! [He's handsome!]
g) Nǐ shì wǒ māma de péngyou ma? [Are you my mom's friend?]
h) Mǎ hé lǎohǔ bù tóng. [Horses and tigers are different.]

3
a) 你妈妈的朋友不是我的朋友。nǐ māma de péngyou bú shì wǒ de péngyou
b) 王老师在吗？wáng lǎoshī zài ma?
c) 我的老师真帅。wǒ de lǎoshī zhēn shuài
d) 我妈妈是北京大学的老师。wǒ māma shì běijīng dàxué de lǎoshī
e) 他是我哥哥的老师的朋友。tā shì wǒ gēge de lǎoshī de péngyou
f) 我是你（的）老师的妈妈的哥哥 wǒ shì nǐ (de) lǎoshī de māma de gēge
g) 猫的心理很不好学。māo de xīnlǐ hěn bù hǎo xué
h) 人和马的爱好不同。rén hé mǎ de àihào bù tóng

4
a) 我姐姐很美。
b) 我妈妈看书。(的 is redundant)
c) 你是不是老师？（吗 is redundant）
d) 我的朋友都爱我的女朋友。
e) 她是我哥哥的朋友。

5
a) 马先生找齐老师。
b) 王小猫妈妈的朋友是北京大学的老师。
c) 是,马先生是新的学生。
d) 齐老师不骑自行车来上课;他骑马来上课。
e) Jerry是王小猫的朋友。

6
a) 你的马也很美。
b) 你的中文很好。
c) 她骑谁的马?
d) 北京大学的中文书很好看。
e) 中国的啤酒不贵。

5

2
a) 我听说你妈妈和你爸爸都学中文。
b) 我女朋友不美。
c) 她妈妈有没有男朋友?/有男朋友吗?
d) 她老说我不帅。
e) 我爸爸喝很多茶。
f) 王小猫和齐老师都看书呢。
g) 算了,学生老骂老师。
h) 我当然爱你,你就是我的爱!你才不爱我。
i) 真丢脸!

3
a) 中国的啤酒不贵。(是 is redundant)
b) 我妈妈有五个好朋友。
c) 我没有筷子。
d) 我的老师很高。
e) 老师没来。(了 is redundant)

4
a) 我爸爸老喝啤酒。
b) 我也是老师。
c) 他骑马来上课。
d) 你的男朋友是哪里的?
e) 她是新的老师

5
a) 马先生是法国人。
b) 马先生叫马王。
c) 马先生当然有女朋友。
d) 王小猫不觉得马先生的女朋友美。
e) 齐老师觉得马先生的女朋友不美。
f) 马先生才不可思议。

6
a) 这位很帅的老师就是我们的中文老师。
b) 哪个同学不爱Jerry?
c) 他下午才来上课。
d) 大家都说马先生爱吃豆腐。
e) 你错了!
f) 你吃饭了吗?
g) 我没吃饭。我很饿。
h) 那个法国学生也上中文课。
i) 我有一个中国的男朋友。
j) 老师不是好人;他没有一个好朋友。(He has no single good friend.)

7
Wǒ xìng Wén, míngzi jiào Měinǚ [My last name is Wen, my name is Měinǚ (Beauty; Beautiful Woman)].
Wǒ shì Hánguórén [I am Korean].
Wǒ de jiā bú dà [My family is not big].
Wǒ yǒu yí gè dìdi, tā yě xìng Wén, kěshì tā bú jiào Měinǚ, tā jiào Shuàigē [I have one little brother, his last name is also Wen, but his name is not Měinǚi (Beauty), his name is Shuaige (Hot Dude).
Wǒ dìdi xué rìwén [My little brother studies Japanese].
Tā de rìwén hěn hǎo [His Japanese is good].
Tā shì yí gè hǎo dìdi [He is a good little brother].

Cultural note: Very disturbingly, both 美女 měinǚ "beauty" and 帅哥 shuàigē "handsome" became popular forms of address in China. People address strangers in the streets using such terms. Korean pop culture became extremely popular in China, and Koreans, especially men, are regarded as the hottest humans alive.

6

2
a) 她有四十二个孩子。不可思议!
b) 我的家很大,有八口人:妈妈,爸爸,两个妹妹,一个哥哥,爷爷,奶奶和我;也有两只小猫和一匹老马。
c) 他不但很奇怪,而且不工作。
d) 我爸爸是商人。
e) 我没有男朋友,可是那没有关系,因为我有很多好朋友。
f) 你爸爸做什么工作?

4
a) 我有两个孩子。
b) 我也爱你!
c) 我弟弟是画家。
d) 你有几个兄弟姐妹?
e) 我不认识齐老师的好朋友。

5
a) 他的爱人很有名 tā de àirén hěn yǒu míng [His spouse is famous]
b) 他不但很有钱而且有三个女朋友 tā bú dàn hěn yǒu qián érqiě yǒu sān gè nǚpéngyou [He's not only rich, but also has three girlfriends]
c) 我爸爸的老朋友是医生 wǒ bàba de lǎo péngyou shì yīshēng [My dad's old friend is a doctor] or 我老朋友是爸爸的医生 [My old friend is dad's doctor] or 医生是我爸爸的老朋友 [Doctor is my dad's old friend] or 我老朋友的爸爸是医生 [My old friend's dad is a doctor] or 我医生是爸爸的老朋友 [My doctor is dad's old friend] or 我老朋友是医生的爸爸 [My old friend is doctor's dad]
d) 画家都有很多情人 huàjiā dōu yǒu hěn duō qíngrén [Painters all have lots of lovers]

6
a) 齐老师的家有两口人。
b) 齐老师的姐姐是马医生。
c) 不知道呀... 他不在北京。
d) 马先生的爸爸难看。
e) Jerry没有家。

7
a) 齐老师和Jerry的关系真有意思。[The teacher's relationship with Jerry is interesting]
b) 这个帅哥就是齐老师。[This hot dude is exactly Teacher Qi]
c) 中文课的同学都说Jerry很帅。[All Chinese language class classmates say Jerry is handsome.]
d) 你也姓王吗？[Is his last name Wang, too?]
e) 有名的画家一定很有钱。[Famous painters are certainly rich]
f) 我们大学只有一匹马。[There is only one horse at our University]
g) 马先生上午不忙，因为他下午才去上中文课。[Mr. Ma is not busy in the morning, because he doesn't go to Chinese language class until the afternoon]
h) 老师老问我这个问题。[The teacher keeps asking me this question]

8
a) 哪个同学是法国的？
b) 她是哪国人？
c) 你女朋友有几个孩子？
d) 谁是司机？
e) 那个帅哥是谁？
f) 你哥哥爱吃什么？

9
a) wǒ àirén bú ài gōngzuò [My spouse does not love to work/hates work]
b) wǒ ài wǒ àirén, kěshì tā bú ài wǒ [I love my husband, but he does not love me]
c) wǒ gēge hěn shuài, kěshì tā de nǚpéngyou bù duō [My elder brother is handsome, but he does not have many girlfriends/his girlfriends are few]
d) wǒ nánpéngyou de àihào jiù shì píjiǔ [My boyfriend's hobby is exactly this: beer]
e) nǐ shàng nǎ gè dàxué? [Which University are you going to]
f) wǒ jiějie shàng Běidà [My elder sister goes to Beida (Beijing University)]

7

2
a) 我要给我医生送什么礼物？
b) 你喝了我的啤酒！你怎么敢！
c) 我弟弟饿了！
d) 你奶奶的生日是几月几号？
e) 你多大？

3
a) 我23岁。(是 is redundant)
b) 你今年多大了？
c) 现在两点半了。
d) 我爸爸也没有钱！
e) 我不知道他叫什么名字。
f) 老师也这样说。

4
a) 下午两点半
b) 下午一点零五（分）
c) 早上三点
d) 下午五点二十（分）
e) 早上七点
f) 下午三点十五（分）／三点一刻

g) 晚上九点差十分
h) 晚上八点差五分
i) 晚上六点十五（分）／六点一刻
j) 中午

5
a) 王小猫今年21岁了。
b) 齐老师今年44岁了。
c) 王小猫的生日四月一号。
d) 马先生来找齐老师。
e) 齐老师在办公室里。
f) 齐老师的生日七月四号。

6
a) 四月十五号
b) 二〇〇一年
c) 一九九七年
d) 一六五三年
e) 一七一一年
f) 一八六八年
g) 二〇〇五年五月二十六号
h) 二〇一七年一月五号
i) 一九七二年七月三十号
j) 二〇四二年二月十四号
k) 三一〇年十月二十号
l) 一九九九年十二月三十一号
m) 一九九三年十一月六号
n) 一八五三年
o) 一九八八年二月十号
p) 三月二号
q) 二〇〇七年九月九号
r) 二〇〇四年六月三十号
s) 二〇一八年三月二十八号
t) 二〇一二年八月三十一号

7
王小猫在老师的办公室里喝啤酒。
齐老师在北京骑自行车。
马先生在中国上长城。
Jerry 在公园里吃花。
马先生在大学学画画儿。

8
a) Wǒ bù guǎn tā xiǎng shénme. [I don't care what she thinks]
b) Lǎoshī cuò le. [Teacher made a mistake/was wrong]
c) Mǎ Xiānsheng zài Běijīng shàng le dàxué. [Mr. Ma went to University in Beijing]
d) Qí lǎoshī tài qíguài le, xuésheng dōu bù gǎn qù zhǎo tā [Teacher Qi is extremely weird, students don't dare to go see him/seek him out]
e) Jerry zuò le hǎo chī de fàn, nǐ zěnme bù chī ne? [Jerry made delicious food, how come you are not eating?]
f) Māma bú ài bàba le. [Mom no longer loves dad]
g) Zhè gè wèntí wǒ yào wèn shéi? [Whom should I ask this question?]
h) Qí lǎoshī bù xiāngxìn Wáng Xiǎomāo huì kàn zhōngwén shū. [Teacher Qi does not believe Wang Xiaomao can read books in Chinese]

9
a) Jerry累了 [Jerry is tired]
b) 我不忙了 [I am no longer busy]
c) 你的主意 不错 [Your idea is not bad]
d) 你 怎么 不认识我？[How come you don't know me?]
e) 我听说Jerry在家里骑齐老师。[I've heard at home Jerry rides Teacher Qi]
f) 没 办法，我们要听老师。[There is no other way, we have to listen to the

teacher]
g) 我们吃饺子吧。[Let's have some dumplings!]
h) 这个看法不行。[This opinion does not work/is unacceptable/is bad]
i) 你怎么会这样说? [How can you say this/so?]
j) 我不管她是谁。[I don't care who she is]
k) 你觉得中文好不好学? [Do you think Chinese is easy to learn?]

10
a) 中国文化很有意思 [Chinese culture is interesting]
b) 谁吃了我的饭?
c) 这个说法很奇怪.
d) 你为什么不学中文?
e) 你怎么有我男朋友的照片呢?

8

1
a) 一年 (个 is redundant)
b) 二〇〇八年一月三号
c) 去年
d) 明年
e) 两天

2
a) Jerry 会去美国。
b) 王小猫不会学法文。
c) 齐老师会给Jerry打一个电话。
d) Jerry 不会给齐老师打电话。
e) 马先生会去商店买高跟鞋和啤酒。
f) 我们都会死。

3
a) (不对) 王小猫平常不上课。
b) (不对) 王小猫去商店买啤酒
c) (对) 王小猫花了很多钱
d) (不对) 王小猫买的花不贵
e) (不对) 齐老师以为王小猫会死。
f) (对) 王小猫昨天很舒服

4
我不知道我哥哥为什么那么爱吃草。我问了他，但是他没告诉我。他说我太小。他每天都吃。今天他不但吃草，而且也吃花了。我以为他会死，可是他没有。我想他一定会生病。我不管，因为我不爱他，可是我觉得很奇怪。我哥哥是不是一匹马?

5
a) 我今天不忙，不去上课，就在家里休息。
b) 一个人过生日很难过。
c) 我没有这么多钱。
d) 我以为他会画画儿。
e) 你会给她什么礼物?
f) 因为我爱人做的饭不好吃，所以我不在家吃饭。

6
a) 妈妈平常打爸爸。
b) 马先生每天都去商店买豆腐。
c) 我明年才可以去中国。
d) 我爱人老说她今天就会死。
e) 老师上午九点上中文课。
f) 那个帅哥今天下午请我女朋友喝茶了，所以我明天去他家打他。

7
a) 猫 (送给你)
b) 高跟鞋 （一百零五块）（钱）
c) 饺子 (十一块) （钱）
d) 自行车 (一千〇四十块)（钱）
e) 摩托车 (两千一百一十七块) （钱）
f) 马先生难看的花儿 (二百五十块) （钱）

Cultural note: 250 二百五 is an expression and means "dimwit" or "moron"

g) 中国饭 (十四块) （钱）
h) 书 (四十二块) （钱）
i) 花 (一百一十六块) （钱）
j) 茶 (两块) （钱）
k) 筷子 (二十二块) （钱）

9

2
a) 王小猫什么时候买自行车了?
b) 学生每天早上几点上中文课?
c) 他们星期几晚上请我们吃饭?
d) 齐老师几天没有睡觉了?
e) 马先生几个星期没有来学校了?
f) 王小猫病了几个月?
g) 她几月几号过生日?

3
a) 爸爸今天有很多事：他得给妈妈做饭，还得去商店买酱油。
b) 我爱人不爱我了，可是我还爱她。
c) 我以为Jerry没有男朋友。
d) -- 王小猫病了多久?
-- 她没有病。

-- 真的吗? 那她为什么没来上课?
e) 我哥哥很高，但是他没有很多女朋友。他是一个男人，可是他找一个男朋友。
f) 你什么时候会有时间给我打电话?
g) 我们去你那儿喝酒吧!

4
a) 我想跟他过夜 [I'd like to spend a night with him]
b) 你今天下午有没有时间? or 今天下午你有没有时间? [Do you have time today in the afternoon?]
c) 我晚上八点有事 or 晚上八点我有事 [I have something to do at 8PM]
d) 你什么时候去美国? [When are you going to America?]
e) 她吃了几个蛋糕? [How many cakes did she eat?]
f) Jerry 早上六点在商店买啤酒 or 早上六点Jerry在商店买啤酒 [At 6AM Jerry is at the store buying beer]
g) 你明白了吗? [Did you get it?]
h) 我不相信你爸爸是一个外星人 [I don't believe your dad is an alien] or 你不相信我爸爸是一个外星人 [You don't believe my dad is an alien]

5
a) 我明年才可以去中国。[all other options work in this case too]
b) 我很想去中国，可是我没有钱。
c) 如果你老吃醋，

249

你会生病。
d) 我觉得你得去看心理医生。
e) 他才13岁，还不能喝啤酒。

6
a) 如果我有钱，我会请大家喝酒。[If I had money, I would invite everybody for a drink]
b) 如果我有时间，我一定给你打电话。[If I have time, I will certainly give you a call]
c) 如果我有事，我会告诉你。[If I have something going on, I will let you know]
d) 如果你累，你得休息。[If you are tired, you must rest]
e) 如果你太忙，你可以/得找新的工作。[If you are too busy, you can/must find a new job]
f) 如果你不会做蛋糕，你可以/得去商店买。[If you don't know how to make a cake, you can/must go get one from the store]
g) 如果你不舒服，你得/可以看医生。[If you are unwell, you must/can see a doctor]
h) 如果你打我，你会后悔。[If you beat me, you will regret]

7
1) 我真笨。I'm really stupid.
没错。That's right.

2) 我爱你。I love you.
我知道。I know.

3) 王小猫做什么呢？What is Wang Xiaomao doing right now?
她休息呢。She's taking some rest.

4) 我不爱我弟弟。I don't love my little brother.
我常常打他。I often beat him.

5) 我的猫不是老虎。My cat is not a tiger.
它太小了。He's too small.

6) 我哥哥没有女朋友。My elder brother has no girlfriend.
他花太多钱。He spends too much money.

7) 我吃的豆腐很好看。The tofu I ate looked very good.
也很香。Also very delicious.

8) 姐姐做了一个蛋糕。Elder sister made a cake.
她给我过生日。She's celebrating my birthday.

9) 我想我哥哥是一个外星人。I think my elder brother is an alien.
他的脸很奇怪。His face is strange.

10) 老师想Jerry。The teacher is missing Jerry.
他不能睡觉。He cannot sleep.

11) 老虎吃小猫。The tiger is eating a little cat.
小猫很不高兴。The little cat is very unhappy.

12) 有人敲门。Someone's knocking on the door.
是谁啊？Who is it?

8
Wǒ jiā yǒu sì kǒu rén, bàba, māma, gēge hé wǒ. Wǒ bàba jīn nián 55 suì. Tā bù gāo. Bàba shì sījī, kěshì tā chángcháng hē jiǔ, suǒyǐ tā bù néng měi tiān dōu gōng zuò. Māma shuō hē jiǔ de sījī bú shì hǎo sījī. Wǒ māma yě 55 suì, tā shì yí gè měinǚ, yīnwéi tā de liǎn hěn piàoliang. Māma shì xīnlǐ yīshēng. Tā chángcháng kàn bàba de bìng, tā yě chángcháng bù gāoxìng. Wǒ gēge jīn nián 23 suì, tā hěn kù. Tā de míngzi jiào Míng Xīng, kě shì dàjiā dōu jiào tā shuàigē. Shuàigē shuō tā shì huàjiā, dànshì wǒ bù xiāngxìn, yīnwéi tā bú huì huà huà'er. Wǒ kàn le tā huà de huà'er, dōu fēicháng nánkàn. Wǒ bù míngbái tā wèi shénme nàme ài huà xiǎo māo ......Shuàigē bù gōngzuò, kěshì tā yǒu liǎng gè nǚpéngyou, hái yǒu yí gè nánpéngyou, suǒyǐ tā hěn máng. Tāmen dōu gěi tā qián, suǒyǐ tā néng mǎi fàn. tā nánpéngyou shì shāng rén. Tā ài qí mǎ. Tā bù niánqīng le, jīn nián 68 suì. Shuàigē shuō nà méi yǒu guānxi, yīnwéi tā hěn yǒu qián, érqiě fēicháng ài shuàigē. Tā lǎo shuō shuàigē bú dàn hěn gāo érqiě hěn shuài. Shuàigē hái yǒu yí gè àihào, jiù shì zuò zhōngguó fàn. Wǒ jīn nián 19 suì. Wǒ shì dàxuéshēng, zài Běijīng xué zhōngwén. Shuàigē chángcháng dǎ wǒ, yīnwéi wǒ bù gěi tā qián. Zuótiān shuàigē hěn shēng qì, yīnwéi tā nánpéngyou gěi wǒ sòng le xīn de shǒujī. Wǒ xiǎng dǎ shuàigē, kěshì wǒ bù gǎn, yīnwéi tā hěn dà.

There are four people in my family: dad, mom, elder brother, and I. My dad is 55 this year. He is not tall. Dad is a driver, but he often drinks alcohol, so he can't work every day. Mom says a driver who drinks alcohol is not a good driver. My mom is 55, too, she's a beauty, because her face is pretty. Mom is a psychologist. She often checks on dad's illness (examines dad's disease), she is also often unhappy. My elder brother is 23 this year, he's cool. He's name is Ming Xing (bright star; superstar), but everybody calls him Shuaige (handsome dude). Shuaige says he's a painter, but I don't believe it, because he can't paint. I saw the paintings he painted, they are all extremely ugly. I don't understand why he loves to paint little cats so much … Shuaige does not work, but he has two girlfriends and also one boyfriend, therefore he's busy. They all give him money, so he can buy food. His boyfriend is a businessman. He loves riding horses. He's no longer young, 68 this year. Shuaige says that doesn't matter, because he's rich, and also he extremely loves Shuaige. He keeps saying that Shuaige is not only tall but also handsome. Shuaige also has another (has one more) hobby, which is cooking Chinese food. I'm 19 this year. I am a college student, I study Chinese in Beijing. Shuaige often beats me, because I don't give him money. Yesterday Shuaige was very pissed, because his boyfriend gave me a new cell phone as a gift. I want to beat Shuaige, but I don't dare to, because he's big.

10

1
a) 十一个病人来看医生。11 patients came to see the doctor.
b) 王小猫有两个心理问题。Wang Xiaomao has 2 mental problems.
c) 十四个学生没有来上课。14 students didn't come to class.
d) 这个老人一百零二岁。This old person is 102 years old.
e) 我的小孩子五岁了。My little child is 5 years old.
f) 马先生的家有七口人。There are 7 people in Mr. Ma's family.
g) 他吃了六个蛋糕。He ate 6 cakes.
h) 我认识二十二个外国人。I know 22 foreigners.
i) 在美国新的手机八百一十二块钱。A new cell phone in the US costs 812 dollars.
j) Jerry有十个麻烦。Jerry has 10 worries.
k) 我有九个情人。I have 9 lovers.

2
a) Jerry 的老朋友住在哪儿？Where does Jerry's old friend live?
b) 你爱听什么音乐？What music do you love listening to?
c) 你想吃什么？What would you like to eat?
d) 我不应该喝什么？What should I not drink?
e) 学生什么时候不用去学校？When do students not need to go to school?
f) 你跟谁一起去商店？Who do you go to the store with?
g) 谁认识他？Who knows him?
h) 你在哪儿做饭？Where do you cook?
i) 我们几点下课？What time do we get off class?
j) 你得去哪儿？Where must you go?
k) 他病了多久？How long was he sick for?

3
a) 我想住在北京 [I'd like to live in Beijing]
b) 我还没有吃饭 [I still have not eaten]
c) 她已经睡觉了 [She already went to bed/to sleep/is sleeping already]
d) 老师已经下课了 [The Teacher finished class already]
e) 我们一起去吧 [Let's go together!]
f) 老师今天一个人去公园看马 or 老师今天去公园一个人看马 [Teacher is going alone to watch horses in the park today]
g) 我也想跟她一起去 [I also would like to go together with her] or 她也想跟我一起去 [She also would like to go together with me]
h) 在公园里做饭很不方便 [Cooking in the park is very inconvenient]

4
a) 你应该给他付钱。
b) 你可以给孩子吃饭吗？
c) 你为什么不给她打电话？
d) 我不想跟猫一起睡觉。
e) 你应该休息休息。
f) (给) 我看 (一) 看。
g) 爸爸常常给妈妈做饭。
h) 你跟我 (一起) 来吧。
i) 孩子很麻烦。
j) (现在) 下雨了。

11

1
a) 书桌，衣柜，椅子，沙发都是家具。[Desks, cabinets, chairs, sofas are all furniture]
b) 卧室，客厅，洗手间，厨房都是房间。[Bedroom, living room, bathroom, kitchen, are all rooms]
c) 里面，外面，上面，下面，左边，右边，还有旁边，到处都有猫；这个地方真奇怪。[Inside, outside, on top, underneath, left, right, and also on the side, there are cats everywhere; this place is really weird!]

2
a) wǒmen hái méi yǒu zuò hǎo zhǔnbèi [We still have not prepared]
b) bù kěnéng [impossible]
c) diànnǎo zài zhuō shàng [the computer is on top of the table]
d) yīguì lǐ yǒu gāogēnxié [there are high heels inside the closet]
e) wǒ qù zhǎo bié rén [I go find someone else]

3
a) (要)
b) (要) (要)
c) (想)
d) (想)
e) (要)
f) (要)
g) (想)
h) (要) (想)
i) Are you going to work? (要) or: Would you like to work? (想)
j) I am going to listen to music (要) or: I'd like to listen to music (想)
k) I am not going to spend a night with you (要) or: I don't wish to spend a night with you (想)
l) She will (is going to) to eat Chinese food. (要) or She'd like to eat Chinese food (想)
m) I am going to China to study Chinese (要) or: I'd like to go to China to study Chinese (想)
n) I am going to go to the park to watch baby alpacas (要) or: I'd like to go to the park to watch baby alpacas. (想)

4
猫在衣柜里
Jerry坐在椅子上
高跟鞋在桌子下
Jerry在老师和王小猫中间
电脑在地上

5
a) 我妈妈做的包子很好吃/很香。
b) 老师骑的马很漂亮。
c) 我在中国学中文的男朋友很有钱。
d) 爸爸给妈妈买的衣服很贵。
e) 我不喜欢不吃豆腐的人。
f) 你做的事不对。
g) 你爱的人很奇怪。
h) 常常去中国的人不一定会说中文。
i) 我买的电视机在哪儿?
j) 每天早上六点给你打电话的人是谁?
k) 我五岁的小弟弟已经有手机了。
l) 没有付钱的人不能进。

6
a) 要是你不给我钱,我（就）不（会）给你看我男朋友的照片。If you don't give me money, I won't show you my boyfriend's picture.
b) 要是你不付钱,我（就会）告诉妈妈。If you don't pay up, I will tell mom.
c) 要是你不洗手,你（就）不能吃饭。If you don't wash your hands, (then) you can't eat.
d) 要是你不喜欢他,（就）不要请他喝茶。If you don't like him, (then) don't invite him to tea.
e) 要是他来,我们（就）可以一起看电视。If he comes, (then) we can watch TV together.
f) 要是床太小,我们（就）不能一起睡。If the bed is too small, (then) it's impossible to sleep together.
g) 要是你觉得这里太贵,我们（就）去找别的地方。If you think here is too expensive, (then) we can go someplace else.
h) 要是天气太冷,我们（就）在家里休息。If the weather is too cold, (then) we (may) stay at home and rest.
i) 要是办公室没有窗户,我（就）不想在这里工作。If the office has no window, then I don't want to work here.
j) 要是沙发上有青蛙,我（就会）坐（在）地（上）。If there is a frog on the sofa, (then) I sit on the floor. (坐地 "sit ground" is just a short version of 坐在地上 "sit present ground on").

7
a) 我喜欢你的男朋友。我想请他喝个酒。[I like your boyfriend, I'd like to invite him for a drink.]
b) 我想去中国。因为我喜欢吃中国饭。[I'd like to go to China. Because I like Chinese food.]
c) 我喜欢做饭。今天我想做包子。[I like cooking. Today, I want to make steamed buns.]
d) 我喜欢看电视。我得买新的电视机。[I like watching TV. I have to buy a new TV set.]
e) 你喜欢喝啤酒吗? 我想跟你一起喝, 怎么样? [Do you like to drink beer? I'd like to drink with you, how about that?]
f) 我喜欢你的家。我想在你的沙发上休息休息，可以吗? [I like your house. I'd like to take some rest on your sofa, is that okay?]
g) 老师喜欢骑马。她想买一匹。[Teacher likes riding horses. She'd like to buy one.]
h) 我喜欢说中文。我想找一个中国男朋友。[I like speaking Chinese. I'd like to find a Chinese boyfriend.]
i) 我喜欢北京。我想在那儿上大学。[I like Beijing. I'd like to go to University there.]

12

2
a) 你说得对 [you're right/what you say is correct]
b) 她/他睡得很晚 [she/he sleeps late]
c) 请你坐一下 [please have a seat]
d) 有的人喝酒喝得太多 [some people drink too much alcohol]
e) 我只吃有机的鸡蛋 [I only eat organic eggs]
f) 老师工作得很忙 [teacher's work is busy/works busily/work makes her/him busy]
g) 我哥哥对我不客气 [my elder brother is unkind/mean to me/treats me bad]
h) 有的时候我给爸爸妈妈打电话 [sometimes I call my parents]

3
a) lǎohǔ bù chī miàn [Tigers don't eat noodles]
b) nǐ kěyǐ bāng wǒ yí gè máng ma? [can you help me out?]
c) tā wèishénme lái de nàme zǎo? [why did he come so early?]
d) nǐ zěnme pǎo de zhème kuài? [why/how come you are running so fast?]
e) yǒu de nǚde bù xǐhuan nánde [some women don't like men]
f) wǒmen yào xiǎng biéde bànfǎ [we must think of something else/another way/find another solution]
g) dàbiàn duì huā yǒu yòng [poop is useful for the flowers]
h) suīrán wǒ gēge hěn kě'ài, dànshì tā méi yǒu yòng [even though my elder brother is cute, but he's useless]
i) nǐ wèishénme duì wǒ nàme bú kèqi? [why are you so impolite/unkind/mean to me?]

4
a)
Q: Jerry喝啤酒喝得多不多?
A: Jerry喝啤酒喝得很多。
b)
Q: 老师喝啤酒喝得怎么样?

A: 老师喝啤酒喝得很醉。

c) Q: Jerry做日本饭做得怎么样？
A: Jerry做日本饭做得好吃。

d) Q: Jerry看电视看得怎么样？
A: Jerry看电视看得很高兴。

e) Q: 马先生洗手洗得怎么样？
A: 马先生洗手洗得不干净。

f) Q: Jerry上课上得早不早？
A: Jerry上课上得很早。

g) Q: 王小猫听音乐听得多不多？
A: 王小猫听音乐听得不太多。

h) Q: 齐老师说法文说得怎么样？
A: 齐老师说法文说得还行。

i) Q: 学生准备中文课准备得怎么样？
A: 学生准备中文课准备得还可以。

j) Q: 妈妈做饭做得怎么样？
A: 妈妈做饭做得还好。

k) Q: 齐老师骂学生骂得怎么样？
A: 齐老师骂学生骂得不好听。

l) Q: 这个人骑自行车骑得怎么样？

A: 这个人骑自行车骑得很慢。

m) Q: Jerry学英文学得怎么样？
A: Jerry学英文学得真不错。

n) Q: 我男朋友炒鸡蛋炒得怎么样？
A: 我男朋友炒鸡蛋炒得很香。

o) Q: 学生在大学过得怎么样？
A: 学生在大学过得开心。

5
a) 老师先刮脸再洗澡 [teacher first shaves then showers]
b) 小猫先洗脸再喝牛奶 [little cat first washes her face then drinks milk]
c) 马先生先喝醉再打人 [Mr. Ma first gets drunk then picks up fights with people]
d) 我哥哥先看电视再睡觉 [my elder brother first watches TV then sleeps]
e) 有的老师先骂学生再问问题 [some teachers first berate the students then ask questions]

6
a) 他吃饭吃得很快。
b) 我的老师不帅。
c) 我的朋友炒鸡蛋炒得很香。
d) 我的书在哪里？
e) 老师的房间很干净。
f) 他说话说得很慢！
g) 他喝我的啤酒喝得很醉！
h) 你女朋友不美，而且她做饭做得不好吃。

i) 我每天都起床起得很早！
j) 老师的厕所没有门！

7
a) 请你看一下。
b) 请你听一下。
c) 请你说一下。
d) 请你问一下。
e) 请你坐一下。
f) 请你吃一下。
g) 可以炒一下。
h) 请你喝一下。
i) 我要方便一下。

13

1
老师和Jerry明年夏天七月四号去韩国 (Hánguó) [Next year in the summer on July 4th Teacher and Jerry are going to Korea]
这个星期一下午Jerry打乒乓球。[This Monday afternoon Jerry plays ping pong]
星期五晚上八点半王小猫和马先生去电影院。[Friday night at 8:30 Wang Xiaomao and Mr. Ma are going to the movies.]
下个星期老师要带Jerry去西班牙餐厅吃饭。[Next week the teacher will take Jerry to a Spanish restaurant]
上个星期六晚上Jerry去酒吧唱歌。[Last Saturday night Jerry went dancing in a bar.]
下个月老师每天都要去游泳。[Next month the teacher will go swimming every day]
Jerry每天上午10点到11点在公园跑步。[Every morning from 10 to 11 Jerry goes jogging in the park]
每个星期四马先生都喝醉 [Every Thursday Mr. Ma is drunk]

2
a) 虽然她每天都工作得很忙，但是她不累。
b) Jerry打乒乓球打得很棒。
c) 我妹妹游泳游得很快。
d) 虽然王小猫学得很努力，但是她中文说得不好（说中文说得不好）。
e) 马先生住得不远。
f) 明天我要起得早（起床起得早）。

3
a) 我不理你 [I'm ignoring you (an expression use often to rebuke someone, e.g. "I don't care what you say/do")]
b) 她/他说得对 [S/he's right]
c) 这家餐厅很贵 [This restaurant is expensive; 家 here is a measure word]
d) 你吃完了吗？[Have you finished eating?]
e) 我们的中文老师很棒。[Our Chinese language teacher is awesome]
f) 他/她来得早 [S/he arrived early]

4
a) wǒ shuì de hěn wǎn
b) tā chī de zǎo
c) māo pǎo chū qù le
d) nǐ yào xǐ yīfu ma?
e) wǒ shuā yá shuā de lèi
f) xǐyījī xǐ yīfu xǐ de gānjìng
洗衣机 **xǐyījī** = wash-

ing machine

5
a) 来了北京以后，我才开始学中文。[Only after coming to Beijing have I started learning Chinese/I did not start learning Chinese until I came to Beijing.]
b) 看完电视以后，Jerry和别的马去公园喝啤酒。[After finishing watching TV, Jerry and other horses go to the park to drink beer.]
c) 吃饭了以后，大家都应该刷牙。[Everybody should brush up teeth after eating]
d) 吃了爸爸做的饭以后，妈妈马上就生病了。[After eating the food that dad cooked, Mom immediately got sick]
e) 除了Jerry以外，我不认识别的会说话的马。[Except for Jerry, I don't know other horses that can talk]
f) 马先生上了厕所以后没洗手。[Mr. Ma did not wash his hands after using the toilet]
g) 王小猫没有付钱，就从商店里跑出去了。[Wang Xiaomao just ran out of the store without paying/did not pay and just ran out of the store]
h) 好学生看完书以后才去睡觉。[Good students sleep only after they finish their studies/ don't go to sleep until they finish their studies]
i) 不好的学生起了床以后马上就上网。[Bad students go online as soon as they get up]
j) 有文化的人先敲门再进去。[People who have culture (well educated people) first knock on the door and then enter]

6
a) 有的人上网的时候不理别人 [Some people, when they go online, they don't pay attention to other people]
b) 生病的时候得休息，喝水，不要喝酒 [When sick, one must rest, drink water, one must not drink alcohol]
c) Jerry看他老朋友的照片的时候老师很吃醋 [When Jerry looks at the picture of his old friend, Teacher is jealous]
d) 有的人上厕所的时候爱听音乐 [Some people love to listen to music when they use the toilet]
e) 齐老师洗澡的时候唱歌 [Teacher Qi sings when taking a shower]
f) 上课的时候不应该用手机 [When in class one should not use the cell phone]
g) 在电影院看电影的时候不要说话 [When watching a movie in a movie theater one must not talk]
h) 老师生气的时候骂学生 [When the teacher is pissed he curses the students]
i) 王小猫难过的时候买花 [When Wang Xiaomao is sad she buys flowers]
j) 忙的人饿的时候吃快餐 [When busy people are hungry they eat fast food]

7
a) 跑进去
b) 跑出去
c) 跑进来
d) 跑出来

So ...

What is going to happen to Jerry?

Why is Jerry leaving?
Will he come back?
What is teacher Qi going to do?

If you want to find out – keep on learning Chinese!

Oh, Jerry! – Part 2 – will be available from 2024.

The ISBN will be 978-3-945174-26-5.

Stay tuned:
www.skapago.eu/jerry/bonus

Would you like to learn more languages?

Skapago can help you even with other languages. What about learning **Swedish** with Alfred the ghost, **Norwegian** with Nils the doll or **German** with Jens and Jakob, the sparrows from Berlin?

More information:
www.skapago.eu

www.ingramcontent.com/pod-product-compliance
Ingram Content Group UK Ltd.
Pitfield, Milton Keynes, MK11 3LW, UK
UKHW060213240426
12048UKWH00031BB/1708